look for
- hours
- conditions
- community
- habits (spending, marriage, etc.)

The
RUSSIAN
WORKER

The

RUSSIAN WORKER

*Life and Labor
under the Tsarist Regime*

Edited, with an introduction
and annotations,

by Victoria E. Bonnell

University of California Press

Berkeley • Los Angeles • London

University of California Press
Berkeley and Los Angeles, California
University of California Press, Ltd.
London, England
© 1983 by
The Regents of the University of California

Library of Congress Cataloging in Publication Data

The Russian worker.

   Bibliography: p.
   Includes indes.
   1. Labor and laboring classes—Soviet Union—History—Addresses, essays,
lectures.   I. Bonnell, Victoria E.
HD8526.R89   1983   305.5'62'0947   83–47856
ISBN 0-520-05059-2 (alk. paper)

Printed in the United States of America

5   6   7   8   9

For G.M.F.

Contents

List of Illustrations

Preface

The idea for this collection originated five years ago when I was conducting research for another book on the politics and organizations of workers in tsarist Russia. While engaged in that project, I faced the problem of comprehending the daily lives and mentality of people far removed from ourselves in time and place. Workers' memoirs and other first-hand accounts of working-class life offered a valuable source for drawing closer to the diverse groups that comprised the laboring population in Russia at the end of the nineteenth and the beginning of the twentieth centuries. This volume is intended to make some of these sources available to an English-speaking audience.

While preparing the collection, I was greatly assisted by Reginald E. Zelnik, whose seminal essay on the biographies of Russian workers helped to inspire the project and whose encouragement and assistance facilitated its completion. Professor Zelnik has translated the selections from the memoirs of Kanatchikov that appear in this volume, and he has prepared the annotations for that chapter.

In translating the works of Timofeev, Pavlov, Oliunina, and Gudvan, I was assisted by Michael Atkin, Gregory Freidin, and especially Lynn Mally.

Lynn Mally also made extensive editorial and research contributions to the manuscript.

Many of the materials in this collection were gathered during a research trip to the Soviet Union in 1977, made possible by grants from the International Research and Exchanges Board and the Fulbright-Hays Faculty Research Abroad Program. A grant from the Translation Program of the National Endowment for the Humanities in 1980 enabled me to complete the project. I also benefited from the support provided by the Institute of Urban and Regional Development at the University of California, Berkeley, under the direction of Professor Melvin M. Webber. The input of the manuscript onto a word processor, as well as editing and formatting, were expertly accomplished by Dorothy Heydt, with assistance from Maureen Jurkowski.

Note on Translations

The five selections in this volume have been chosen and translated from longer works originally published in Russian. In the interest of continuity, especially because I wished to emphasize themes pertaining to everyday life and workplace conditions, I have omitted some passages from the Russian text. These omissions will not be indicated in the translations that follow. Those wishing to consult the original version will find the translated selections, with some deletions, on the following pages:

S. I. Kanatchikov, *Iz istorii moego bytiia*, Book 1 (Moscow and Leningrad, 1929), pp. 8–11, 14–20, 42–56, 62–68.

P. Timofeev, *Chem zhivet zavodskii rabochii* (St. Petersburg, 1906), pp. 3–6, 11–23, 28–34, 78–85, 91–100, 110–114.

F. P. Pavlov, *Za desiat' let praktiki (otryvki iz vospominanii, vpechatlenii i nabliudenii iz fabrichnoi zhizni)* (Moscow, 1901), Author's Preface and pp. 10–16, 51–61, 74–79, 98–123.

E. A. Oliunina, *Portnovskii promysel v Moskve i v derevniakh Moskovskoi i Riazanskoi gubernii. Materialy k istorii domashnei promyshlennosti v Rossii* (Moscow, 1914), pp. v, 22–23, 31–32, 39–40, 47–48, 170–177, 188–200, 202–205, 217, 233–254, 257–262, 266–271.

A. M. Gudvan, *Ocherki po istorii dvizheniia sluzhashchikh v Rossii* (Moscow, 1925), pp. 122–128, 131–141, 150–152, 155–158, 160–163, 165, 170–177, 185–189.

Notes marked with an asterisk appeared in the original. All other notes were prepared for this volume. Subtitles within chapters are provided, for the most part, by the editor.

Note on Dates and Transliteration

All dates refer to the Old Style (Julian) calendar in use in Russia until February 1918.

The system of transliteration used here is the Library of Congress system. Names and places that are well known are presented in their more familiar English form.

Introduction

It was not until the closing decades of the nineteenth century that Russia entered the industrial age. Only then, under the impact of favorable government policies, did traditional Russian society begin to undergo a rapid transformation. Vast rural areas were soon converted into factory villages, and urban centers expanded to absorb new factories, shops, and residential districts. But most significant of all, a new and greatly enlarged working population was formed as tens of thousands of peasants migrated from the countryside, forsaking their plows for jobs in cities and towns.[1]

Labor force statistics testify to the magnitude of the changes that took place in the 1890s, a period of accelerated economic growth. More than

[1]On the history of Russia's industrialization, see William L. Blackwell, *The Beginnings of Russian Industrialization 1800-1860* (Princeton, 1968); M. I. Tugan-Baranovsky, *The Russian Factory in the 19th Century* (Homewood, Ill., 1970); Alexander Gerschenkron, "Problems and Patterns of Russian Economic Development," in *The Transformation of Russian Society: Aspects of Social Change Since 1861*, ed. Cyril E. Black (Cambridge, Mass., 1967), pp. 42–71; Theodore von Laue, *Sergei Witte and the Industrialization of Russia* (New York, 1963); Reginald E. Zelnik, *Labor and Society in Tsarist Russia: The Factory Workers of St. Petersburg 1855-1870* (Stanford, 1971). James H. Bater, *St. Petersburg: Industrialization and Change* (London, 1976) offers a valuable account of changes in the composition of the labor force and the impact of industrialization on the capital.

1

one million men and women—most of them peasants—entered the industrial labor force between 1887 and 1900, bringing the total number of factory and mine workers at the turn of the century to 2.4 million. But industrial employment represented only one aspect of the growing non-agricultural economy. During the 1890s, thousands of peasants found jobs in artisanal trades and in an expanding network of putting-out industries in cities and the countryside. Still others earned a livelihood in commercial firms and in the flourishing service, construction, transportation, and communications sectors of the economy. Another large group joined the ranks of day laborers. In all of these categories combined, there were 6.4 million hired workers in the Russian Empire in 1897, the year of the country's first national census.[2]

The Russian working class consisted of heterogeneous elements employed in many different occupations and industries. Together these diverse groups were destined to play a crucial role in the country's future, and by 1900 they were already showing signs of volatility and a propensity for collective action that could not be ignored. In the 1890s, factory groups in the capital, St. Petersburg, mounted the first large-scale city-wide strikes in Russia, and less than a decade later, during the 1905 revolution, workers throughout the Empire joined in upheavals that decisively challenged the autocratic system, forcing the government to give in to demands for constitutional reform. When the old regime finally collapsed during the February Revolution, workers once again moved to the forefront of the popular movement, this time helping to bring the Bolshevik party to power in October 1917.[3]

[2]*Chislennost' i sostav rabochikh v Rossii na osnovanii dannykh pervoi vseobshchei perepisi naseleniia Rossiiskoi Imperii 1897 g.*, 2 vols. (St. Petersburg, 1906), I, pp. viii-xx.

[3]On the period before 1917, see Victoria E. Bonnell, *Roots of Rebellion: Workers' Politics and Organizations in St. Petersburg and Moscow, 1900-1914* (Berkeley and Los Angeles, 1983); Laura Engelstein, *Moscow, 1905: Working-Class Organization and Political Conflict* (Stanford, 1982); John L. H. Keep, *The Rise of Social Democracy in Russia* (Oxford, 1963); Ezra Mendelsohn, *Class Struggle in the Pale: The Formative Years of the Jewish Workers' Movement in Tsarist Russia* (Cambridge, 1970); Solomon M. Schwarz, *The Russian Revolution of 1905: The Workers' Movement and the Formation of Bolshevism and Menshevism* (Chicago, 1967); Gerald Dennis Surh, "Petersburg Workers in 1905: Strikes, Workplace Democracy, and the Revolution," Ph.D. diss., University of California, Berkeley, 1979; Allan K. Wildman, *The Making of a Workers' Revolution: Russian Social Democracy,*

Russian workers were exceptionally active during the final decades of autocratic rule, participating in three revolutionary upheavals in a dozen years. Yet little is known about the daily lives of workers, their experiences at the workplace and outside of it, their social relations, and aspirations. These important but neglected aspects of working class life provide the subject for the memoirs and first-hand accounts by contemporaries that appear in this volume. My aim in the introductory essay is to place the selections in an historical context and to acquaint the reader with some of the major issues and themes in the study of Russian labor.

THE LABOR FORCE

The program of state-sponsored industrialization that got under way in Russia at the end of the nineteenth century brought about many changes in the nonagricultural economy, but none was so dramatic and fateful as the proliferation of factories and the appearance within them of a large and highly concentrated group of industrial workers.[4] As elsewhere in Europe at an earlier time, the advent of a factory system was inextricably connected to the expansion of two major industries: textiles and metalworking.

With more than half a million workers, the textile industry (cotton, silk, wool, and linen) was the largest single employer of factory labor in the

---

1891–1903 (Chicago, 1967). On 1917, see William Henry Chamberlin, *The Russian Revolution*, 2 vols. (New York, 1935); Diane Koenker, *Moscow Workers and the 1917 Revolution* (Princeton, 1981); Alexander Rabinowitch, *Prelude to Revolution: The Petrograd Bolsheviks and the July 1917 Uprising* (Bloomington, Ind., 1968); Alexander Rabinowitch, *The Bolsheviks Come to Power:: The Revolution of 1917 in Petrograd* (New York, 1976); John L. H. Keep, *The Russian Revolution: A Study in Mass Mobilization* (New York, 1976).

[4] The precise definition and classification of the factory worker need not detain us here. Suffice it to note that before 1901 the government designated a "factory" any manufacturing enterprise that employed fifteen or more workers or utilized engine-powered machinery. In 1901, the definition of a factory was changed to include only manufacturing enterprises with twenty or more workers, regardless of the type of machinery. These criteria were not, however, applied consistently by the government. See S. N. Semanov, *Peterburgskie rabochie nakanune pervoi russkoi revoliutsii* (Moscow, 1966), pp. 6–17, esp. p. 7, n. 4.

ιpire in 1897. Textile mills could be found in many parts of
the industry was heavily concentrated in the cities and factory
villages of the Central Industrial Region, an area encompassing six
provinces in the heart of European Russia. Metalworking, the second
largest employer of factory labor, accounted for about 414,000 workers at
the end of the 1890s.[5] This industry was centered in Petersburg province in
the northwestern region of the country and, to a lesser extent, in Moscow
province.[6]

Both the textile and metalworking industries in Russia were distinguished by their unusually high concentration of workers per enterprise;
in both branches there were many firms that employed more than one
thousand workers. But here the similarities end, for the composition of the
labor force in the two industries differed greatly. Whereas textile mills
relied mainly on unskilled and semiskilled labor, there was a predominance
of skilled workers in metalworking plants at the turn of the century. As
many as four out of every five workers in some metalworking enterprises
belonged to the ranks of skilled labor. Furthermore, the textile mills employed a large number of women and children; the labor force in metalworking, by contrast, was almost entirely male.

There were many differences between metal and textile workers—
differences that are described in the selections that follow. Yet these two
groups of workers shared one common characteristic that distinguished
them from other segments of the urban laboring population. Most metal
and textile workers were employed in enterprises that the government
classified as "factories," and by the end of the nineteenth century factory
workers were subject to a special set of laws and regulations setting them
apart from the rest of the labor force.

As early as 1835, the tsarist government enacted legislation regulating
the terms and conditions of factory employment, but implementation and

[5]*Chislennost' i sostav*, I, pp. viii-ix. Included in the Central Industrial Region were the
provinces of Moscow, Vladimir, Tver, Iaroslavl, Nizhnii-Novgorod, and Kostroma.
Some definitions also include part or all of Tambov, Riazan', Tula, Kaluga, and Smolensk
provinces.

[6]For a valuable discussion of the Petersburg metalworking industry, see Heather Jeanne
Hogan, "Labor and Management in Conflict: The St. Petersburg Metal-Working Industry, 1900–1914," Ph.D. diss., University of Michigan, 1981, Chs. 1, 2.

enforcement of this law proved ineffectual.[7] A similar fate befell the law of 1845, which banned factory night work for children under twelve years of age. In 1882, new legislation was promulgated restricting the work time of children and juveniles in factory enterprises. This law also established a Factory Inspectorate whose responsibilities included surveillance of firms to ensure compliance with government legislation. In 1885, additional laws were enacted prohibiting children under seventeen years of age and women from night work in cotton, linen, and wool mills. Further legislation the following year expanded government regulation of the labor contract, strengthened criminal sanctions for violations, and enlarged the role of the Factory Inspectorate.

A decade later, widespread labor unrest in St. Petersburg prompted the government to enact another major labor law. The legislation of June 2, 1897, restricted the length of the workday in factory enterprises to a maximum of eleven and a half hours for all adult workers on weekdays and to a maximum of ten hours on Saturdays and on the eves of holidays. Although overtime work was subsequently ruled permissible, this law— together with its predecessors—gave factory workers a degree of protection and regulation that was not extended to any other segment of the laboring population.

By the turn of the nineteenth century, factory workers, with their special juridical status, occupied a growing place in the manufacturing sector of the Russian economy. But in some branches of manufacturing, factories were still relatively undeveloped, and most production was carried on in small workshops based on traditional artisanal trades. Artisanal workers represented a broad and amorphous group in Russian cities around 1900.

[7]On the history of labor legislation in Russia, see Tugan-Baranovsky, *Russian Factory,* Chs. 5, 10; Zelnik, *Labor and Society;* I. I. Shelymagin, *Zakonodatel'stvo o fabrichno-zavodskom trude v Rossii 1900-1917* (Moscow, 1952); V. Ia. Laverychev, *Tsarizm i rabochii vopros v Rossii (1861-1917 gg.)* (Moscow, 1972); Gaston V. Rimlinger, "Autocracy and the Factory Order in Early Russian Industrialization," *Journal of Economic History,* 20 (1960); Jacob Walkin, "The Attitude of the Tsarist Government Toward the Labor Problem," *American Slavic and East European Review,* 13 (1954); Theodore von Laue, "Factory Inspection Under the 'Witte System:' 1892–1903," *American Slavic and East European Review,* 19 (Oct. 1960), 347–362; Lynn Mally, "Russian Workers and Factory Legislation 1882–1900." Seminar paper, University of California, Berkeley, Spring 1978.

No official data are available on the total number of artisanal workers in the country as a whole, though in key cities they represented a very sizable and diverse group. Thus, in St. Petersburg around the turn of the century there were 150,709 artisanal workers compared with 161,924 in factory enterprises. In Moscow, the country's second largest urban and manufacturing center, artisanal workers (151,359) outnumbered the factory population (111,718).[8]

Within the artisanal labor force, the largest single group was employed in the apparel trades. The 1897 census reported that there were 346,000 garment workers in the Russian Empire as a whole, nearly all of them employed in small firms that did not qualify as "factories" within the terms of government regulations. In cities such as St. Petersburg and Moscow, about one out of every three artisanal workers was employed in the apparel trades.[9] Other large contingents of artisanal workers could be found in leather and shoemaking, woodworking, printing, metal and machine tool building, and in the skilled construction trades.

The large and variegated group of artisanal workers in urban Russia included many craftsmen who labored for long hours under sweatshop conditions in subcontracting shops and garrets, as well as a much smaller contingent employed in workshops that retained many of the features of preindustrial handicraft production. Among the latter group were some craftsmen who still belonged to an artisanal guild at the beginning of the twentieth century.

Introduced into Russia in the early eighteenth century by Peter the Great, Russian guilds never attained extensive jurisdiction over production and distribution or the exclusive corporate privileges of their counterparts in Western Europe.[10] When industrialization gathered momentum in the second half of the nineteenth century, Russian guilds maintained their

[8]Bonnell, *Roots of Rebellion*, Table 1.

[9]*Ibid.*, Tables 2 and 3. The studies devoted to tailors include E. A. Oliunina, *Portnovskii promysel v Moskve i v derevniakh Moskovskoi i Riazanskoi gubernii. Materialy k istorii domashnei promyshlennosti v Rossii* (Moscow, 1914); S. M. Gruzdev, *Trud i bor'ba shveinikov v Petrograde 1905-1906 gg.* (Leningrad, 1929); N. Shevkov, *Moskovskie shveiniki do fevral'skoi revoliutsii* (Moscow, 1927).

[10]On the origins and history of Russian guilds, see Zelnik, *Labor and Society*, pp. 12, 15; and K. A. Pazhitnov, *Problema remeslennykh tsekhov v zakonodatel'stve russkogo absoliutizma* (Moscow, 1952).

juridical status but suffered a steady decline. By 1900, only 28 percent of the artisans in St. Petersburg still belonged to a guild, and a mere 16 percent in Moscow.[11] For most handicraft workers at the turn of the century, therefore, guild organizations and regulations had little practical consequence.

Whereas the government regulated the terms and conditions of labor for factory workers, artisanal groups lacked comparable protection at the beginning of the twentieth century. This situation, discussed in Oliunina's study, had especially grave consequences for those employed in the large apparel industry where pressure for increased production led to the proliferation of subcontracting shops producing on a putting-out basis for wholesale and retail marketing firms.

Apart from the large segment of factory and artisanal workers there was a substantial group employed in sales and clerical occupations. These occupations can be divided into five major subgroups: salesclerks, cashiers, bookkeepers, clerks, and apprentices. Although their number in the Russian Empire cannot be ascertained on the basis of available data, in St. Petersburg there were more than 109,000 sales-clerical workers at the turn of the century and in Moscow about 86,000. Salesclerks represented the largest single category, with nearly 60,000 in St. Petersburg and more than 40,000 in Moscow.[12] Thus, approximately one-half of the sales-clerical

[11]*Remeslenniki i remeslennoe upravlenie v Rossii* (Petrograd, 1916), p. 32. Only journeymen and apprentices are included in this calculation; master artisans have been excluded because most were workshop owners.

[12]Bonnell, *Roots of Rebellion*, Table 6 and Ch. 1. My data on the number of sales-clerical workers, based on the municipal censuses conducted in St. Petersburg in 1900 and in Moscow in 1902, are considerably lower than figures found in various Russian and Soviet studies on the subject. The principal works on sales-clerical groups include D. V. Antoshkin, *Ocherk dvizheniia sluzhashchikh v Rossii* (Moscow, 1921); S. S. Ainzaft, "K istorii professional'nogo dvizheniia torgovo-promyshlennykh sluzhashchikh," *Vestnik truda*, 2 [39] (1924): 222–230; V. M. Anufriev, P. I. Dorovatskii, and N. I. Roganov, *Iz istorii profdvizheniia rabotnikov torgovli* (Moscow, 1958); A. Belin [A. A. Evdokimov], *Professional'noe dvizhenie torgovykh sluzhashchikh v Rossii* (Moscow, 1906); M. Gordon, ed., *Iz istorii professional'nogo dvizheniia sluzhashchikh v Peterburge. Pervyi etap (1904–1919 gg.)* (Leningrad, 1925); K. Muromskii, *Byt i nuzhdy torgovo-promyshlennykh sluzhashchikh* (Moscow, 1906); M. Rozen, *Ocherki polozheniia torgovo promyshlennogo proletariata v Rossii* (St. Petersburg, 1907).

workers in these cities were employed as salesclerks in retail, wholesale, industrial, and cooperative firms. About 90 percent of them were male.

Toward the end of the nineteenth century, expansion of the economy led to a proliferation of commercial establishments. Just as there was a growing concentration of capital and labor in large factory enterprises, so the world of commerce witnessed the appearance of the first large retail establishments: department stores such as Muir and Merrilees. Similar trends can be discerned in other facets of commerce. But despite growing concentration, most transactions at the turn of the century still took place in small shops, sprawling public markets, street stalls, and by means of vendors and peddlers whose horse- and hand-drawn carts formed a colorful part of the urban landscape.

APPRENTICESHIP

Around 1900, most Russian workers had been born in the countryside and had spent their early years in a village. The sojourn from the countryside to the city or factory was a familiar occurrence in European Russia.[13] Rural poverty, overpopulation, and land scarcity drove peasants from their native villages in search of work; still others migrated in the hope of finding opportunities for a better life. Departure from the countryside frequently took place for the first time at an early age. The reminiscence of one such journey by Kanatchikov opens this volume. A sixteen-year-old peasant from a village in Moscow province, Kanatchikov entered a factory apprenticeship in 1895.

At the turn of the century, an apprenticeship system existed in virtually

[13]On this subject, see Barbara Anderson, *Internal Migration During Modernization in Late Nineteenth-Century Russia* (Princeton, 1980); Robert E. Johnson, *Peasant and Proletarian: The Working Class of Moscow in the Late Nineteenth Century* (New Brunswick, N.J., 1979); Joseph Crane Bradley, Jr., "Muzhik and Muscovite: Peasants in Late Nineteenth-Century Urban Russia," Ph.D. diss., Harvard University, 1977; Reginald E. Zelnik, "The Peasant and the Factory," in *The Peasant in Nineteenth-Century Russia*, ed. Wayne S. Vucinich (Stanford, 1968); Theodore von Laue, "Russian Peasants in the Factory, 1892–1904," *Journal of European History*, 21 (March 1961): 61–80; Theodore von Laue, "Russian Labor Between Field and Factory, 1892–1903," *California Slavic Studies*, 3 (1964): 33–64.

all skilled occupations, occupying a far more important place in working-class life than is generally acknowledged in the literature and exerting a formative influence over workers' conceptions of class and status in Russian society. Apprenticeship remained mandatory in virtually all artisanal trades and in numerous other skilled occupations carried on in a factory setting, in sales establishments, and in other sectors of the economy.

Many different types of workers served an apprenticeship in tsarist Russia, though the nature and conditions of this training were far from uniform. Kanatchikov's apprenticeship in patternmaking, like most craft training in a factory setting, proceeded on a more or less informal basis over a two-year period. At the end of that time, Kanatchikov had become sufficiently adept to demonstrate his mastery of the patternmaking craft and qualify as a skilled worker.

Apprenticeship in apparel and other artisanal trades and in sales occupations generally began earlier in life than factory training and lasted for a longer term. As disclosed by Oliunina and Gudvan, it was not unusual for ten-year-old boys and girls to serve an apprenticeship in workshops or commercial firms. An oral contract concluded between parents and the shop owner committed these children to the employer's tutelage and authority for a period normally lasting from three to five years. When this term had been completed, an individual was entitled to perform adult work. The traditional certification procedure in artisanal trades, involving a formal demonstration of craft skills, applied only to the small minority of guild members at the beginning of the twentieth century.

For tailors, salesclerks, and many other artisanal, commercial, and service occupations, the function of apprenticeship had undergone a subtle but important change in the closing decades of the nineteenth century. Shifts in production processes, an increasingly complex division of labor, and the spread of subcontracting and commercial activity induced many shop owners to rely increasingly on the unpaid labor of apprentices as a surrogate for adult labor while at the same time diminishing the instructional aspect of apprenticeship.

Whereas some peasant youths entered an apprenticeship when barely into their teens, there were many others between the age of twelve and fifteen who performed unskilled factory work without the prospect of advancing to a more skilled and specialized occupation. As in Western

Europe, child labor was especially prevalent in the textile industry where many production tasks could easily be accomplished by boys and girls.

For youths recruited fresh from the countryside, early entry into the labor force had diverse effects. Those who entered an apprenticeship were more likely than others to find themselves inducted into the adult subculture of the factory or shop and to develop, albeit gradually and perhaps tenuously, a new self-image that corresponded to their growing skill as "a patternmaker," "a tailor," or "a salesclerk." To a far greater extent than child and juvenile laborers in factories and mills, young apprentices developed an awareness of their position as urban workers, a self-image still comparatively rare in Russia at the turn of the century. As a result of these experiences, youths such as Kanatchikov began to acquire a new identity as urban workers, in contrast to the peasantry from which most had come.[14]

The process of identity formation was, of course, extremely complex in a society that officially discouraged the creation of a permanent stratum of urban workers, disengaged once and for all from their peasant roots. Thus, a great many workers maintained some connection with the countryside at the beginning of the twentieth century, and nearly all of them had to come to terms in one way or another with the vexing problem of their continuing ties to the village—its traditions, expectations, and social networks. The way in which a worker dealt with this problem depended, in large measure, on the position that he or she occupied in the *urban* work hierarchy.

STRATIFICATION OF THE LABOR FORCE

Peasants entering the workplace for the first time encountered a highly stratified arrangement. Above them stood various authority figures. The factory director, as described by Pavlov, wielded vast power over his employees, controlling the destiny of hundreds or even thousands of individuals. The shop owner was no less powerful, however, and within the confines of the workshop or sales firm the employer could be a merciless tyrant—a situation noted by Oliunina and Gudvan. In addition to bosses

[14]For an extended discussion and analysis of Kanatchikov's evolution as an urban worker, see Reginald E. Zelnik, "Russian Bebels: An Introduction to the Memoirs of Semen Kanatchikov and Matvei Fisher," *Russian Review*, pt. 1, 35 (July 1976): 249–289; pt. 2, 35 (Oct. 1976): 417–447.

and managers, many firms (both large and small) employed intermediary figures of authority that included supervisors and technical personnel, foremen, assistant foremen, and work crew leaders. In a factory, the foreman occupied a unique place in the worker's everyday life. As Timofeev puts it, "The foreman represents that lever which presses on the worker the hardest."[15] Workers were thus subordinated to many different types of direct and indirect authority at the workplace.

The labor force itself was highly stratified, primarily along the lines of skill and occupational specialization. Hierarchical subdivisions existed among various industries and trades. In St. Petersburg and Moscow, the sharpest contrast in the factory milieu was between the two major industrial groups: metalworkers and textile workers. "The world of the textile factory is completely different from that of the large metalworking plant," Timofeev observes, ". . . [and] these two groups of workers should never be confused."[16] Status differences between the two groups were keenly discerned by contemporaries, as illustrated by the recollections of another Petersburg metalworker, Aleksei Buzinov:

Metalworking plants and textile mills were concentrated in our Nevskii district. At that time [about 1900], the difference between metal and textile workers was like the difference between the city and the countryside. . . . Metalworkers considered themselves aristocrats among other workers. Their occupations demanded more training and skill, and therefore they looked down on other workers, such as weavers and the like, as an inferior category, as country bumpkins: today he will be at the mill, but tomorrow he will be poking at the earth with his wooden plough. The superiority of the metalworker and everything that it implied was appreciated by all.[17]

Each industry or occupation also had an internal labor hierarchy. At the summit stood a small but highly skilled substratum such as metal pattern-makers, fabric cutters in the garment industry, and clerks in fashionable retail stores catering to a prosperous and exclusive clientele. Below them were ranged a variety of skilled occupations—metalfitters, lathe operators, and smelters in metalworking, tailors employed in custom-made men's and

[15]See below, p. 75.
[16]See below, p. 73.
[17]A. Buzinov, *Za Nevskoi zastavoi. Zapiski rabochego* (Moscow, 1930), p. 20.

women's tailoring shops, clerks in jewelry shops, and machinists in textile mills. They were followed by semiskilled and unskilled workers.

The labor force in skilled occupations was further subdivided into apprentices (*ucheniki*) and qualified adult workers. In artisanal trades, the latter group was further subdivided into journeymen (*podmaster'ia*) and master craftsmen (*mastera*). This arrangement still remained in effect at the turn of the century in both guild and nonguild workshops despite the fact that most journeymen could anticipate only lateral mobility and not vertical ascent into the ranks of workshop owners.

Prior to the 1880s, several designations for adult factory workers were utilized by the government, factory management, and the workers themselves. The term *masterovoi* (derived from the guild designation *master*) referred to the skilled worker whereas *rabochii*[18] applied to semiskilled and unskilled workers alike. Among skilled metalworkers the word *rabochii* had such pejorative connotations that it was often used as a term of opprobrium.

Workers attached enormous importance to these designations and were bitterly opposed when factory management sought to alter them by eliminating the category of *masterovoi*, reclassifying skilled groups as *rabochie*, and applying the term *chernorabochie*[19] to the remainder. One such episode is discussed at some length by Timofeev, but the workers' preoccupation with matters of status differentiation emerges from all of the selections below. Social interaction among individuals was determined, in large measure, by one's position in the status hierarchy. Thus, Kanatchikov recalls that when he was still a mere apprentice, the metalturner Rezvov would not condescend to socialize with him. This situation changed, however, when Kanatchikov himself became a fully qualified craftsman.

Highly attentive to nuances of difference among occupational specializations, Petersburg metalworkers responded to a 1908 survey with a list of

[18]The word *rabochii* is etymologically a descendant of the Old Church Slavonic word *rab"*, meaning servant, servitor, or slave; see Max Fasmer, *Russisches etymologisches Wörterbuch* (Heidelberg, 1950–1958), "Rabochii." The unpleasant connotations of the word, which still carried a distant echo of *rab"* or slave, may have contributed to the workers' resistance to this designation.

[19]The prefix *cherno*, meaning "black," was affixed to the word *rabochii* to signify the lowest position within the ranks of workers.

more than one hundred separate occupational categories to identify their place in the industry.[20] That workers keenly felt these differences can be documented from memoirs such as Buzinov's account of his apprenticeship at the Nevskii shipbuilding plant in St. Petersburg in the late 1890s:

The more I grew into the factory family, the clearer became to me its heterogeneity, even within the boundaries of one plant. Soon I began to realize that workers in the machine shop—the metalfitters and lathe operators—looked down on me. After this, the inferior position of workers in the "hot" shops—the smelting, rolling, and blacksmith shops—became obvious. . . . I was especially struck by the absence of equality among workers. Now it seems a minor matter, something not even worth remembering. But at the time, it painfully wounded my pride. I didn't want to be worse than the others. I thought that if only I could master the skills of metalfitting and lathe operating, everything would fall into place.[21]

The hierarchical subdivisions within the laboring population acquired particular significance for contemporaries in part because the minority of skilled workers stood out so sharply from their unskilled and semiskilled counterparts. In appearance and demeanor, skilled workers exhibited their differential status. Kanatchikov describes the urbanized patternmakers who wore fancy clothes and whose bearing conveyed their consciousness of their own worth. In a similar vein, Oliunina observes that tailoring shop workers and subcontract workers dressed quite differently. Whereas the former wore suits, stylish boots, and different coats according to the season, the subcontract workers could often be found wearing nothing but a calico shirt, faded pants, and long underwear.

The visibility of status differences shaped the ways workers thought of themselves and related to others, as well as their treatment by managerial personnel. The external appearance of the job applicant, Timofeev reports, affected the foreman's disposition. "His form of address will depend on your clothes. If you are well dressed, he might address you politely."[22] There were many pressures on workers, moreover, to discard their peasant

[20]*Materialy ob ekonomicheskom polozhenii i professional'noi organizatsii Peterburgskikh rabochikh po metallu* (St. Petersburg, 1909), pp. 94–96.
[21]Buzinov, *Za Nevskoi zastavoi*, p. 21.
[22]See below, p. 87.

attire and to assume the clothing and demeanor of the urban milieu. A worker newly arriving in the city from the countryside could not fail to discern the status and dignity associated with an urbanized appearance. Kanatchikov recalls that "skilled workers looked down on me with scorn, pinched me by the ear, pulled me by the hair, called me a 'green country bumpkin' and other insulting names." Workers (including some skilled elements) who retained their peasant clothing—they "wore high boots, traditional cotton-print blouses girdled with a sash, had their hair cut 'under a pot,' and wore beards that were rarely touched by the barber's hand"— were called "gray devils" by their more urbane and sophisticated co-workers.[23]

Even in the remote factory villages of the Central Industrial Region observed by Pavlov, workers were highly sensitive to exterior propriety and eager to purchase perfume, fine soap, fashionable jackets, and patent leather shoes. These pressures mounted in occupations that required regular contact with the general public. Thus, workers in sales and clerical jobs required attractive urban attire to obtain and maintain their employment, a situation that drove some women to seek supplementary income through prostitution.[24]

By the turn of the century, a growing group of workers in all sectors of the economy had succeeded in acquiring specialized skills and an appearance and demeanor that betokened their status and position in the world of the factory or shop. Yet a majority of these skilled and urbanized workers remained tied in various degrees to their native villages. The persistence of these ties represents a distinctive feature of the formative period in the development of the Russian working class.

THE SIGNIFICANCE OF RURAL-URBAN TIES

The relation between the worker and the village assumed a variety of forms, ranging from permanent urban workers with no ties whatsoever to the countryside to semipeasant workers with ongoing ties to their native villages. In general, workers with the highest levels of occupational special-

[23]See below, pp. 47–48.

[24]On prostitution, see Richard Stites, *The Women's Liberation Movement in Russia: Feminism, Nihilism, and Bolshevism, 1860-1930* (Princeton, 1978), pp. 182–185.

ization and skill were the least likely to have continuing ties to the countryside.[25] Seasonal industries such as tailoring present a partial exception to this pattern since many skilled tailors departed annually for their villages when production subsided. Even here, however, the rate of seasonal return to the village was lower among the relatively more skilled retail tailoring shop workers than among subcontract workers.

The number of permanent urban workers was steadily increasing by the turn of the century. Data for Moscow show that Moscow-born workers comprised a minority of the labor force in 1902 (7 percent of the factory workers, 10 percent of the artisanal workers, and 20 percent of the sales-clerical employees). A considerably larger group had migrated to Moscow and spent ten years or longer in the city (34 percent of factory workers, 37 percent of artisanal workers, and 34 percent of sales-clerical employees). Combining the two groups, we find that 41 percent of the factory workers, 47 percent of the artisans, and 54 percent of the sales-clerical employees either were permanent residents or had spent a decade or more living and working in Moscow by 1902.[26]

Some of the workers, moreover, may have lived in more than one city. Kanatchikov is a case in point. After working for several years in Moscow, he moved to St. Petersburg, where he remained for fifteen months until illegal political activities led to his arrest and exile. There were numerous workers with a history of interurban migration,[27] and though it is not possible to establish their exact number, these workers typically spent a prolonged period in various urban centers and had relinquished most of their ties to the countryside. De facto if not de jure, they had become a permanent part of the urban population.

Transitional workers with attenuated ties to the countryside comprised a

[25]By way of illustration, 65 percent of the highly skilled Moscow typesetters had no ties to the village in 1907. Among the less skilled lithographers and bindery workers, only 24 percent and 28 percent, respectively, had relinquished their connection to the village; see V. A. Svavitskii and V. Sher, *Ocherk polozheniia rabochikh pechatnogo dela v Moskve (po dannym ankety, proizvedennoi obshchestvom rabochikh graficheskikh iskusstv v 1907 godu)* (St. Petersburg, 1909), pp. 8–9.

[26]*Perepis' Moskvy 1902 goda*, chast' 1, vyp. 2 (Moscow, 1906), p. 10.

[27]In 1907, one out of six Moscow typesetters had worked in two cities, and one out of sixteen had spent time in three; Svavitskii and Sher, *Ocherk polozheniia*, p. 11.

very substantial group in the Russian labor force. Their involvement with rural life was limited to the possession of a house or parcel of land (cultivated by family members or rented out) and the provision of monetary assistance to family members in the countryside. They did not themselves engage in agricultural cultivation, and in many cases their immediate family lived in the city or the factory village. It was not unusual for such workers to work in a factory or shop for ten, twenty, or even thirty years while continuing to hold a rural passport and to pay taxes for land in the village.

As Timofeev observes, transitional workers frequently had an ambivalent attitude toward the village. Many skilled workers, for example, regarded their ties as an encumbrance and wanted to sever their connections to the village once and for all. But a variety of circumstances prevented them from doing so. Above all, the village served as a form of social security for workers in the absence of state or employer assistance for unemployment, illness, injury, and old age. Thus, even though skilled workers often felt that the village was more of a hindrance than a help, they nevertheless held onto a house or land or sent money to relatives in order to protect themselves against adversity. For transitional workers, contact with the village had been sharply curtailed but not yet ruptured altogether. After long years in a factory or shop, many of them belonged, for all practical purposes, to the urban working class and viewed themselves as such.

The semipeasant worker, by contrast, maintained close and continuing relations with the village. By 1900, only a small percentage of the factory labor force in St. Petersburg and Moscow returned seasonally to the countryside to participate in cultivation. Regular returns to the village were a more frequent occurrence among workers in seasonal occupations such as tailoring where the off-season coincided with the agricultural cycle. Oliunina's survey conducted in 1910–1911 reveals that more than one-half of the tailoring shop workers and 78 percent of the subcontracting workers made three to five visits to their native village each year, remaining there for weeks or even months at a stretch.

The location of a worker's family was an important determinant of rural ties. Immediate family members (spouse and children) of male skilled workers were more likely to reside in the city than the family members of unskilled and semiskilled workers. In 1897, 69 percent of the married workers in the capital's metalworking industry maintained a wife and/or children in the countryside, whereas the corresponding figure for textile workers was 87 percent.[28] The unskilled workers who predominated in industries such as textiles generally had insufficient earnings to support a family that had been transplanted from the village although, as Pavlov observes, entire families sometimes went to work in the mills, including children.

In sum, workers' relations with the countryside showed considerable variation. Some segments of the labor force remained closely tied to the village, "and their conversations," as Kanatchikov recalls, "were mostly about grain, land, the harvest, and livestock."[29] In appearance, outlook, and family life they were still very much part of the rural environment. Gradually, however, some of these workers were becoming assimilated into the urban or factory milieu, with a corresponding attenuation of their links to the countryside. Finally, the urban workers—both city-born and those who had relinquished all connection to their native villages—comprised a small but growing group in Russian society. Kanatchikov eventually belonged to this category, as did many of his fellow patternmakers at the Gustav List factory who were "family men and were related to various petty bourgeois strata."[30] So, too, were the female seamstresses in Moscow tailoring shops, nearly all of them city-born, together with many clerical employees and others.

THE POSITION OF WOMEN WORKERS

By the turn of the century, women comprised a large and growing proportion of the nonagricultural labor force in Russia, occupying the lowest-skilled and lowest-paid positions in many different sectors of the economy. Manufacturing enterprises, both factory and artisanal, employed tens of thousands of women workers throughout the Empire. In 1900, slightly more than one out of every four factory workers was female. The number

---

[28]*Istoriia rabochikh Leningrada, 1703-fevral' 1917* (Leningrad, 1972), I, p. 184.
[29]See below, p. 48.
[30]See below, p. 47.

of factory women increased rapidly from 1905 on and by the outbreak of the First World War in 1914 they accounted for 31 percent of the industrial labor force.[31] Industrialists deliberately recruited female workers—sometimes as replacements for men—because they provided a cheap and compliant source of labor.

The textile industry was the largest single employer of female factory labor in Imperial Russia. As early as 1897, two out of five textile workers were women.[32] In factory villages of the Central Industrial Region described by Pavlov, entire families often entered employment in the mill. Wives and daughters would be found in relatively low-skilled occupations such as spinning or carding, while male workers were employed as machinists or fabric printers.

Female labor was also widespread in some artisanal trades. The large apparel industry attracted many women workers, both in urban workshops and in rural villages where putting-out arrangements were rapidly proliferating. Two out of three garment workers in St. Petersburg and Moscow were female at the turn of the century.[33] As in the textile industry, women in the apparel trades were concentrated in relatively low-skilled jobs and they earned lower wages than male workers, even when they did identical work. Thus, women subcontract workers received 85 percent of the wages paid to male workers; women in tailoring shops earned a mere 55 percent.

This pattern can be discerned in virtually all industries and occupations where women were employed at the beginning of the twentieth century.[34] Comprising about one-tenth of the salesclerks in St. Petersburg and Moscow, women characteristically held jobs in food stores and other retail establishments where wages, hours, and working conditions were least desirable. In St. Petersburg and Moscow, the wage rates for female shop

[31]A. G. Rashin, *Formirovanie rabochego klassa Rossii. Istoriko-ekonomicheskie ocherki* (Moscow, 1958), pp. 225, 236. For a comprehensive discussion of working women in tsarist Russia, see Rose L. Glickman, *Russian Factory Women: Workplace and Society, 1880–1914* (Berkeley and Los Angeles, 1984).

[32]Glickman, *Russian Factory Women*, Table 5.

[33]*Perepis' Moskvy 1902 goda*, chast' 1, vyp. 2, pp. 68–72; *S.-Peterburg po perepisi 15 dekabria 1900 g.*, vyp. 2 (St. Petersburg, 1903), pp. 112–115, 117, 119–121.

[34]Rose L. Glickman, "The Russian Factory Woman, 1880–1914," in *Women in Russia*, ed. Dorothy Atkinson, Alexander Dallin, and Gail Warshofsky Lapidus (Stanford, 1977), p. 69.

clerks were only about one-half those of their male counterparts and in Odessa, 41 percent.

Working-class life in Russia was harsh for men and women alike, but women faced exceptional hardships as a consequence of their confinement to low-skilled, low-paying, and low-status jobs, and their multiple burdens as workers, housewives, and mothers. "Female labor," observes Gudvan, ". . . deserves to be considered as a separate subject because of its unique features."[35] The special difficulties experienced by women are recounted in this volume by Oliunina and Gudvan, whose studies of garment and sales-clerical workers brought them into contact with some of the most defence-less and downtrodden segments of the female labor force. Sexual abuse was commonplace in the tailoring firms where young female apprentices were victimized by shop owners and male workers. Impoverished female shop clerks and clerical workers were often expected to provide sexual favors for employers as a condition for hiring or continued employment; in some cases, they turned to prostitution. Situations such as these were not, of course, restricted only to artisanal, sales, and clerical occupations. Factory workers, domestic servants, and many other women workers faced similar depredations.

STANDARDS OF LIVING

Workers occupied a wide range of positions in the labor hierarchy, and they experienced correspondingly diverse standards of living. Wages, of course, showed considerable variation depending on such factors as skill, geographical location, gender, and age. Differential earnings corresponded, in turn, to different consumption patterns and contrasting levels of material well-being. But in Russia as elsewhere, living standards involved more than just lodging, food, apparel, and the recreational and cultural activities a worker could procure. These were, to be sure, critical aspects of a worker's life, and contemporaries attached enormous importance to their quality and availability. Yet there was another, less tangible consideration that profoundly affected living standards: the extent to which the individual could exercise control over the everyday decisions of his or her life.

[35] See below, p. 193.

ı this connection, a sharp distinction must be drawn between employer-provided lodging and/or food and the arrangements made by a worker independently of employer supervision. As all the selections in this volume attest, workers who depended on the employer for lodging and/or food were subjected to a strict regimen, both on the job and during their free time. They forfeited their autonomy during nonworking hours and became subordinate to the whims and regulations of the employer, whose unbridled authority in these matters was seldom tempered by paternalistic considerations.

Lodging

At the beginning of the twentieth century, many Russian workers depended upon their employer for housing. In artisanal, sales, and service occupations, workers frequently lived on the very premises where they labored during working hours. This situation was widespread among such groups as tailors (as described by Oliunina), bakers, shoemakers, and other urban craftsmen for whom the small workshop remained the characteristic unit of production. Saleclerks, too, sometimes lived in or adjacent to the shops where they worked, often sleeping on wooden planks in the kitchen or pantry, an arrangement observed by Gudvan.

Workers obliged to live on the premises of the shop had to endure the continual surveillance of the employer, who often endeavored to control not only working hours but leisure time as well. In some small shops, employers locked the doors at the end of the workday to prevent workers from departing.[36] Owners sometimes imposed curfews on workers and required regular church attendance. Thus, even during nonworking hours, the employees in these shops had little control over their lives.

The situation was scarcely better for factory workers living in employer-provided housing. In 1897, two out of every five factory workers in Russia still lived in a company dormitory or in barracks.[37] This arrangement was more prevalent in factory villages—the large manufacturing centers in rural Russia—than in major urban centers. Nevertheless, Kanatchikov notes

---

[36]On this point, see the discussion of small bakeries in *Professional'noe dvizhenie Moskovskikh pishchevikov v gody pervoi revoliutsii*, (Moscow, 1927), I, pp. 102, 147.

[37]Iu. K. Kir'ianov, *Zhiznennyi uroven' rabochikh Rossii* (Moscow, 1979), p. 227.

that the Mytishchensk railroad car factory, which opened in Moscow in 1896, included both little wooden houses and enormous barracks for bachelors. Timofeev describes a workers' dormitory operated by a small metalworking factory in St. Petersburg. Only 10 percent of the capital's factory workers occupied employer housing, however. Most of the workers in employer housing were in industries such as textiles where the labor force included many semipeasant elements.[38]

In the factory villages of the Central Industrial Region, by contrast, about one-half of the workers were housed on company premises. A survey conducted in Moscow province in 1904, for example, disclosed that 56 percent of the factory labor force occupied employer-provided lodging.[39] Another study of workers' budgets conducted in the Bogorodsk textile district of Moscow province in 1908 showed that married workers spent an average of 15 percent of their earnings on factory housing, whereas single workers spent an average of 3 percent.[40] The latter group inhabited barracks of the type described by Pavlov, where rental charges were as minimal as the comfort and privacy they afforded. The workers in these rural factory districts who did not live in company housing either rented accommodations outside the factory gates or lived in their own cottages nearby.

The evidence indicates that many workers were far from satisfied with company housing. As Pavlov observes, factory lodgings usually resembled military barracks or a prison with their bleak uniformity, cramped conditions, lack of privacy, and regimentation. To be sure, some workers could recall even worse conditions in factories of an earlier decade, and for some peasants even the dismal dormitories and barracks represented an improvement over the peasant hovels they had left behind. Yet there were many others who longed for a cottage of their own, with a barn and garden beside it. Individual dwellings, as one worker put it to Pavlov, provided privacy and the freedom to do as one pleased.

[38]*Ibid.*, ch. 4.

[39] Other surveys confirm this general trend. A survey conducted in 1897 in Vladimir province showed that 42 percent of the workers occupied company housing; a survey of the Bogorodsk district in Moscow province in 1899 showed that the proportion was 49 percent. *Ibid.*, p. 228.

[40]N. K. Druzhinin, *Usloviia byta rabochikh v dorevoliutsionnoi Rossii (po dannym biudzhetnykh obsledovanii)* (Moscow, 1958), p. 107.

Contemporary investigations confirm the impression conveyed by Pavlov that workers sought to flee company housing whenever possible and to move into the private sector. Those who rented private accommodations faced several options. Some joined an artel (*artel'*), a cooperative living arrangement. The artel was most frequently encountered among male workers from the same or neighboring districts in the countryside. United by a common bond as *zemliaki* (fellow countrymen), they pooled their resources to rent an apartment, purchase food, and prepare common meals.[41] When Kanatchikov first arrived in Moscow to begin apprenticeship training, his father placed him in one such artel under the supervision of a fellow villager. Timofeev emphasizes the close bonds among the *zemliaki,* most of them semipeasant workers holding unskilled or semiskilled jobs. Once a worker became more fully and permanently integrated into the urban milieu, he generally withdrew from the artel and sought other types of housing that afforded greater privacy.[42] Thus, the young Kanatchikov, after obtaining his first job as a fully qualified patternmaker, left the artel and moved into the apartment of a fellow worker and his wife.

In major urban centers, the housing supply failed to keep pace with the rapid growth of the laboring population, and accommodations for workers were scarce and costly. At the turn of the century, few workers could afford the luxury of a private apartment, and entire families often occupied a room or even half a room, while single workers commonly rented a corner of a room (*ugol*) or merely a cot (*koika*). A survey conducted in St. Petersburg in 1900 revealed that in the city as a whole, there were 1.7 persons per room in apartments, 3.2 people per room in one-room flats, and 3.4 people in cellars. Another survey taken in St. Petersburg in 1904 showed that it was not uncommon for six people to occupy a single room and for five or more people to share a bed.[43]

Expenditures on housing generally represented one of the largest items in a worker's budget. St. Petersburg workers who rented lodging outside the factory or shop, for example, typically spent 21 percent of their earnings for this purpose if they were married, 15 percent if they were single.[44]

[41]For a discussion of the artel, see Johnson, *Peasant and Proletarian,* pp. 72–73, 91–92.
[42]Kir'ianov, *Zhiznennyi uroven',* p. 228.
[43]Bater, *St. Petersburg,* p. 336.
[44]Druzhinin, *Usloviia,* p. 116; the data apply to 1908.

In exchange for their hard-earned money, however, workers usually found themselves housed in filthy slums that were overcrowded, damp, and cold. Mariia Pokrovskaia, a doctor who investigated housing conditions among Petersburg workers around the turn of the century, has summarized her findings:

> The general impression I had of the housing of Petersburg workers can be stated briefly. In these dwellings there is dampness, filth, darkness, foul air. Frequently there is no running water or flush toilets, which constitute an essential part of any comfortable dwelling. In the vast majority of cases, tenants use the primitive outhouses which contaminate the ground and spread stench in backyards and apartments.[45]

Notwithstanding the deplorable conditions in workers' housing, those who lived outside the factory or shop enjoyed one important advantage: the freedom to dispose of their nonworking time as they pleased. Living in private lodgings gave workers considerably more contact with city life than they would have had in company housing and far greater discretion over their activities. In stores and taverns, on trams and in the crowded streets, workers came into contact with many different segments of the urban population. Some of them—typically the more skilled, literate, and prosperous workers with shorter hours and higher wages—took advantage of the cultural, recreational, and educational options available in a big city. But even in a factory village, workers who inhabited a cottage beyond the factory gates had certain freedoms and pleasures unavailable in the dormitory or company barracks. They often kept a garden and raised some livestock, and, most important of all, they could conduct themselves as they pleased, without submitting to onerous regulations or enduring the prying eyes of fellow workers.

Food

Expenditures for food (excluding alcohol) represented the largest item in every worker's budget, consuming 31 to 48 percent of total earnings if

[45]M. I. Pokrovskaia, *Po podvalam, cherdakam i uglovym kvartiram Peterburga* (St. Petersburg, 1903), p. 31.

the worker was single and 38 to 52 percent if married.[46] Many workers—
even some who did not live in employer-provided housing—depended on
the employer to provide meals. In artisanal trades, shop owners often
furnished meals, deducting the cost from workers' wages. This arrangement could be found in numerous subcontracting shops where, as
Oliunina observed, workers and the owner sometimes ate out of one large
earthenware or enamel pot.

Some factories also served meals to employees, but this arrangement
was encountered far less frequently than in workshops. A 1908 survey of
Petersburg factory workers found that only 38 out of 632 respondents (6
percent) took their meals at the employer's facility.[47] More commonly,
factory workers had their main meal either at an artel, their place of
residence, or in a local tavern or canteen. In still other cases, workers
brought along food that was eaten cold on the premises of the firm. The
type of arrangement depended, above all, on the distance between a
worker's lodging and place of employment.

The midday meal break generally lasted one and a half hours, and by
Russian custom this was the major meal of the day. Normally it was a hot
meal that included soup as well as kasha or potatoes. Together with bread,
these were the staples in the Russian worker's diet. One study of workers'
budgets revealed that as much as one-half of the expenditures on food
were allocated for starch; 9 to 19 percent of the food budget typically went
for meat and meat products.[48] The lack of sufficient meat in the diet
sometimes gave rise to complaints by workers. As related by Oliunina,
striking tailors in 1911 demanded that their employer provide beef twice a
week and that each worker be supplied with an individual plate.

Alcohol

Alcohol consumption was a major aspect of the Russian worker's daily
life—both at the workplace, where it was an intrinsic part of many rituals

---

[46]Druzhinin, *Usloviia*, p. 107. These data are based on three surveys conducted in 1908
involving a sample of Petersburg textile workers, workers in a factory in the Bogorodsk
district of Moscow province, and workers in a factory in Kostroma province.

[47]S. N. Prokopovich, *Biudzhety Peterburgskikh rabochikh* (St. Petersburg, 1909), p. 12.

[48]Druzhinin, *Usloviia, p. 112.*

and customs, and outside the workplace, where drinking was the inevitable accompaniment of social occasions and a convenient escape from the dreary and monotonous work routine. Expenditures on alcohol sometimes represented a considerable part of a worker's budget. Surveys conducted in St. Petersburg and the Central Industrial Region disclosed that textile workers spent 2 to 10 percent of their wages on alcohol.[49] Oliunina's study of Moscow tailors indicates that in some cases expenditures were far higher.

All of the selections in this volume illustrate the ubiquitousness of alcohol consumption and widespread drunkenness among male workers. The communal aspects of drinking deserve special attention. There was scarcely an event in working-class life that did not culminate in communal drinking. By way of illustration, the new worker on the shop floor, the newly promoted foreman, and the newly elected shop elder were all expected to buy a round of drinks. On paydays (Saturdays), workers frequently went from the factory or shop to the local tavern. Still suffering from the aftereffects of protracted drinking when work resumed on Monday, many workers continued their carousing on the job.

The authors in this collection offer various explanations for the widespread consumption of alcohol. Kanatchikov and Timofeev focus on the social pressure to participate in drinking bouts. Oliunina and Gudvan emphasize the attractions of alcohol for workers with harsh, often confining, conditions in their daily lives. Pavlov draws attention to the lack of alternative forms of leisure time activities in factory villages. Boredom, he suggests, impelled many workers to turn to alcohol as a means of diversion from an otherwise monotonous and routine existence.

Leisure Time Activities

The workday for most Russian workers lasted at least eleven hours and in some cases far longer. Typically, a worker was on the job six days a week, and some segments of the labor force—such as salesclerks—were required to work seven days a week. Yet despite the limited number of nonworking

[49]*Ibid.*, pp. 36, 107. The highest expenditure in these surveys was by single male workers in the Petersburg textile industry.

hours available for leisure time activities, workers found many different ways of occupying themselves when not at the workbench, the machine, or the sales counter.

The selections in this volume illustrate the kinds of activities in which workers engaged during nonworking hours. Visits to the local tavern provided, as we have seen, a widespread form of recreation, as did alcohol consumption generally. Many workers found relaxation in card games and various forms of gambling. Organizations, including clubs and mutual benefit societies, held social dances that enjoyed great popularity among younger workers. Kanatchikov's earnest efforts to acquire social graces and dance instruction from a "how-to" book reflect the mentality of young better-off worker-aristocrats in the urban labor force who were eager to emulate their social superiors.

Not all leisure time activities were frivolous, however. Kanatchikov recalls visiting museums in Moscow, and some workers attended theatrical performances and concerts as well. Church attendance was widespread among workers. An ethnographic study conducted in the 1920s reported that 70 percent of the male workers and 85 percent of the female workers who were interviewed had attended church prior to the 1917 revolution.[50]

Some workers devoted their nonworking hours to self-improvement, including intellectual pursuits. In 1897, 74 percent of the male workers in St. Petersburg and 40 percent of the females were classified as literate. This was higher than in the Russian Empire as a whole where only 52 percent of the working population (both male and female) could claim basic literacy in that year.[51] Literacy was correlated, above all, with skill and age. Industries and occupations with a high proportion of skilled workers, such as metalworking, showed a correspondingly high rate of literacy. In St. Petersburg, 73 percent of the metalworkers were literate compared with 44 percent in textiles.[52]

Although no systematic data were collected on the proportion of liter-

[50]E. O. Kabo, *Ocherki rabochego byta. Opyt monograficheskogo issledovaniia domashnogo rabochego byta* (Moscow, 1928), I, p. 132.

[51]*Chislennost'*, I, Table 3, p. 2; II, Table 3 *(prilozhenie)*, p. 16.

[52]U. A. Shuster, *Peterburgskie rabochie v 1905-1907 gg.* (Leningrad, 1976), p. 52.

ate workers in artisanal trades, we know that some trades made basic literacy a prerequisite for entry into apprenticeship.[33] Oliunina's study of Moscow tailors reveals that in tailoring shops, 89 percent of the male workers and 90 percent of the female workers were literate in her sample. By contrast, only 73 percent of the men in subcontracting shops and 67 percent of the women were literate. Among salesclerks, literacy was often a requirement for the job, and according to Gudvan, nearly 88 percent of the country's clerks had attained literacy at the beginning of the twentieth century.

In assessing these data, it must be kept in mind that literacy often entailed little more than a very rudimentary ability to read. But if many literate workers were unable to read anything but the simplest text, there was a small but growing group of cultivated workers who sometimes attained a high level of intellectual development. Pavlov professes his amazement at discovering worker-intellectuals in the textile mill where he was employed in the 1890s. Such individuals were far more prevalent in other industries such as metalworking or printing. The two worker-authors in this volume, Kanatchikov and Timofeev, exemplify the new type of worker-intelligentsia that was emerging in Russia at the beginning of the twentieth century.

Apart from a small stratum of worker-intellectuals, there was a far larger group of literate workers. They have been described by Jeffrey Brooks:

Though their reading habits were in some respects similar to the peasants', the workers, concentrated in the cities with a high rate of literacy, formed the core of a new lower-class reading public for whom the written word was increasingly the dominant means of articulating social values and developing class consciousness. Unlike the countryside, the city was an environment filled with printed words. In the streets, in the shops, in places of work, announcements, signs, newspapers and books beckoned those who were able to read. Workers had

---

[33]By way of illustration, completion of rural primary school was a requirement for entry into apprenticeship in precious metalworking; see N. Mamontov, "Dvizhenie rabochikh po obrabotke blagorodnykh metallov v Moskve v 1905 g. (po lichnym vospominaniiam)," *Materialy po istorii professional'nogo dvizheniia v SSSR*, (Moscow, 1927), V, pp. 180–181.

more money to spend than peasants and, small though their expenditures on 'culture' were, they were still significant.[54]

The new working-class reading public was attracted to adventure and morality tales, much like their counterparts who remained behind in the countryside. Tales such as these were published both in book form and as serials in leading newspapers. Kanatchikov recalls that he and other members of his artel were fascinated by the lurid installments of stories published in *Moskovskii listok* (Moscow Sheet); they even shared a common subscription to the newspaper.

It was not until after the Revolution of 1905 that a new type of newspaper emerged, geared explicitly to the growing urban lower-class reading public. The so-called "kopeck" newspapers first made an appearance in St. Petersburg and then spread to Moscow and other cities.[55] Named for their low price, these newspapers swiftly acquired a huge circulation drawn mainly from the working population. A legal trade union and radical press appeared beginning in 1905, and it, too, was directed to a working-class audience. Although the circulation of these newspapers was far less impressive than that of the "kopeck" papers, they nevertheless had considerable appeal among workers. Their emphasis on political topics, in many cases approached from a socialist perspective, attracted a readership among the more sophisticated and activist segments of the labor force.

THE ASPIRATIONS OF WORKERS

"In the ten years that I have lived with workers," Timofeev wrote in 1905, "I have rarely met anyone who did not dream of changing his occupation."[56] All of the selections in this volume touch upon the issue of workers' aspirations, that is, their hopes and dreams and their visions of an alternative to the present. For some, this vision centered around a return to rural life, stripped of the painful features that had compelled many to flee the

---

[54]Jeffrey Brooks, "Readers and Reading at the End of the Tsarist Era," in *Literature and Society in Imperial Russia 1800–1914*, ed. William Mills Todd III (Stanford, 1978), p. 142.
  [55]*Ibid*, pp. 146–147. Petersburg's *Gazeta Kopeika* first appeared in 1908.
  [56]See below, p. 101.

countryside for factories and shops.[57] Others envisioned a blend of rural and factory life that combined the best features of both worlds. This image is illustrated by Krasnov, the skilled and well-paid metalfitter in a textile mill who dreams of a factory village in which workers inhabit individual huts, each with a barn, a vegetable garden, livestock, pigs, and chickens.

For another group of workers, the primary aspiration was to achieve mobility and prosperity within the factory itself. For a blue-collar worker, there were several channels for upward mobility. Some workers advanced into the ranks of work crew leaders, assistant foremen, and even foremen. The foreman occupied the highest position a worker could attain in terms of wages, status, and responsibility within the enterprise. Consequently, as noted by Timofeev, there were always workers who aspired to this position and who were prepared to take whatever steps were necessary to achieve it. If some aspired to join the ranks of low-level supervisory personnel, still others sought to advance from unskilled or semiskilled jobs to a skilled trade. As we have seen, the aspiration to become a *masterovoi* in the factory involved not only economic considerations but issues of status and dignity as well.

There were some, however, who sought to flee the bosses and to set themselves up as independent workers. In artisanal trades, garret-masters found a certain measure of independence from direct supervision when they began working at home, often with the aid of other family members. Enterprising artisans sometimes even set up shop as subcontractors or, more rarely, on a retail basis. The dream of becoming one's own master and owning a shop had not been entirely dissipated by the beginning of the twentieth century although in reality few artisanal workers could succeed in this endeavor.

Many salesclerks, as Gudvan observes, harbored the vision of becoming shop owners. They came to believe early on that money would free them from the deprivation and humiliation they had known since childhood, making them master over others. Consequently, some clerks tried to accumulate sufficient savings to open a small stall or a shop of their own. By the

[57]For a penetrating discussion of workers' images of alternative arrangements, see Barrington Moore, Jr., *Injustice: The Social Bases of Obedience and Revolt* (White Plains, N.Y., 1978), pp. 208–216.

end of the nineteenth century, however, large retail establishments and department stores intensified the competition for small firms, sharply curtailing the opportunities for independent entrepreneurship by working people.

One theme predominates in the discussions of workers' aspirations: the strong desire among workers to achieve more control over their lives, both at the workplace and outside it. In some cases, this meant the relative independence of the peasant proprietor. For others, it signified independent entrepreneurship or elevation into the ranks of managerial personnel. During the Revolution of 1905, another conception of the future gained currency among workers—the image of a new kind of society altogether. Partly under the influence of radical intellectuals, partly as a consequence of their own struggles with employers and the government, some workers began to envision an entirely new form of social organization in which they would attain dignity, civil and political rights, and the control over their everyday lives that most were denied under the prevailing order.

A NOTE ON THE AUTHORS

The authors in this collection speak, as it were, with different voices. Their accounts illustrate the complex and varied contemporary perceptions of the workers' milieu as well as the diversity of experiences and conditions within the laboring population. Exemplifying three major groups on the Russian labor scene—workers, technical and managerial personnel, and intelligentsia sympathizers and activists—they allow us to enter the world of Russian workers and to gain new understanding of life and labor during the final years of the tsarist regime.

With the exception of Kanatchikov, regrettably little is known about the life histories of these authors—their backgrounds, their careers, and their fate in the years following the October Revolution. Semen Ivanovich Kanatchikov alone among them went on to attain a prominent position in the post-October regime, thereby preserving for posterity an historical record of his life.

Kanatchikov was born in 1879 into a peasant family in Moscow province and arrived in Moscow to begin an apprenticeship in 1895. At this point he began the long journey from peasant to "conscious" worker and political activist.[58] His first contacts with the radical underground took place in 1899, following his move to St. Petersburg. There he joined an illegal Social Democratic circle, where he received his first systematic exposure to socialist ideas. As a result, he was soon arrested and sent into exile in the provincial town of Saratov. It is unclear when Kanatchikov formally joined the Russian Social Democratic Workers' Party (RSDRP)—one Soviet source erroneously dates his entry into the party in 1898[59]—but following the party's factional split into Mensheviks and Bolsheviks (1903), Kanatchikov sided with the Bolsheviks, to whom he remained loyal throughout his career.

During the 1905 revolution, Kanatchikov joined the RSDRP's Moscow Committee (Bolshevik), a step that launched his career as a "professional revolutionary."[60] During the next half-decade—until his arrest in 1910—he carried on party work in several different cities. Between 1908 and 1910 he was one of the few Bolshevik activists in the capital to become deeply involved in the trade union movement, participating both in the Petersburg metalworkers' and woodworkers' unions.

Following the February Revolution, Kanatchikov resumed his party activities, and after October he emerged as one of the prominent worker-Bolsheviks in the new regime. In 1919 he became the dean of the Communist University in Petrograd, retaining this post for five years. He then directed the press section and the party history section of the Central Committee of the Communist Party. In 1926 he was sent to Czechoslovakia as a correspondent for the Soviet news agency Tass, a position he held for two years. After returning to the Soviet Union in 1928, he served in various capacities as an editor and journalist. He died in 1940.

Kanatchikov's memoirs were first published in 1924—though parts were almost certainly drafted considerably earlier—and reissued in 1929 and 1934. At the time of the original publication of the memoirs, the

---

[58]See Zelnik's "Russian Bebels" for an illuminating discussion of Kanatchikov's psychological development as well as an account of his career before and after 1917. Also on his career, see the entry in the *Bol'shaia sovetskaia entsiklopediia*, 3rd ed. (Moscow, 1973), XI, p. 321.

[59]*Bol'shaia Sovetskaia entsiklopediia*, 3rd ed., XI, p. 321.

[60]Zelnik, "Russian Bebels," pt. 2; the following description of Kanatchikov's career draws upon this source.

atmosphere in Russia was still relatively tolerant, and Kanatchikov's account is notable for its candor and lack of ideological rhetoric.

Far less is known about the second author, P. Timofeev (pseudonym for P. Remezov). Like Kanatchikov, Timofeev acquired a skilled trade (probably metalfitting) in the 1890s. He, too, was attracted to the illegal underground Social Democratic circles that functioned in the capital at the end of the 1890s. According to his reminiscences, the circle that he joined

> was considered social democratic, but not because we all knew Marx and shared the SD party program, but simply on the basis of the popularity of the word "social democrat." In it we discerned an oppositional spirit, a symbol of struggle, and not the struggle of one against many, but an organized comradely struggle. Our student propagandist called himself a social democrat, and could we, his students, have labeled ourselves any differently?[61]

Unlike Kanatchikov, however, Timofeev did not join the SD party. Indeed, his writings suggest that Social Democratic ideology never fully appealed to him. He belonged to the ranks of those educated workers who instinctively bridled at the involvement of radical intellectuals in the workers' milieu. Together with many others like him, Timofeev resented what he took to be the haughty attitude of radical intellectuals, sensing that they lacked a true knowledge or understanding of working-class life.[62] He also experienced a good deal of discomfort in the presence of radical mentors from the educated classes—a problem familiar to other worker-intellectuals.[63]

Timofeev eventually gravitated to the Socialist Revolutionaries (SRs), though it is unclear whether he actually joined this pro-peasant party or simply remained a sympathizer. Nor is it possible to determine if his attraction to the SRs was due to his strong peasant background and ties or to some other—perhaps ideological—consideration. In any event, he had entered into close contact with the SRs by 1906. His writings appeared in *Russkoe bogatstvo* (Russian Wealth), a journal with pronounced SR leanings, and he himself made a point of stressing the positive features of this

---

[61]P. Timofeev, "Rabochie i politika," *Russkoe bogatstvo*, 8 (Aug. 1906): 172.

[62]*Ibid.*, pp. 172–174.

[63]On this important issue, see Wildman, *Making of a Workers' Revolution;* and Zelnik, "Russian Bebels," pt. 2.

"socialist" party. Nothing is known of Timofeev's subsequent career or even, for that matter, the date of his death.

Fedor Pavlovich Pavlov (pseudonym for A. N. Bykov), the third author, was an engineer by profession. During the 1890s he spent six years working at textile mills in the Central Industrial Region. His departure from the region was the result of a series of disagreements with his employer over issues relating to workers' grievances. In 1897 Pavlov went to France where he visited a shipbuilding factory in Toulon and the silk manufacturing district of Lyon. Upon returning to Russia, he wrote his impressions of factory life in the Central Industrial Region and in France. These observations were published first in the Moscow newspaper *Moskovskie vedomosti* (Moscow Gazette) and then in book form in 1901.

By sensibility, Pavlov belonged to the liberal-minded elements in Russian society at the end of the nineteenth century, those groups in the cities and countryside who felt growing dismay at the widespread misery and brutalization of the lower classes. The six years he spent in Russian textile mills helped to awaken his social conscience, and his subsequent trip to France fortified his critical attitude. Pavlov displays particular animosity toward the factory director at the mill, whose quest for profits made him impervious to elementary human rights and the material and spiritual well-being of the thousands of workers subject to his control. The factory inspector, by contrast, is presented in a highly favorable light. Indeed, one finds a sensibility very similar to Pavlov's in the memoirs of S. Gvozdev, a factory inspector in the Central Industrial Region from 1894 to 1908.[64] Both Pavlov and Gvozdev maintain a sympathetic, if somewhat distant, attitude toward workers while deploring contemporary conditions and looking for ways to establish a more humane and rational organization of factory life.

E. A. Oliunina was a student at the Higher Women's Courses in Moscow, a postsecondary institution for female students. She studied under the supervision of one of the school's leading faculty members—Iosif Gol'dshtein—and it was in his seminar on political economy that Oliunina undertook her study of Moscow tailors in 1910–1911. But Oliunina was not simply a disinterested observer of the garment workers.

[64]S. Gvozdev, *Zapiski fabrichnogo inspektora, iz nabliudenii i praktiki v periode 1894–1908 gg.* (Moscow, 1911). Gvozdev refers to Pavlov's account at the outset of his book.

During the Revolution of 1905, she had been one of the leading intelligentsia activists who assisted Moscow tailors to organize their first trade union.[65] Although the evidence is scanty, it appears that she was a Menshevik sympathizer in 1905. Oliunina evidently remained active on behalf of the garment workers following the October Revolution. In 1927, she published a book on the formation of the all-Russian union of tailoring workers in the Soviet Union.[66]

The final author in the collection, A. M. Gudvan, lived in Odessa and was obviously a person of considerable education when he embarked on his research into the subject of sales-clerical workers in 1899. He began collecting survey data on sales-clerical workers in Odessa as part of a crusade to achieve government regulation of working hours in commercial establishments. In 1901 he represented Odessa salesclerks and bookkeepers in deliberations at the Ministry of Finance over laws limiting the worktime of sales and clerical personnel. When Odessa shop clerks formed a trade union in 1906, Gudvan was elected to the first directing board of the new organization. The union proved short-lived, but in 1907 Gudvan was again active in the campaign for government regulation of the worktime of sales-clerical employees.[67]

Gudvan's first publication appeared in 1903, a book-length study of Odessa salesclerks. This was followed by a series of publications focusing on the plight of sales-clerical groups not only in Odessa but in Kiev, Warsaw, St. Petersburg, Moscow, and elsewhere in the Russian Empire. In all, Gudvan published nine books between 1903 and 1925 (the date of his last known publication) and eleven articles. Only one publication appeared in the post-October period: his survey of the history of sales-clerical workers (1925) from which our selection is taken. This comprehensive and detailed study of sales-clerical groups, drawing upon two and a half decades of research and personal observation, marks the end of Gudvan's career as a writer. His subsequent fate is not known.

---

[65]For a discussion of the formation of this union, see Bonnell, *Roots of Rebellion*, Ch. 3.

[66]E. A. Oliunina, *Organizatsiia vserossiiskogo soiuza rabochikh shveinikov* (Moscow, 1927).

[67]N. Luninskii, "Soiuz prikazchikov Odessy (1905–1917 gg.)," in *Professional'noe dvizhenie sluzhashchikh Ukrainy (1905–1907 gg.) Sbornik* ed. I. S. Stepanskii (n.p., n.d.), pp. 70, 74–75.

Part One: Metalworkers

I

S. I. Kanatchikov

From the Story of My Life†

$\mathbf{M}$y departure was invested with a
certain solemnity. In the morning Father gathered the entire family in the
cottage and lit the icon lamps in front of the images of the saints. Everyone
sat on the benches in solemn silence and waited. Then Father arose and
began to pray to the icon. The entire family followed his example. When
the prayer was over, Father addressed me with his parting words, once
more reminding me not to forget God, to honor my superiors, to serve my
employer honestly, and, above all else, to be mindful of our home.

In the spring of 1895, when I was sixteen years old, Father drove me to
Moscow where he placed me into apprenticeship at the Gustav List
engineering works.[1] Since there was no place in the pattern shop, I began in
the painting shop.

---

†Translated and annotated by Reginald E. Zelnik.

[1]The List engineering works, founded in 1863, was a moderately large machine-
construction plant (550 workers in 1890, 800 in 1897), located on the southern bank of
the Moscow River, just below the Kremlin. It specialized in the manufacture of steam
engines, fire-fighting pumps, and scales.

IN THE ARTEL[2]

I remember what a stunning impression Moscow made on me. My father and I, sitting in our cart, walked our gray horse along the brightly lighted streets. Huge multistoried houses—most of them with lighted windows—stores, shops, taverns, beer halls, horse-drawn carriages going by, a horse-drawn tramway, and all around us—crowds of bustling people, rushing to unknown destinations for unknown reasons. I was not even able to read the signboards. What struck me most was the abundance of stores and shops: for every house, there was one store after another.

1. Moscow street, Gazetnyi pereulok, around the turn of the century.

[2]The artel (*artel'*) was an ancient Russian folk institution with roots dating back to the medieval period. The term is sometimes rendered in English as "cooperative," but by the end of the nineteenth century it was applied to so wide a variety of institutions as to defy any single, uniform translation. Here Kanatchikov is using the term to describe a cooperative living arrangement among workers, some of whom came from the same village or region. Members of the artel shared the costs of rent, food, fuel, and the cook's wages.

"Who buys all these goods?" I asked my father. "Why, there are more stores here than there are people!"

"Mother Moscow, she feeds all of Russia. Our tradesmen also come here for merchandise," Father responded, coughing and moaning from shortness of breath.

Compared with our village hovels, what struck me about the houses of Moscow was their grandiose appearance, their luxury.

"Am I to live in a house like that?" I asked with delight.

"You'll find out in due course."

And sure enough our gray horse soon turned into a side street, and the wagon entered the gates of a huge stone house with a courtyard that looked like a large stone well. Wet linens dangled from taut clotheslines all along the upper stories. The courtyard smelled of an acrid stench and carbolic acid.[3] Throughout the courtyard glittered dirty puddles of water and discarded vegetables. In the apartments and all around the courtyard people were crowding, making noise, yelling, cursing.

My delight was beginning to turn into depression, into some kind of inexplicable terror before the grandiose appearance and cold indifference of my surroundings. I felt like a small insignificant grain of sand, lost in the unfamiliar and hostile sea of people that surrounded me.

On the evening of the same day, my father and I, together with our countryman[4] Korovin, who had arranged my job at the factory,[5] went to a tavern. Father ordered tea for three, with rolls and a pint of vodka.

Korovin—tall, round-shouldered, wearing a goatee, in a faded, knitted jacket worn over his shirt—adopted the strict, preceptorial attitude of a teacher with me. But when the pint had taken effect, he began to brag

---

[3]Probably from coal tar, accumulated in the yard.

[4]In Russian, *zemliak*, the equivalent of the German *Landsmann*. Normally the term was used to refer to persons who hailed from the same village, clearly the meaning intended here. It could also be used, however, to refer to natives of different, usually neighboring, villages in the same region. For a discussion of the importance of the community bonds linking immigrant countrymen residing in Moscow, see Robert E. Johnson, *Peasant and Proletarian: The Working Class of Moscow in the Late Nineteenth Century* (New Brunswick, N.J., 1979), Ch. 4.

[5]It was customary for workers employed in urban factories to assist their newly arrived countrymen, either by prearrangement or upon their arrival, to obtain work at their factories. On this point, see the memoirs of P. Timofeev, Ch. 2, below.

about his closeness to the foreman, his knowledge of his craft, his high wage, and his plan to build a two-story house in the village.

Father sat quietly, nodding his head in approval, occasionally offering advice on the building of the house. At the end of the evening Father asked Korovin to treat me strictly, to keep me from consorting and getting into mischief with the wrong kind of people. And he again admonished me to be obedient to my bosses and superiors and have faith in God.

On the following day, early in the morning, Father departed for the village, and I remained alone. Two feelings were struggling in my soul. I longed for the village, for the meadows, the brook, the bright country sun, the free clear air of the fields, and for the people who were near and dear to me. Here, in the hostile world of Moscow, I felt lonely, abandoned, needed by no one. While at work in the painting shop to which I'd been temporarily assigned, which smelled of paint and turpentine, I would remember pictures of our village life, tears would come to my eyes, and it was only with great effort that I could keep from crying. But there was another, more powerful feeling that gave me courage and steadfastness: my awareness of my independence, my longing to make contact with people, to become independent and proud, to live in accordance with my own wishes, and not by the caprice and will of my father.

Awkward, sluggish, with long hair that had been cut under a round bowl,[6] wearing heavy boots with horseshoes, I was a typical village youth. The skilled workers looked down on me with scorn, pinched me by the ear, pulled me by the hair, called me a "green country bumpkin" and other insulting names.

Our workday at the factory lasted eleven and a half hours, plus a one-and-a-half-hour lunch break. In the beginning I would grow terribly tired so that as soon as I got home from work and ate dinner, I would fall into my filthy, hard, straw-filled sack and sleep like a dead man, despite the myriads of bedbugs and fleas.

I roomed and boarded not far from the factory, in a large, smelly house inhabited by all kinds of poor folk—peddlers, cabmen, casual laborers, and

---

[6]The hair of village boys was frequently cut *pod kruzhok,* i.e., by placing an inverted bowl or comparable round object over their heads and trimming all around beneath the rim.

We rented the apartment communally, as an artel of about fifteen ne were bachelors, others had wives who lived in the village and ran households. I was put in a tiny, dark, windowless corner room; it was dirty and stuffy, with many bedbugs and fleas, and the strong stench of "humanity." The room contained two wooden cots. One belonged to Korovin, my countryman and guardian; the other I shared with Korovin's son Vanka,[7] who was also an apprentice and worked in the factory's pattern shop.

Our food and the woman who prepared it were also paid for communally. The food was purchased on credit at a shop; our individual shares were assessed twice monthly. Every day at noon, as soon as the factory's lunch bell rang, we would hurry back to the apartment and sit right down at the table where a huge basin full of cabbage soup was already steaming.

All fifteen men ate from a common bowl with wooden spoons. The cabbage soup contained little pieces of meat. First, they would ladle out only the soup; then, when the soup was almost all gone, everyone tensely awaited a signal. A moment later someone would bang his spoon against the edge of the soup basin and say the words we were waiting for: "Dig in!" Then began the furious hunt of the spoons for the floating morsels of meat. The more dexterous would come up with the most.

Avdotia, the cook, her sleeves tucked up and the hem of her calico-print dress pulled back, would look steadfastly at the bottom of the soup basin, saying:

"Should I throw in some more, fellows?"

"Throw it in Duniakha,[8] throw it in!" several voices would sing out in unison.

Avdotia would carry the basin to the oven, refill it with cabbage soup, and return it to the table. After the soup came either buckwheat kasha with lard or fried potatoes. Everyone was hungry as a wolf; they ate quickly, greedily.

After lunch everyone—except for the youngsters—would throw himself on a cot to rest without removing his boots or workshirt.

---

[7]A diminutive form of Ivan.
[8]A diminutive form of Avdotia.

Twice a week—on Wednesday and Friday—Avdotia would prepare the fast-day food: cabbage soup with a fishhead and kasha with vegetable oil.[9]

Twice a month, on the Saturday paydays,[10] our artel indulged in wild carousing. Some, as soon as they had collected their pay, would go directly from the factory to beer halls, taverns, or to some grassy spot, while others—the somewhat more dandified types—first went back to the apartment to change clothes.

Somber, cross, often bruised, and in some cases still in a state of undiluted intoxication, the inhabitants of our artel would return home late at night or on Sunday morning.

In the wintertime, when the Moscow River was frozen, we would go to the wall of the dike and have fistfights with workers from the Butikov factory.[11] In the evening we would return home with our black eyes and our broken bloody noses.

But we also had our "cultural" amusements. The artel subscribed to the boulevard newspaper *Moskovskii listok* (Moscow Sheet),[12] in which what interested us the most were the chronicle of criminal cases and the

kellylxay

[9]According to strict Russian Orthodox observance, believers were expected to eat no meat or dairy products on Wednesdays (the day of the betrayal of Christ) and Fridays (the day of the crucifixion). Hence Avdotia prepared the soup with fish instead of meat and the kasha (gruel) with vegetable oil instead of grease, butter, or milk.

[10]Payday in Russian factories was almost always on a Saturday afternoon (a six-day week was the norm, with Saturday as a half-day), either once or twice a month.

[11]The Butikov factory was a large mechanized textile mill specializing in the weaving of woollen cloth. It employed approximately 1,100 workers in 1890.

[12]*Moskovskii listok,* published from 1881 to 1917, was a "scandal-mongering paper that covered the family affairs of prominent merchants, advertised pianos and tools, and convinced its readers to pay seven and a half rubles a year [roughly half the monthly pay of a semiskilled worker] . . . on the strength of its regular serial novels, [which were] potboilers. . . ." See Jeffrey Brooks, "Readers and Reading at the End of the Tsarist Era," in *Literature and Society in Imperial Russia, 1800-1914,* ed. William Mills Todd III (Stanford, 1978), p. 144. Brooks describes the main clientele for this and similar papers as "merchants, the petty bourgeoisie, and the service people with whom they had contact," but Kanatchikov's account suggests that factory workers were not immune to its attractions.

feuilletons. At that time the paper was running a long, serialized novel called *Bogdan Khmelnitskii*, in which the entire artel became engrossed.[13]

On Sundays we sometimes went to look at the pictures at the Tretiakov gallery and the Rumiantsev museum.[14]

In addition, we never missed a Moscow fire, and, no matter how tired, we would run at breakneck speed to see these free spectacles.

2. Religious ceremonies on the shop floor, such as this one at a metalworking plant in the Urals, were commonplace in factories throughout Russia at the beginning of the twentieth century.

[13]Bogdan Khmelnitskii (or, in Ukrainian, Bohdan Khmelnytskii) was a renowned Cossack military leader who led Ukrainian Cossacks in a series of uprisings against their Polish overlords in the mid-seventeenth century, which led indirectly to the incorporation of the Left Bank Ukraine (east of the Dnieper) into Russia in 1667. The novel serialized in *Moskovskii listok* no doubt presented Khmelnitskii as a larger-than-life Russian Orthodox hero in a struggle against Polish Catholic domination.

[14]The Rumiantsev Art Museum was located on Tver Street, the site of Moscow's main administrative and cultural institutions. The Tretiakov gallery housed the country's

Once a year, on a winter Sunday, my employer would organize a public prayer meeting at the factory. In the enormous machine shop, a large rostrum was erected which was ascended by all the authorities of the factory: the owner, the director, the chief engineer, the foremen of the various shops, and the clergymen in their gilded vestments. Through the dense crowd of workers, the older workers elbowed their way forward and took their places at the tribune, under the eyes of the authorities. They crossed themselves with fervor, kneeled, and bowed down to the ground, especially when the priest prayed for the long life of the factory owner. When the prayers were over, the priest delivered an emotional, moralizing sermon about a negligent slave and a zealous lord. Then we came up to the priest and kissed the cross.

IN THE PATTERN SHOP

After working for a month in the painting shop, I was transferred to the pattern shop, where I was placed under the authority of an unskilled worker named Nikifor. My duties for two or three months were to prepare the glue, paint the pattern models, run to the storehouse for nails, help Nikifor sweep up the shop, and "pay attention" to how the job of patternmaking was carried out.

Nikifor treated me in a comradely fashion—he would always joke with me or tell me things about himself, and when he noticed that I was beginning to pine for the village, he would cheer me up.

Nikifor had once been a fine wood engraver; he had worked in the best furniture workshops, but after repeatedly straining his eyes in bad light, he began to lose his vision. He was compelled to abandon engraving and to look for some other kind of work, something not requiring good eyesight. Subsequently, he worked as a sweeper, a janitor, watchman at a cemetery (or, as he liked to put it, watchman over the closed-eyed ones, i.e., the dead), until finally he got a job as an unskilled laborer at the List factory, for

---

greatest collection of Russian paintings, donated to the city of Moscow by the wealthy Moscow merchant and art collector Pavel M. Tretiakov in 1892. It was located within easy walking distance of Kanatchikov's quarters.

sixty kopecks a day. With a family to support, his life wasn't easy, but he never lost heart.

On the Mondays following payday, when half the workers in our shop were hung over with splitting headaches,[15] Nikifor would become everyone's idol. Early in the morning a pilgrimage to him would begin. With a swollen red face, with glazed eyes, one of the "sufferers" would usually come up to him and ask mysteriously in a drunken bass:

"Well, Nikisha,[16] have you brewed the tea?"

"No, not yet. I'll go to the storeroom in a little while and get a nice fresh pot."

"Great, old boy, but make it quick. I can't endure it much longer, my head is splitting so!"

Nikifor would make a compassionate face, shake his head sympathetically, and say consolingly:

"All right, all right, just show a little patience and your thirst will grow."

The sufferer would walk off with hope. After him Nikifor would have several more visitors, with wistful, imploring eyes, asking him to hurry with the "teapot."

After they went away, Nikifor would reach behind the boards under a workbench, pull out a tin can filled with an alcohol-based varnish, which had been prepared on Saturday for painting the models, drop a certain amount of salt into it, shake it, and return it to its secluded spot.[17]

"In the morning these damn bastards sure make it hard for you! Just let them get drunk before lunch and the foreman will catch the scent and ask where they got the drink," Nikifor would grumble.

After lunch half the shop would be drunk. Some would loaf on other people's workbenches; others would sit it out in the lavatory. Those whose morning-after drinking had gone too far went to sleep in the drying room or in the shop shed.

[15]Mondays were generally unproductive days in the factory, as workers returned hung over—and often late—from their weekend drinking and carousing. This was the cause of numerous petty conflicts between workers and their supervisors. For further discussion of this phenomenon, see below, Ch. 4, pp. 170–171, 181.

[16]A diminutive form of Nikifor.

[17]Nikifor was clearly attempting to make the "tea," i.e., the alcohol-based varnish, more palatable to the workers who would soon be drinking it.

On such days the lavatory would be transformed into a loud and lively "club." The latest gossip about all kinds of happenings was shared there, people quarreled, insulted each other, or played tricks on someone. The unelected president of the "club" was almost always its most frequent visitor, the driller Ivan—a prankster, boisterous and foul-mouthed.

After I had been at the factory about four months, Bogdan Ivanovich, a German foreman, summoned me to the office and said: "Simon, your painting been satisfactory. Go now to joiner's bench. You soon get used to work."[18]

I thanked the foreman and, pleased and delighted, I went to Nikifor to share my happiness.

"Well, Semen, that means you've risen in the world. You'll be a pattern-maker—remember me, a poor sinner," Nikifor said half-jokingly, as he accompanied me to the workbench. "Let's have a drink to your new wages."

My wage had been twenty-five kopecks a day, but now it was going up to forty kopecks. My spirits were rising. I liked the work in the pattern shop, which had a great attraction for me.

In those days patternmakers still worked with their own tools. A good patternmaker, when he started work at a new factory, was expected to bring a case of tools along, and some factories even required that he have his own workbench. My first act was to begin to fashion myself a joiner plane and a chisel out of strong beechwood. At first my tools were not completely satisfactory, but they were good enough to use. My hands were still poorly trained; they lacked the dexterity and strength to cut hard wood with care and precision.

I also learned how to use a turning lathe. This work absorbed me greatly since I soon learned to carve all kinds of wooden knickknacks—wine-glasses, little tumblers, eggs, pencilcases, and so on. True, sometimes my excessive love for knickknacks cost me a whack across the head from the foreman, but that didn't bother me very much.

After a year's experience at the workbench, I already knew how to draw and could design a pattern if it wasn't very complex. My confidence in my

[18]The German foreman speaks in broken Russian in the original text. The broken English here is meant to approximate the original.

3. Patternmaking shop in a Petersburg shipbuilding plant, 1903.

own powers was growing stronger. But at the same time, my faith in my old principles was declining. I was becoming bolder and more definite in my opinions. The authority of my "elders" was beginning to lose its effect on me. I already had a critical attitude toward everyday, conventional morality.

The pattern shop was considered to be the "aristocratic" workshop. Most of the patternmakers were urban types—they dressed neatly, wore their trousers over their boots, wore their shirts "fantasia" style, tucked into their trousers, fastened their collars with a colored lace instead of a necktie, and on holidays some of them even wore bowler hats. They cut their hair "in the Polish style" or brush-cut. Their bearing was firm, conveying their consciousness of their own worth. They used foul language only when they lost their tempers and in extreme situations, or on paydays, when they got drunk, and not even all of them at that.

It is hard to understand why it was that the patternmakers gained such an "aristocratic" reputation. True, our work was mentally challenging, and literacy was an absolute requirement, but patternmakers earned much less than, for example, smelters or metalturners. The basic contingent of patternmakers almost never changed: they had been working at the List factory for ten, fifteen, and even twenty years. Most of them were family men and were related to various petty bourgeois strata. Some of them had put away savings "for a rainy day."

In general, our lives were peaceful and harmonious, a small paradise. Only one thing was wrong—our workday was too long: eleven and a half hours. But even that problem was soon removed without a struggle. After the St. Petersburg weavers' strike of 1896, our sagacious employer, Gustav Ivanovich List, immediately introduced the ten-hour day at his factory.[19] After that our group of skilled workers began to live as well as could be.

How we experienced those events will be discussed later.

Among the patternmakers there was one group whose appearance set them off from the rest—the patternmaker peasants, whose ties with the village were still strong. They wore high boots, traditional cotton-print blouses girdled with a sash, had their hair cut "under a pot," and wore beards that were rarely touched by a barber's hand. Every payday without fail they would send part of their money back to the village. They lived in crowded, dirty conditions and behaved stingily, denying themselves everything in order to accumulate more money for the village. They were always

---

[19]In the spring of 1896 a citywide strike of unprecedented size and tenacity took place in the St. Petersburg textile industry. It was followed by a similar strike in January 1897. One of the strikers' principal demands was the introduction of a ten-and-a-half hour workday. Although this demand was never met, the strikes did lead indirectly to the promulgation of the law of June 2, 1897, which limited the length of the workday for adult male factory workers to eleven and a half hours on normal workdays and to ten hours on Saturdays and on the eves of twelve official holidays. These strikes and their historical significance are discussed in Allan K. Wildman, *The Making of a Workers' Revolution: Russian Social Democracy, 1891–1903* (Chicago, 1967), Ch. 3, and Richard Pipes, *Social Democracy and the St. Petersburg Labor Movement, 1885–1897* (Cambridge, Mass., 1963), Ch. 6. Kanatchikov is of course suggesting that List was frightened by the news from St. Petersburg and introduced a shorter workday to head off a possible strike movement in his own factory. By the end of the year, several other Moscow factories had done this, either under pressure from the actions of their own workers or out of fear of such pressure in the future.

looking for a free drink. On holidays they attended mass and visited their countrymen, and their conversations were mostly about grain, land, the harvest, and livestock. When they weren't able to return to their village on visits, the "missus," that is, their wives, would come to town to visit them; these were fat, big-bosomed women in woolen skirts, in bright red calico sarafans,[20] with whom the men would go to the tavern on holidays to be entertained and listen to the music "machine."

The other patternmakers did not like these peasants, called them "gray devils," and made fun of them on every possible occasion. Most of the peasant patternmakers had never passed through a factory apprenticeship but had been village carpenters under a contractor and had done only simple, rough work with an axe. They became patternmakers only by accident or through someone's protection—either they did some foreman a "favor" or one of their countrymen set them up.

These village patternmakers had yet another bad trait. They tried as hard as they could to compensate for their ignorance of their craft with extra "zeal." Stalwart and powerful fellows, they would work all the time, never leaving the workbench or straightening their backs.

"Pavlukha! Enough of this drudging! Take a break! The foreman won't see you. He went away," one of the patternmakers would say in a mocking tone.

But Pavlukha, ignoring the derision, continued to "drudge," for he knew full well that the eyes and ears of the foreman remain in the workshop even in his absence. Of course the shop aristocrats could not forgive the villagers for all of this.

In the workshop one could often hear the following joke, illustrating the carpenter origin of the village patternmaker.

One mocker turns to another and says:

"Vaniukha, Vaniukha! Did you cut off a length of board?"

"Sure I cut it, but it came out too short!"

"By very much?"

"Just by a straw."

"Well, that's all right, it can be stretched with a nail."

"It can't be stretched."

---

[20]A sarafan was a brightly-colored sleeveless dress, usually of printed linen.

"How come?"

"I cut the board that it fits against a straw too short too."

All this is spoken in the restrained dialect of Vladimir province. Everyone roars with laughter.

Another equally popular scene was often performed: how the contractor dismisses the workers he does not need in the fall.

"Look, fellows, a bear is crawling on the roof," says the contractor, rushing toward the window.

"What kind of bear is that! It's a cat!" retort some doubters.

"No, it's a bear!"

"It's a cat!"

"You say it's a cat, I say it's a bear. Whoever thinks I'm wrong is fired!"

THE BEGINNING OF MY WANDERINGS FROM FACTORY TO FACTORY

Two years of my apprenticeship at the List factory passed. By now I was already an accomplished draftsman and designed uncomplicated patterns on my own. I loved my craft, and I put a lot of spirit and initiative into it. As everyone knows, the pattern is made for casting the iron and bronze parts of a machine, which is also constructed from forged iron or steel parts that are made in different workshops in accordance with a strict division of labor. In order to acquaint myself with the entire process of producing a complete machine, I often made the rounds of the factory's various shops, where I spent hours standing and watching how this or that part of a machine was made.

I especially enjoyed visiting the foundry where the patterns were sent after being completed in our shop. In the huge, tall foundry building, which was covered by soot and dust, dirty, dark-colored people, whose blackened, soot-covered faces revealed only the whites of their eyes, rummaged like moles in the earth and dust of the earthen floor. The roar of the enormous lifting cranes, of turning gears, the clattering of the thick chains, and the mighty breathing of the cupola furnace where the pig iron was smelted—all these sounds constantly filled the foundry building with their din.

In the evening, when the casting began, the foundry would turn into a veritable hell. Pouring out of the furnace on a chute would be an enormous, heavy fire-red stream of molten pig iron, which spewed forth large blazing sparks and illuminated the dark faces of the smelters standing nearby. One after another the molten pots of pig iron were quickly filled, and, two at a time, the smelters carried them on an iron handbarrow across the huge floor, which was littered with moulds ready for the casting. The dark floor of the shop would be brightly illuminated by a large number of fire-red points with tails resembling little blazing comets. Then the smelters slowly poured the molten pig iron from the pots into the earthen moulds. The heat near the pots and the furnaces was unbearable, and the clothes of the smelters would repeatedly catch fire and have to be doused with water.

On the following day I would watch how the iron parts of the future machines, cast but still not cooled down, were cleansed of earth and cleared of knobs and patches of pig iron by unskilled workers.

Then, after a few more weeks or months, depending on the size of the machine, I could see the workers in the assembly shop painting the powerful beauty—with its polished bronze and steel parts sparkling—the completed steam engine.

Workers would look with a loving glance at its massive iron body as they passed by. As for me, I began to be gripped by the poetry of the large metal factory, with its mighty metallic roar, the puffing of its steam-driven machines, its columns of high pipes, its rising clouds of black smoke, which sullied the clear blue sky. Unconsciously, I was being drawn to the factory, to the people who worked there, who were becoming my near ones, my family. I had the feeling that I was merging with the factory, with its stern poetry of labor, a poetry that was growing dearer and closer to me than the quiet, peaceful, lazy poetry of our drowsy village life.

Christmas was approaching. During these holidays the factory would close down for almost an entire week. A large number of workers had ties with their villages: these were the workers from the areas of Mozhaisk, Tula, Riazan, and Volokolamsk.[21] They would await the coming of the holidays

---

[21]Mozhaisk and Volokolamsk were the westernmost districts of Moscow province, located at fairly easy commuting distance from the city of Moscow. Tula and Riazan were neighboring provinces located to the south and southeast of Moscow province, respectively. Kanatchikov himself came from a village in Volokolamsk.

with impatience—they saved their money to buy things for themselves and for their village hosts. When it came time for the great departures to the countryside—which happened both at Christmas and at Easter—we were subjected to a medical examination at the factory. It was carried out quite primitively and crudely, and it yielded almost no results. On payday, in the paymaster's office, a doctor would be seated next to the bookkeeper while he paid us. We would line up, undo our pants, and show the doctor the part of our bodies he needed to see.[22] The doctor, after tapping it with a pencil, would tell the bookkeeper the results of his "examination," whereupon the bookkeeper would hand us our pay. Although there were probably quite a few workers at the factory who were infected by venereal disease, I do not know of a single instance when the doctor found such a person during these medical examinations.

After the medical "examination" I was given my pay and, along with other workers, I too departed for my village. But this time my voyage turned out to be a fateful one. This is what happened. Korovin had decided that, come what may, he would marry off his son Vanka—who was a year older than me—during this holiday vacation. Korovin decided to carry out all the preliminary marriage procedures—the showing of the bride, the striking of hands, etc.—during the holy period when priests cannot perform the actual weddings.[23] Then, after the holy period, he would take off three or four additional workdays for the wedding itself. Whether he had received permission from the foreman for this extension in advance or whether the foreman authorized the illegal absence of Korovin and his son after the fact I no longer remember. In any case they were not penalized. For me, however, the story was to have an unhappy ending.

I played a very active role in Vanka's marriage preparations in the village:

[22]This was obviously a genital examination. The practice was widespread in Russian industry and was often the cause of humiliation and unrest on the part of the workers.

[23]This is the festive holiday or Yuletide period from Christmas Eve to January 6. For a description of the typical procedures and ceremonials that surrounded a marriage in the villages of the Moscow region, see Mary Matossian, "The Peasant Way of Life," in *The Peasant in Nineteenth-Century Russia*, ed. Wayne S. Vucinich (Stanford, 1968), pp. 25–29. Matossian also describes the intense celebrations and other activities of the Yuletide season (pp. 32–33). The "striking of hands" mentioned in the text refers to the final sealing of the marriage bargain by the fathers of the bride and groom.

I went to parties with him, accompanied him to the showing of the bride, and finally, after we had selected a bride for him, I was his best man at the wedding. In general I had a great time in the village on this visit, though my merrymaking almost led me into getting married myself, to the sister of Vanka's bride. But once again, when all my other arguments had proven useless, and vanished into smoke before the verbal onslaught of my sisters and aunts, I was rescued by my impending military service.

From Korovin's point of view, Vanka's marriage was very successful. It seems that he got a dowry of some two hundred rubles and all sorts of fine clothing. What is more, the bride herself wasn't bad. Although her face was not pretty, her body was splendid—broad-boned, stately, and tall. As our workers would say when she later came to visit her husband in Moscow: "That's not a girl, it's a city!"

But what pleased Korovin the most was that his daughter-in-law was the daughter of a rich kulak,[24] a man of renown in our district. To be sure, this was of no major material benefit to Korovin, either then or later, but it was still very nice to become the kin of a rich man, and it gave him some hope for the future.

Vanka, the real hero of the festivities, was in seventh heaven. He had never even dreamed he might have a wife like that! People now began to call him Ivan Ivanovich.[25]

At this point I shall make a small digression and say a few more words about Vanka, whom I hardly ever saw again for the rest of my life. At work he was a diligent, assiduous fellow, obedient to the factory administration, deferential to his superiors. His father had known how to bind him to his home and instill in him obedience to his parents. And Vanka, without even stopping to think—if he was capable of thinking at all—submitted to all of Korovin's wishes and blindly followed in his father's footsteps.

Korovin himself, I was later told, ended up as follows: When Bogdan Ivanovich, the old foreman in the pattern shop, died, Korovin replaced him as foreman. In that position he soon became universally disliked and made a lot of personal enemies. He died in a very sad manner. It seems that one

[24]A relatively well-to-do peasant. The word *kulak* means "fist" and suggests a person who is miserly, greedy, and acquisitive.

[25]His formal first name and patronymic, indicating that the marriage had earned him new respect from his neighbors.

day the factory administration had arranged some kind of celebration for the workers. At the festivities, many workers became extremely drunk. Then, when the celebration was in full swing, one of Korovin's "well-wishers" flung a glass of vodka at him, terrifying Korovin so greatly that he died on the spot. I have never been able to learn any more of the details of this story.

Korovin's son Vanka is still alive and well. He is working at the very same factory, having inherited his father's post as foreman and having acquired all his virtues: he never misses a single mass, goes to confession every year, takes Communion, and is very concerned about maintaining the splendor of the neighborhood church.

And now let us return to my own youth. Having celebrated young Korovin's marriage with lots of din and uproar and a good deal of drinking, we headed back to our factory. As I already said, we were three days late. The Korovins got away with it, but the old foreman Bogdan Ivanovich declared categorically that I was fired with two weeks notice.[26] Korovin and I pleaded with him, but all in vain. The prospect of unemployment confronted me. I became depressed, and my work deteriorated. I was frightened by the unknown.

"Cheer up, Semen, you'll pull through," Savinov[27] said to me with compassion as he slapped me on the back, having come up behind me unobserved.

"How can I, Vasilii Egorych,[28] when I have nowhere to go?"

"You sure have been worrying! Don't be afraid. With good hands and a head on your shoulders, you can always find work!" He looked at me with his clear, invigorating gaze and added in a stern, businesslike tone: "Semen, stop feeling sorry for yourself and let's talk some sense instead."

---

[26] According to the existing factory legislation, both employer and employee were obligated to give two weeks notice in order to terminate a contract. If the employer wished the worker to leave immediately, he was required to give the worker two weeks additional salary as severance pay.

[27] Vasilii Egorevich Savinov, a twenty-seven-year-old patternmaker whom Kanatchikov had recently befriended. Savinov, who was antireligious and politically aware, had been instrumental in launching Kanatchikov's apostasy from Christianity and had introduced him to his first socialist literature.

[28] Egorych is the shortened, conversational form of the patronymic Egorevich.

"Vasilii Egorych, I always ask your advice about everything," I answered meekly, while feeling reassured.

"Well then, everything will be fine. Don't come to work here tomorrow. Instead, go to the entrance of the big Bromlei factory[29] first thing in the morning and ask the foreman for a job. I've heard they need patternmakers there."

On the next day I packed my tools in my beloved gray toolbox and, after all sorts of kind parting words from my friendly fellow patternmakers, I abandoned the Gustav List factory, filled with joy about the present and anxiety about the future.

I AM AN ADULT

With fear and trembling, for the first time in my life I am standing at a joiner's bench as an adult! I lay out my tools and begin to study the designs for the work that has been assigned me as a test of my skills in the pattern shop of the "Old Bromlei" factory. The design—which is for a bearing— turns out to be uncomplicated, and, without any help from the older patternmakers, I am able to cope with the task by myself. Then I hand the completed pattern to the foreman. I wait in a state of excitement, my heart pounding, while the foreman, using calipers and measure, tests the accuracy of the pattern I have made.

In my later wanderings from factory to factory, when I had already acquired real skill in my work as well as confidence in myself, I never experienced any special feelings of agitation. But this time, when my future as an independent craftsman[30] was being decided, I literally trembled like a puppy dog as I stood by the workbench and waited for the foreman to complete his examination of my work.

[29]The Bromlei Brothers' engineering works (founded in 1857), often called the "Old Bromlei" to distinguish it from a second Bromlei factory, was one of the larger engineering works in Moscow, with over 900 workers at the end of 1896.

[30]Kanatchikov is not using the term *independent* to suggest an intent to set up his own shop. More likely, he is trying to convey the skilled, "qualified" worker's sense of personal achievement and autonomy. Successful completion of the kind of test of the quality of his work that Kanatchikov is describing was a sort of rite of passage, leading from apprenticeship to professional adulthood. Distant echoes of the medieval guild notion of completion of a *chef d'oeuvre* can be heard in this factory ritual.

From stories I had heard from experienced workers, I knew that foremen always preferred to hire reliable, older patternmakers and would pay them higher wages even if they were less skillful than the younger men. In general, my youthful appearance—I not only had no beard, I did not even have a moustache—was very distressing to me and, at that time, was the source of many unpleasant moments for me. For one thing, the young women—stockingmakers, milliners, dressmakers—with whom my older-looking contemporaries were so successful, refused even to acknowledge me as an adult man. At times like that I regretted very much that I had not taken care of this problem much earlier and corrected my natural deficiency, as my more experienced comrades had advised me, by artificial means: the application of baked onions, at night, to the spots where I wanted to encourage the growth of facial hair.

To my delight, however, this time things worked out all right even without the "baked onions." The foreman summoned me to the office, announced good-naturedly that my work was of acceptable quality and, right on the spot, gave me the drawings for another pattern. Flushed and excited with embarrassment and afraid that other workers would notice my unrestrained joy, I proudly and confidently marched to my workbench with the new drawings in hand, trying to look as if all of this was the most normal routine for me.

"Well, Kanatchikov, did you make it?" my neighbor asked with curiosity.

"I made it," I answered, trying in vain to conceal my joy with a tone of indifference.

"What'll you be earning, about seventy kopecks a day?"

"Who knows?"

"Listen, if you had a beard, you can be sure the foreman would have offered you a full ruble," said my neighbor, hitting me on my sore spot.

At that time, after the forty kopecks I had been getting at List's, seventy kopecks wasn't a bad wage for me. Secretly, however, I dreamed of more. My neighbor, Sherstiannikov, was much older than me; he was one of those patternmakers who had been a village carpenter, still had problems in reading a design, and was making only eighty kopecks a day. It was obviously his envy that prevented him from admitting that the foreman could pay more than seventy kopecks to a young greenhorn like me.

There was still a week until payday. I was consumed with impatience to learn just how high a wage the foreman would assign me. It was not that I was greedy for money; the size of the wage concerned me not so much for material as for moral reasons, as an appraisal of my worth as a socially useful person, as measured in money by strangers who did not know me. Of course, given the level of my intellectual development at that time, I was not capable of formulating the feelings and mood that possessed me as clearly as I am doing now, but I distinctly recall that they were something like that.

The size of my wage was also of concern to the other patternmakers, who loved a free drink and were anxiously awaiting payday for me to "treat" them, the size of the treat depending upon the size of my wage.[31]

At last the long-awaited Saturday payday arrived. The timekeeper began to distribute the paybooks.[32] He placed mine on the workbench. Trembling, I opened it up. On the first page were my first and last names and my occupation: "patternmaker."

"This means I am no longer just a little apprentice; I'm a real patternmaker!" I said to myself proudly. With trembling hands I licked the tips of my fingers, turned to the next page, and read: eighty kopecks per day! I was filled with so much joy that I could hardly breathe, and my head began to throb.

"How much?" Sherstiannikov asked me.

---

[31]It was common practice in Russian factories for a newly hired or newly promoted worker to treat his fellow workers to drinks. A number of metaphors were used to describe this custom, roughly comparable with "wetting down" an agreement in English.

[32]*Raschetnye knizhki* (paybooks or workbooks) were partially modeled on the French *livrets d'ouvriers*. They contained the terms of the worker's contract, his official title or grade, a running record of all financial transactions that affected him, and a list of all the factory regulations. Intended as a means of protecting workers from abuses of their contracts by their employers, these workbooks were formally required by law in 1835. The law remained largely unenforced, however, and workbooks were continually discussed as a necessary aspect of labor legislation until they were made mandatory in the important law promulgated on June 4, 1886. See Reginald E. Zelnik, *Labor and Society in Tsarist Russia: The Factory Workers of St. Petersburg* (Stanford, 1971), pp. 33–34, 125–129, 141, 358–359; and Mikhail I. Tugan-Baranovsky, *The Russian Factory in the 19th Century* (Homewood, Ill., 1970), pp. 327–332.

Instead of answering I silently handed him the paybook, attempting to conceal my excitement.

That evening, after drinking a cup of tea (I had not yet learned to drink vodka) and treating the others to drinks in a tavern, I hauled my scanty possessions over to the apartment of Sherstiannikov, who had offered to rent me half a room, and parted with Korovin forever.

As I have already said, Sherstiannikov, whose apartment in the Zamoskvoreche district[33] I moved into, was also a worker at Bromlei's and earned eighty kopecks a day. He was married and was expecting an addition to the family in the near future. It was hard enough for two of them to live on eighty kopecks, and now, to add to their misfortunes, there was a child in prospect. Hence they were very pleased to provide me with room and board and thereby add to their income. Sherstiannikov was a quiet, subdued, poorly educated fellow. His wife Grusha was his exact opposite—a glib, saucy, tough-talking city girl;[34] she had once been the housekeeper of some great "lords," a source of enormous pride to her. She considered her marriage with Sherstiannikov a failure and was not ashamed to say as much to his face.

"You boor, you lout! You don't even have any education! Why there were once real gentlemen who wanted to marry me!" she would often cry out in a fit of rage.

"Well, then you should have married a gentleman," Sherstiannikov would answer sullenly.

"Precisely! What a fool I was to disgrace myself with a dope like you. You're not even good enough to clean my shoes. You ought to get down on your knees before me for going for such a lout!"

The more Sherstiannikov would answer back, the more incensed Grusha would become. For this reason he would usually keep quiet during such incidents, and Grusha would gradually calm down.

---

[33]The large area south of the Moscow River, heavily inhabited by workers.

[34]The Russian word *meshchanka* is the feminine form of *meshchanin* (plural: *meshchane*). The term usually refers to the lowest legally constituted segment of the urban population, corresponding roughly to the concept of petty bourgeois. It is sometimes used with the same negative connotations as the latter term. Here we translate *meshchanka* as "city girl" because this appears to be the point Kanatchikov wishes to stress.

4. Corner of a room rented by a Petersburg metalworker and his family in the 1890s.

From time to time Grusha would entertain her girl friends in the apartment. These were workers from the Einem candy factory. They would sit around and drink tea. I would then be invited to join them. Embarrassed and blushing in the presence of girls, I would silently but seriously drink my tea and curse myself in my heart for my incapacity to deal with women. After tea they would move the bed, table, and chairs into a corner and begin to dance without music, either a quadrille or a "pastoral" waltz. Then I would feel my helplessness even more keenly: I simply lacked the real polish of an accomplished dancing partner.

How I used to envy my comrade Stepka, an apprentice turner at the List factory! When he visited me with his fiddle or guitar, our entire apartment would come alive and would soon be filled with the sounds of laughter and merriment. Stepka was a rather good-looking fellow—taller than average, slender, blond, with curly hair and lively, laughing eyes. He played the fiddle and the guitar pretty well, danced all the latest dances, knew a lot of anecdotes, and was able to tell all kinds of entertaining, funny stories.

Naturally, he enjoyed enviable success among our young ladies, and, as we used to say, he was "the first fellow in the dancing ring." Not a single party, not a single wedding celebration among the workers we knew could take place without Stepka. He was always a sought-after guest, always the life of the party. In female company he seemed like a fish in water, and he would "pick the flowers of pleasure" unceremoniously. He had no interest whatever in politics and preferred to read the more humorous magazines, from which he drew his witty material. Nor was he especially religious, which meant it would eventually prove relatively easy for me to dissolve the last remnants of his religious prejudices.

It is true that each of us had his own assessment of the harmfulness of religion. At that time I viewed religion as a fabrication contrived by priests, which prevented people from growing intellectually and workers in particular from creating the heavenly kingdom here on earth. Stepka viewed the problem differently. "What others do is not my business," he would say, "but I don't like religion because it bores me: you have to go to church, observe the fast days, keep a somber look on your face, and spend your whole life in fear of being hung by the tongue or by the feet in your afterlife. I prefer to live and to enjoy myself."

My frequent and close relations with Stepka were bound, of course, to have some influence on me, especially since there was no one around to counteract his influence. Vasilii Egorych Savinov, my former teacher, had recently grown very sad about something; he resigned his job at List's and departed for somewhere in the Ural region, probably Orenburg. I began to devote more attention to my appearance. I bought myself a stylish jacket with mother-of-pearl buttons, a "fantasia" shirt, and a visored cap with a velvet band and a leather crown. In order to master the art of dance, I began to go to a dancing teacher.

The business of worldly self-improvement was now so attractive to me that I secretly began to search for books on these matters. "Indeed," I thought, "why shouldn't there be books like that? Why, there are even books on how to write letters!" I had bought just such a book on letter writing, one that I used with some success and that rendered great service to me.

One day, as I was walking by a store on Nikolskaia Street, I noticed in the window display a little book with a poorly painted cover, on which were depicted a lord and lady dancing. The book was entitled: *Self-Teacher of Dance and Good Manners.* I do not remember the author's name. "This is just what I need!" I said to myself with joy. I entered the store and asked to see the book. The price was reasonable—fifteen kopecks. I ran home with the book at full speed in order to learn the secrets of "good manners" without delay. But, alas, the book contained very little that was useful to me. It said that when seated at table, one should not wipe one's nose with the napkin, roll the bread into little balls, eat fish with a knife, or gnaw at the bones of a grouse. It explained how to eat an artichoke or an asparagus. In short, the book dealt with subject matter I had never even encountered; in fact, I did not even know if these things belonged to the animal, vegetable, or mineral world.

The only part of the book of any value to me was the one that contained some pointers on the "theory" of the art of dance. But it did not make me any less timid or any more resourceful in my relations with the women, notwithstanding the steadfast assistance of my friend Stepka.

In general, I spent that winter quite happily, in a manner that befit an adult craftsman: I attended wedding celebrations, went to parties, danced, did the Kamarinskaia,[35] and recited humorous couplets. And at one wedding party, I even took an active part in a brawl, from which I emerged with honor, ending up with some minor bruises under my shirt. In those days such brawls at weddings and parties were a common occurrence. They broke out at the slightest pretext—even without very much drinking. All that was needed was for two rival groups of young men who were competing for the same girls to run into one another, and a battle was sure to begin. Then, on the next day, decorated with "shiners"[36]—as we liked to call our black eyes—the bearers of these "distinguishing" marks became the targets of everyone's mockery and wisecracks at the factory. The usual, predictable response to the foreman's indiscreet inquiry into the origins of these "facial decorations" was this:

[35]The Kamarinskaia was a lively Russian folkdance.
[36]The Russian slang expression *fonar'*—here translated as "shiner"—literally means "lantern."

"On Saturday when I was at the baths[37] I stepped on the soap, slipped and banged my snout against the washtub."

"Hey, what happened? Stepped on the soap again, eh?" These were the ironic words that usually greeted the embarrassed fellow with the shiner as he entered the lavatory to have a smoke.

"No, it's a little spot that came off somebody's fist."

"What kind of spot is that? More like a sledgehammer!"

Passing my time in this heady atmosphere, I had failed to notice that the long Easter holidays were again approaching. Grusha would wash and scrub clean the room, scream, scold her phlegmatic husband Afanasii, and send him off on errands to bazaars and shops, never allowing him any peace and quiet. I too began to prepare for the holidays. I bought a barrel of red wine and all kinds of sweets, with the intention of organizing a little get-together at my place. I had decided not to return to the village this time but to emancipate myself from my parental home once and for all.

At this point I should make a brief disgression in order that the reader not be left with the impression that, carried away by my good fortune, I had lost all interest in political ideas. Despite my strong attraction to the worldly pleasures of city life, the little ember of political awareness that Savinov had implanted in me continued to smolder. This was expressed by the fact that, in the plant, I openly preached my still rather shapeless socialist ideas, engaged in arguments with the older workers, made fun of religion, spoke abusively about the factory administration, and so on. Of course all these speeches were no secret to the foreman. He heard about them through his informers, and for a certain period of time, he remained quiet and observed what was happening.

As usual, I loved to read, and I would look to books for answers to all the questions that excited me. I loved to walk to Sukharevka[38] and rum-

---

[37]The weekly visit to the public steam baths, usually on Saturday afternoons (when work ended earlier than on weekdays), was almost a universal practice among Russian workers.

[38]Sukharevka was a large open-air market situated in Sukharevskaia Square along the outer ring of boulevards on the north side of the city center. The market "included both a more respectable section for the sale of real and imitation antiques, books, and the like, and a plebeian [section] . . . where petty profiteers bought and sold all sorts of old

mage in the book piles, looking for something, but not even knowing what it was. Along with song books, letter-writing manuals, and the like, I sometimes got hold of books with a "point of view." I would choose these books at random, by their titles, which, of course, did not always correspond to their contents. Using this method, I once bought the book *The Black and the White Clergy*,[39] which did not live up to my expectations. Another time I bought a thick old book called something like *Collection*. This time I was luckier: it contained verses in translation about the exile of Dante as well as a fable by Franko[40] called "The Little Tail." As a rule, I did not read journalistic articles since they were too difficult for me to understand.

The Easter holidays arrived. The first day in our apartment went rather badly. From the crack of dawn there were big arguments between Sherstiannikov and Grusha about their religious disagreements. When Grusha insisted that Afanasii go off to church to have their Easter cakes blessed,[41] he refused. Then a stormy scene transpired. Grusha scolded her husband with foul language, screamed, stamped her feet, and cried. But Sherstiannikov was unmoved. Grusha understood that I was the cause of Afanasii's apostasy, but she still decided not to extend her anger to me. The rest of the day was passed in painful silence.

After lunch on the following day, arrayed in my holiday best, I went to the Moscow River to watch the ice float by. I recall that the weather was springlike—clear, sunny. The riverbank was filled with holiday animation: laughter, joking, people nibbling on sunflower seeds, and here and there one could hear the cursing of drunkards. I ran into Stepka, and we began to

---

clothing and miscellaneous trash." See Robert Gohstand, "The Internal Geography of Trade in Moscow from the Mid-Nineteenth Century to the First World War," 2 vols. Ph.D. diss., University of California, Berkeley, 1973, II, p. 538.

[39] "Black" clergy refers to members of the monastic clergy, who were forbidden to marry; "white" clergy were members of the secular clergy, who were expected to marry. The white clergy comprised the rank and file of Russia's parish priests.

[40] Ivan Franko, a popular Ukrainian poet of the nineteenth century.

[41] Reference is to the *kulich*, a very rich, sweet cake, and the *paskha*, a rich mixture of sweetened curds, butter, eggs, and raisins. At Eastertime, believers would have these ritual cakes, together with their colored Easter eggs, blessed by their parish priest.

wander together without any particular goal. Somehow holidays always seemed to derail us. We would drift aimlessly from street to street until we finally ended up in some beer hall or tavern. And so it was on that day. When it grew dark, we ran into the turner Rezvov, a jolly joker and an old ⟨illegible⟩. When I had been working in the List factory as an apprentice, Rezvov would never condescend to socialize with me. But now I was a skilled craftsman.

The tavern was stuffy, full of smoke, and noisy. But this was all drowned out by the powerful, ringing metallic sounds of the "orchestrion"—the so-called music machine. We sat down at a small table. Rezvov would have liked to order a half-bottle of "Smirnovka," but I proudly announced that I did not drink pure vodka, and we agreed to order ashberry brandy. But Rezvov began to demonstrate so cunningly that there was no real difference between pure vodka and brandy, that the only distinction lay in their strengths—namely, you had to drink more of the one than of the other in order to get nice and tipsy—that I dropped my objections. Today I cannot say for sure whether I had lost my sense of taste or whether Rezvov was actually right, but in point of fact I discovered no essential difference between the ashberry brandy and the purified vodka.

After we had finished the vodka, Rezvov bought a pack of cigarettes and treated us to a smoke. At the time I still did not smoke, but for the company's sake I did not refuse the cigarettes, and I began to puff courageously. This excessive mixing of alcohols, in combination with the cigarettes, had a stupefying effect on an "inexperienced" youth like me. I still cannot recall what we talked about at the table, under what circumstances we separated, or how I left the tavern.

I came back to my senses when I felt the fresh air out on the street as I headed back toward my home. As I was later told by Stepka and Rezvov, they had not even noticed any special change in me, for I was able to stand firmly on my feet for the entire time. I lived on the fifth floor. As I ran quickly up the stairs, I could feel my head turning round in circles and sat down on one of the stone steps. But I had barely closed my eyes when I was caught in such a terrifying, dizzying whirlwind that I felt that the building, the stairway on which I sat, everything had begun to spin and whirl around in circles while I was hurtling into some kind of abyss. I gripped the bannisters tightly. Inside of me something began to stir and turn about, as if, within my gut, a huge sickening snake had made its lair and was now coming up into my throat and trying to crawl out of me. For a while I either fell asleep or blacked out. When I came to, I had a strong headache and a tortured, remorseful conscience. I knocked on the door of the apartment and tried my best to appear sober. Then I walked through to my room. Grusha had opened the door, it seemed, without noticing anything. I felt relieved. I was especially afraid of losing my authority with her, for—in view of my sober lifestyle—she called me a "neat little mirror," forgave me my free-thinking, and always held me up as an example to her husband Afanasii, who suffered breakdowns from his drinking bouts. And now, suddenly, she might see this "little mirror" in a drunken stupor. Just the thought of this consumed me with shame. Fortunately, however, everything turned out well.

I woke up early the next morning with an unbearable noise crackling in my head. Then I put my dirty outfit in order, destroyed the traces of my crime that had been left on the stairs, and only after that, feeling much more relaxed, did I tell the Sherstiannikovs the story of my first fall into sin. In the wake of this shock I then took a solemn oath never again to touch any vodka. Of course I did not keep to this vow fully and completely, but at least I never again was to find myself in that condition.

The holidays ended badly for me in one other respect. Every year the "Old Bromlei" factory would undergo a cleansing of "unsuitable," "unreliable," and generally "undesirable" elements. This operation was carried out rather simply. When the Easter holidays came round, all the workers would be dismissed. Then when the holiday was over the foremen of the various shops would hire their workers anew.[42] In this manner all the workers whom the foremen found objectionable were left outside the factory gates. This was the category I now found myself in. The whole

---

[42]Labor contracts were often drawn up so as to expire with the coming of the Easter holidays, in part because some workers with close ties to the countryside wished to return to agricultural work at that time of year. Since the contract had expired, the Bromlei factory was not bound at this time by the requirement for two weeks notice (see n. 26 above), and the dismissals were therefore legal. Technically, in fact, they were not dismissals at all; the administration would simply refuse to rehire the "undesirables" whose contracts had expired.

situation was so stupid that you could not even learn the reason for your dismissal. Not that many were interested in knowing.

This time, however, I did not grow sad, the way I had the previous time. First, because I already knew my own worth; second, because it was spring, and in the summer, as we used to say, "every little bush can give you shelter for the night"; and third, because this was a time when industry was beginning to flourish—new factories were being constructed everywhere and workers were in great demand. There were, of course, no labor exchanges in those days, but in spite of this we were very well informed as to where workers were needed.

So this time, taking along my traditional toolbox, I boarded a train and headed for the Mytishchensk railroad car factory, which had just been built.[43] That morning I "stepped up" to the foreman and was hired.

AT THE MYTISHCHENSK FACTORY

The new, bright-colored, spacious Mytishchensk factory sparkled like a toy. It was pleasant to look at from every angle. And the roar of its mighty Herculean whistle, with which the trumpets of hosts of archangels could not compare, resounded through the distant meadows and forests, frightening the animals and awakening the shabby, gray villages from their deep, centuries-old slumber. In and around the factory construction work was still in full swing—new factory buildings were being erected, workers' housing was going up in disorder—both little wooden houses and, for the bachelors, enormous barracks.

Our pattern shop was situated on the upper floor, above the machine shop, inside a huge, tall building. The shop contained the characteristic monotonous metallic din of regularly operating turners' lathes, planing and milling tools, and the rustling sound of an entire cobweb of sliding driving belts. Now and then the screech of a circular saw cutting into strong dry wood would burst into this rhythmic noise.

Since the factory had been functioning for only a few months, no musty

---

[43]The Mytishchensk factory was located near the village of Mytishchi, twenty kilometers northeast of Moscow. In 1903, the factory employed 1,367 workers.

workshop traditions had been able to take shape.[44] There were few older
workers; merry, cheerful, freedom-loving young men were predominant. I
felt at home from the very first day. By now I was not in the least bit
troubled by having to perform tests of my skill. I handled these examinations without the slightest difficulty. Despite my youth (I was eighteen), the
foreman set my daily wage at a ruble sixty, that is, double what I was paid at
Bromlei's. I was, as they say, in seventh heaven.

One evening I returned home from work to find a "guest" awaiting me.
It was my father. When he saw me, he rose to greet me, embraced me, and
kissed me three times. In his long, fading pleated waistcoat, with his beard
grown white and his dark thinning hair streaked with gray, he had somehow become stooped, pinched, and aged over the past few months. His
voice had grown quiet. I felt sorry for him. The two of us sat together in my
room all evening (Volodia Ozeretskovskii[45] was working the night shift that
week). Coughing intermittently and breathing heavily, my father spoke in a
low voice about the village, about the bad flax harvest, about the loss of
two sheep, about our family difficulties, about his quarrel with my older
brother, and so on. I understood that in all the family problems it was my
father himself, with his authoritarian, despotic character, who was guilty,
while my brother was the victim. But as I heard his soft, penetrating speech,
I was infected involuntarily by my father's mood. I felt an interminable pity
for him, for this lonely, suffering old man, forsaken by everyone. But how
could I help him? By returning to the village to become a peasant? No, that
was out of the question. Even my father understood my state of mind and
therefore uttered not a word about my returning to the village.

He stayed at my apartment for three days. He paid close attention to our
style of life. All in all, he seemed pleased with me.

My comrades were very attentive to my father. Wishing not to hurt the
old man, Volodia even decided to conceal our free-thinking: on Saturday
evening he lit the lamp before the icon that hung in our closet, although in
general it was never illuminated, and on Friday he quietly asked the land-
lady to prepare lenten fare for us. Such precautions were superfluous, for

[44]Kanatchikov's expression here is "a tradition of . . . *tsekhovshchina*," by which he
means an excessive devotion to or pride in one's own workshop, craft, or some other
limited, parochial unit.

[45]Ozeretskovskii, one of the five tenants of the cottage, shared Kanatchikov's room.

my father understood full well that I had "not returned to the Christian faith," that I had indeed become even firmer in my free-thinking. And I myself did not conceal this.

Soothed and touched by my attentiveness, Father returned to the village. As we parted, I gave him ten rubles. Evidently, this kind of attention was particularly pleasing to him. Many years later people in the village would tell me how proud of me my father had been. It was not the money as such that was important to him as much as the fact that I had made my own way in life and become independent.

Yet at the same time, judging from his letters and from the accounts of fellow villagers, Father was constantly tortured by some kind of dim anxiety about me and about the fate that awaited me.

"I am amazed at the kind of child I have fathered: he drinks no vodka, smokes no tobacco, doesn't play cards, and doesn't care at all about the peasant," he would say with sadness about me to his friends and neighbors.

"It's all right, Ivan Egorych, he'll turn out right when he gets older," they would answer to console him.

The end of the summer was approaching imperceptibly. I was beginning to think about finding a winter apartment, since our dacha was not suitable for winter living. I did not wish to part from Klushin,[46] so we discussed these problems together. In short, all my thinking was channeled toward my winter amenities. I felt solidly ensconced at the factory: the foreman was well disposed toward me and satisfied with my work; I made no errors in my work and arrived at work on time, missing no days. So it seemed to me.

But one day it happened that the foreman assigned me a very simple task: to make a pattern of the most ordinary straight piece of pipe with flanges. The foreman drew the sketches for the pattern by hand. When the pipe was finished, he came up to me, measured the mould with calipers, and declared that it would have to be thrown away because I had erred by an inch. Then he added that I would be fired because of this. Deeply upset not so much over the announcement of my dismissal as over the insult to my professional pride, I rushed to the workbench to get the sketch and

[46]Kanatchikov rented living space in a dacha, or summer cottage, belonging to Vasilii Klushin, a politically radical, older metalworker, who became a new authority figure for Kanatchikov.

shove it in his face, to prove it was his error and not mine. But, alas, the drawing was not on the bench, and I searched for it in vain. The foreman's sketch, the only proof that I was right, had disappeared, vanished without a trace. The foreman made no effort to locate it, which I found suspicious. And when my anger and resentment had subsided somewhat, everything became clear to me.[47]

After being paid off and saying good-bye to my friends, I headed back to Moscow to find a new job.

WORKING FOR A "GRATER"[48]

Once again I did not remain without work very long. I found a job at a rather small machine works near the Krestovsk gate. I believe it was called Vartts and Mak-Gil.[49] At first everything went smoothly and well there. I passed the test, bought everyone a round of drinks, made new friends among the patternmakers, and even gained a bosom buddy, whom I later brought to Piter.[50]

Vania Maiorov was my new friend's name. He was my age but still worked as an apprentice. He had a very keen interest in social questions, liked to argue, and struggled passionately against any kind of "injustice." We hit it off in no time at all and soon were sharing a single room.

Not a month had gone by since I joined the Vartts factory when I was fired once again, this time without even getting two weeks notice. I endeavored to obtain "justice" from the factory inspector, but absolutely

---

[47]The clear implication is that Kanatchikov had been "set up." The real reason he was fired was his effort to propagate his radical religious and political views.

[48]The Russian word is *rashpel'* or *rashpil'* (from the German *Raspel*), which can be translated as either "grater" or "rasp," a kind of rough-edged filing tool. The term is used here pejoratively in reference to a notoriously hard-nosed type of small employer in specialized crafts who worked on subcontract for factories or larger workshops. The first time Kanatchikov uses the expression, his parenthetical explanation is a single word, *khoziaichik*, meaning a subcontractor.

[49]He is referring to Vartse and McGill. See Laura Engelstein, *Moscow, 1905: Working-Class Organization and Political Conflict* (Stanford, 1982), p. 30.

[50] "Piter" was the popular, colloquial term for the capital city, St. Petersburg.

nothing came of this.[51] Vania Maiorov was dismissed at the same time I was. Dark and difficult days of unemployment followed. Our savings were running out. We would arise earlier in the morning than usual, walk to some outlying area of the city, and stand at the gates of a factory awaiting the appearance of a foreman. We had long since stopped riding on the horse-driven trolley, which we could not afford. We lunched in soup kitchens for five kopecks on left-over pieces of tripe and lung. And in the evening we drank tea with bread.

All our efforts to find some sort of job at a factory were fruitless. We were forced to turn to a "grater." The latter greeted us with distrust and suspicion. Usually the people who came to him for work were inveterate drunkards, ruined from drink, who appeared at work dressed in tattered clothes that "barely covered their privates"; now there suddenly show up two young fellows in nice trousers and high boots, in fancy caps with rivets, and without any signs of unrelieved drunkenness on their faces! This was truly an amazing sight to behold! Winking mischievously with his left eye and looking us over unceremoniously from head to toe, the "grater" picked at his nose with self-importance, scratched himself below the back and asked:

"Do you know how to work?"

"We sure do."

"Show up to work tomorrow then."

Filled with joy, after nearly a month of unemployment, we took our places at the joiner's bench with great delight and set to work with zeal. The "grater" was pleased.

There were only a few workers in the Maliavkin (the "grater's" name) workshop: the two of us, the owner's younger brother, who had just returned from the army—he was a powerful fellow, formerly a joiner and now learning the patternmaker's trade—and two young apprentices.

---

[51]A Factory Inspectorate was established in 1882 and confirmed and expanded by the major legislation of 1886 as part of a government program to introduce effective labor laws into Russian factories. It was the job of the inspectors to listen to the complaints of workers, report on violations of the labor laws, and maintain surveillance over other aspects of factory life, such as working conditions and labor disturbances.

Maliavkin's pattern shop was located in Marinaia grove on the basement level of a filthy wooden two-story house. The "grater" Maliavkin—a man of medium height, broad-shouldered, with tiny, constantly squinting eyes that seemed to be taking aim at something, a man with the demeanor of a Iaroslav bartender—did not work in the workshop himself, but rushed about somewhere on the outside, getting orders and making all kinds of other arrangements along the way.

Strictly speaking, Maliavkin's "enterprise" could be called a "pattern shop" only with great reservations since we obtained very few patternmaking orders, and therefore we mainly carried out the "assignments" of various "inventors."

For a while we worked on a solution to the then-fashionable problem of inventing a "nonsplashing" tire: we built various tire covers—shields and casings for the wheels—carving different kinds of notches into them, which, according to the inventors, would hold the mud near the wheel and keep it from splashing on pedestrians.

For a long time we also worked on the "invention" of an armchair toilet seat, with various hidden compartments and shelves that were supposed to give it the appearance of a normal elegant armchair while curtailing the smell. Whether this invention ever brought glory and money to its authors I cannot say, but our "grater" certainly made some money from this affair.

Officially, our workday was supposed to be eleven hours; but to our misfortune, the "time problem" was decided not by us but by our inventor-entrepreneur, who, with the aid of his categorical imperative, also dictated the rules of our behavior. Hanging on the wall of the workshop was a dusty, fly-blown clock, which, obedient to Maliavkin's will, accelerated its pace at the beginning of the workday and slowed down at the end, thereby transforming our eleven-hour workday into twelve hours. Our wage was eighty kopecks a day, a sum we could only accept temporarily. Given my professional ambition and the standard of living I had already attained, I could not be satisfied with a wage like that.

Unfortunately, our "grater" tried to reduce even this meager sum. Always short of money, we were forced to borrow small amounts from Maliavkin in the interval between paydays. On such occasions he would be unusually accommodating and even, it seemed to us, generous. When we asked him for two or three rubles before payday, he usually replied:

"Take even more, my boys—we'll work it out later. For you I always have money." Sometimes the suggestion that we borrow from him came from Maliavkin himself.

Then payday would come around. Maliavkin would "balness" the books, as he put it, and there would always be an underpayment of one and a half or two rubles for each of us. We would try by means of frank discussion to establish the rights of objective truth; however, although we were the majority, the "grater's" subjective truth always gained the upper hand, and the two of us, furious, clenching our fists and cursing his "virtues," would return to our wretched hovel. Then we would discuss at length the inadequacies of the existing social order, building up our stock of spite and indignation.

Winter was approaching. Our life at the "grater's" was becoming unbearable. Tired, angry, we would get home late, drink our tea in silence, and go to sleep. We arose early, dressed hastily, hurriedly ate our breakfast while still half asleep, and rushed to work. So it went from day to day. Each of us on his own, at length and tenaciously, was thinking of how he could break away from the powerful clutches of the "grater." But where to go? In Moscow I was already known at many factories. To get work at some tiny plant was difficult and not even interesting. I would dream passionately of moving to St. Petersburg. I pictured that city as "the promised land," where the majority of workers were "conscious" and lived a cordial, comradely life, supporting one another in their struggle against foremen and owners.

We soon came to a firm decision to move to Piter. I would go first, and then, as soon as I found work, Vania Maiorov would follow.

Having sold my entire wardrobe for next to nothing, I collected my money for the trip and, in the autumn of 1898, I moved to Piter.

II

P. Timofeev

What the Factory Worker Lives By

INTRODUCTION

In recent years, the Russian worker
has persistently forced our society to take note of his existence. More and
more often, the smoldering undercurrent of discontent on the shop floor
has risen to the surface in the form of disorders, strikes, and street demon-
strations.[1] Despite all the repressive measures used to crush such disorders,
disturbances within the factories have not subsided. What is the cause of
this unrest? Many people are trying to answer that question, but it is not
easy; the worker's life is too isolated and jealously guarded from outside
observers by the interested parties. Nor do the demands that workers put
forward during their mass actions give a complete picture of the wishes and
aspirations of the majority of workers as individuals. Consequently, anyone

---

[1]Beginning in the mid-1890s, labor unrest increasingly threatened the social stability of
Imperial Russia. The most dramatic example was the 1896 textile strike in St. Petersburg
(see Ch. 1, n. 19). Major labor disturbances occurred again in St. Petersburg in 1901 and
in the southern industrial region in 1903, spreading from the Baku oil fields to many
other cities in the South. Timofeev's essay, which was published in 1906, may also be
referring here to the labor upheavals that took place during the Revolution of 1905. See
above, Introduction, n. 3, for a list of works on the period 1891–1905 in Russian labor
history.

wishing to study the daily life of Russian workers will find many obstacles in his path.

For the simple reason that I have no other material to rely on than my own personal experiences and observations, I make no claim that the following "sketches" present a detailed study of the worker's life. My task is far more modest. I would merely like to acquaint the reader, if only slightly, with life on the shop floor and to throw some light on those problems most often confronted by the Russian factory worker. The reader should not imagine that I intend to describe the entire class of factory workers. Rather, I will restrict myself to those parts of working-class life that I know best. In what follows, I will be speaking mainly about workers in metalworking enterprises and, specifically, those employed in large plants.

The world of the textile factory is completely different from that of the large metalworking plant.[2] The textile factory has its own unique characteristics. Since the work and the wages are very different for a textile worker than for a worker in heavy industry, these two groups of workers should never be confused. Though they do have certain characteristics in common, the differences in their working conditions are very great.

STRATIFICATION ON THE SHOP FLOOR

A large metalworking plant is like a world in miniature. Some factories contain up to two hundred different workshops. Large factories are usually

[2]Timofeev uses the Russian terms *zavod* (translated here as "metalworking plant") and *fabrika* (translated here as "textile factory") in this context to contrast the two main branches of St. Petersburg industry, metalworking and textiles. The Russian terms, which have no precise English equivalents, designate large and variegated categories of manufacturing enterprise. *Zavod* can be applied not only to metalworking but also to leather manufacturing, sugar refineries, and breweries, to mention only a few. The term *fabrika*, a variant of which exists in most European languages, is used, *inter alia*, for paper mills and most branches of food processing, as well as for textile factories. It is also normally used as the generic term for factories of all kinds. "Engineering works" (*mekhanicheskii* or *mashino-stroitelnyi zavod*) is itself a broad term, encompassing plants for the manufacture of engines, machines, machine tools, railway cars, and locomotives. The St. Petersburg metalworking industry described below by Timofeev had five major branches: munitions, shipbuilding, railroad construction, machine building, and electrical engineering.

5. Shell shop in Petersburg's giant Putilov plant in the early 1900s.

broken up into several divisions, such as the metallurgical department, the foundry, the locomotive department, and the railroad car department. And if we take in turn any one department, say the railroad car department, it will contain a lumberyard, a carpentry shop, a painting shop, an upholstery shop, a roofing shop, a machine shop, a wheel shop, a tire shop, a forge, a foundry, a pattern shop, and so on. Working conditions are by no means the same in the different workshops.

Standing at the head of the entire factory is the general administration with its lower-level management personnel. Each department is under the direction of a special department head, who is usually a specialist technician. Finally, every shop has a foreman with his assistants, and sometimes there may be several foremen, with the senior foreman serving as supervisor. The foreman represents that lever of factory life which presses on the worker the hardest, and the worker's whole existence intimately depends on him.

Even the workers in a single shop by no means constitute a homogeneous group. To begin with, they can be divided into two large groups that differ sharply from one another. There are the so-called skilled or specialized workers [*masterovye*], and the unskilled workers [*chernorabochie*]. The terms "skilled worker" [*masterovoi*] and "worker" [*rabochii*] are now often used completely interchangeably. However, the word "worker" as it is understood by the intelligentsia has actually penetrated the working-class milieu only recently. Not too long ago, it was a gross insult to refer to a skilled worker simply as a worker since he possessed skills which had taken him from three to six years to acquire. Even now, when a friend of a skilled worker feels the need to swear at someone, he does not use ordinary insults but instead says, "Oh, you worker you!" And for a skilled worker that is like calling a count's coachman a "carter."[3] About twenty years ago in one of the railway workshops, I think it was the Korov factory, the workers even rioted over precisely this issue.

This is what happened. In those days, workbooks containing factory regulations had not yet been introduced at factories.[4] Then one fine Saturday such books were distributed to the workers.

"Good Lord! Am I fired? What will I do now?" But when the workers looked inside and discovered that everyone was referred to simply as a "worker," they began to go wild right then and there.

"So we're just workers, are we!" they shouted as they went out through the factory gates. "We're *skilled* workers [*masterovye*], not just workers [*rabochie*]. They want to turn us into common workers now, boys! Well, we're not going to let them get away with it!"

So they decided to go on strike. However, the strike did not last long. Soon the soldiers arrived on the scene, and starting from around two o'clock in the morning of the third day, the "demoted" skilled workers, trying to conceal themselves from one another, stealthily began to make

[3]The reference here is to status differentiations within the lower classes. A common cart driver, or carter, had a much lower status than someone who drove a coach for a nobleman.

[4]On workbooks, see Ch. 1, n. 32.

their way back into the factory. It was then that the factory office came to their assistance. The management had also encountered problems from the elimination of the term "skilled worker" since they, too, needed some way to classify the workers. Formerly, on all the notice boards and information bulletins a distinction had been made between skilled workers and others. But now that the skilled workers had been banished and renamed simply "workers," a new word had to be found for those workers whose job it was to do all the dirty work. Consequently, the latter were now called "unskilled workers" [*chernorabochie*]. This is the way it was not so very long ago. Now, however, much has changed in the world of the factory.

Factory workers can be divided into two large groups, the skilled and the unskilled, each one very different from the other in terms of both their earnings and their attitudes. Numerically, the skilled workers are in the majority in metalworking plants. On the average, for every thousand skilled workers there are two hundred unskilled, although it all depends on the nature of the factory. For example, if the factory contains iron-working shops with Bessemer or Martin furnaces, rolling mills, and so forth, then the number of unskilled workers is far greater. First of all, there is a lot more material to be moved around. Secondly, the iron production process itself, by virtue of its uniformity and its demand for a complex division of labor, makes it easy for an unskilled worker to get used to a specific task. Incidentally, in such cases, one can no longer really refer to the workers as unskilled since they would be earning more money and their work would have to meet the specific requirements of the foreman.

Sometimes such workers can even become department heads (a position normally filled by a trained engineer), although I personally would not recommend that anyone work under them. I have never once seen them show the slightest sign of solidarity with the milieu from which they had come, except that sometimes they become big local patriots, hiring only those people from the same region as themselves. There is one factory in St. Petersburg in which an entire department is filled with workers from two districts in Tver province, Startskii and Novotorzhskii, where the two shop managers were born.⁵

---

⁵Russia's industrial labor force was composed largely of peasants who migrated to industrial regions from the countryside. Tver province, located to the southeast of St.

UNSKILLED WORKERS

In the life of the plant, the unskilled workers are an almost completely insignificant group. They have no say in what transpires on the shop floor, and they passively submit to the common voice of the skilled workers. As day laborers who are paid low wages at the end of each day, they develop no strong ties to the factory and can leave at any time to look for work elsewhere. Unskilled labor is required in almost all the workshops; but usually such workers make up the so-called "menial" or "courtyard brigade" or, as they are jokingly referred to by the skilled workers, "the courtiers."[6] The daily wage of these workers is only sixty to seventy kopecks, and it is paid out every evening. This system of payment is a severe handicap to the worker. Since his wages are always in kopecks, he is deprived of the opportunity of ever possessing sums of money large enough to buy clothing or footwear. Admittedly, savings banks do accept small coins, but their hours are not always geared to the worker's free time. Even when that is not the case, the worker often does not want to waste his precious leisure time inside a bank. More importantly, we are simply not accustomed to using such institutions.

When he arrives in the city from the countryside and settles down at

---

Petersburg, suffered from a surplus of rural labor. As a result, many peasants from this area migrated to St. Petersburg to seek employment in factories and other sectors of the urban economy. In 1910, Tver province was the leading source of peasant workers in St. Petersburg. See James H. Bater, *St. Petersburg: Industrialization and Change* (London, 1976), pp. 143, 146–149, 304. As Timofeev shows, workers who came from the same area of Russia developed a kind of local patriotism and helped one another out as best they could. A person in a position of authority, such as a foreman, sometimes preferred to hire people from the same province, district, or even village as himself. As a result, certain shops, enterprises, and occupations had high concentrations of workers from the same area of Russia. See Robert E. Johnson, *Peasant and Proletarian: The Working Class of Moscow in the Late Nineteenth Century* (New Brunswick, N.J., 1979).

[6]Timofeev is making a pun here on the Russian word *dvor*, which means both courtyard and royal court. The adjective *dvorovyi* means literally "of the courtyard" or "menial" and is used to describe the "menial brigade" of unskilled workers. The word *pridvornye*, however, which has the same linguistic root, means "courtiers." Thus, through a slight modification of words, the skilled workers had created a facetious title for their unskilled fellow workers.

some factory or other, the unskilled worker almost always feels that he is in a suspended state. The first question he has to deal with is his relationship to the village. Of course, as long as his wife remains in the village, it is impossible for him to cut all ties. But even when he has managed to bring his wife to live with him, his position is still not completely resolved. He knows that he is not a "skilled worker," that he can be thrown out at any time, and that it will be much more difficult for him to find a job again than it would be for a skilled worker. His awareness of all these things makes him unwilling to give up his ties to the village, where he can always find a crust of bread that will let him survive until the spring, when the factories start to pick up again. Survive until the spring. . . !

But you would think that in the spring his labor would be needed in the village. That is when all the field work begins. If the village lets him go away in the spring to look for work, this itself is a sign of the poverty and shortage of land which makes his labor superfluous there.[7] It also means that every ruble he can send back to the village from the town is a far more important contribution to the village economy than his work in the fields would be. But how can he save a ruble when he makes only seventy kopecks a day? He has to send money, but where will he get it? The only answer is to economize, to scrimp and save on food, housing, and clothes.

Once I went to visit an unskilled worker whom I knew. He lived in an artel[8] with seventeen other men. The apartment consisted of one large smoke-blackened room with two windows. At one time, wallpaper had covered the walls, but now it was torn away, revealing the plain board walls underneath. Hordes of cockroaches were crawling along the walls. I couldn't help asking my friend, "How come you've got so many cockroaches here?"

---

[7]According to the Emancipation Act of 1861, control over the peasants' internal mobility was vested in the village commune. The commune held a peasant's passport (see n. 12, below), and in order to leave the countryside the peasant had to secure the permission of the commune. Peasants were not permitted to leave the village permanently until their share of the redemption payments had been paid, thereby fulfilling the terms of the emancipation settlement. Some communes, particularly those in poor agricultural regions, allowed members to depart seasonally to look for work elsewhere on the condition that they sent money back to the village.

[8]On the artel, see Ch. 1, n. 2.

There were about twelve people in the room at the time, and they all burst out laughing. One of them replied, "A cockroach is nothing, he doesn't hurt you. A bedbug—that's different. He bites. But a cockroach, he's like part of the family."

"Do you have bedbugs too?" I asked.

"Plenty!" my friend replied. "Fewer than cockroaches, of course, but more than enough for us folks. We've got all kinds of critters in here."

The walls were lined with wooden bunks, obviously the main haven of the bedbugs. In the center of the room was a long trestle table and two equally long benches. There was a small kerosene lamp hanging between the windows. Underneath the lamp was a cheap print of the Tsar's family. A holy icon, blackened with age, hung in the corner. The kitchen, which also served as an entrance hall, was off to one side of the room and contained the cook's bed. That was all the furniture for eighteen people.

I sat down on one of the benches and started up a conversation. At that time I was very interested in workers' ties to the village, and so I immediately turned the conversation to that topic. Eleven of the eighteen men there were married, and all their wives lived in the village. Only one of them had been visited by his wife recently, and before that she hadn't seen her husband in four whole years. One of them had lived there for five years without seeing his wife.

"Why don't you bring your wives here?" I asked.

"How could we do that? Today we're here, but God knows where we'll be tomorrow. So that's how we live—each by himself."

Each member of the communal apartment sent no more than three to five rubles a month back to the village. That sum is by no means insignificant when you consider that even if a worker is *constantly employed*, a wage of seventy kopecks a day comes to no more than sixteen to seventeen rubles a month. A wife could not come without the children, which would mean having to rent a separate room at a cost of six to eight rubles a month. In addition, the cost of food, clothing, and footwear would not only be doubled, but even quadrupled. Obviously sixteen rubles a month would not be enough. Finally, the worker would have to stop sending money to the village and would lose this last refuge during times of unemployment once and for all. This final point was confirmed after I talked to some unskilled workers who had brought their families to live with them in the town. They had broken all their ties to the village and were entirely at the mercy of fate.

The members of an artel always elect one of the group to take on the position of elder,[9] a job that mainly involves buying provisions for the whole cooperative and settling accounts with the cook and the landlord. Some of the workers also give their money to the elder for safekeeping, and for this reason the workers choose someone for the job who is known and trusted by all. If the elder has to lose a day's work, or more often half a day's work, by taking care of the cooperative's business, then he is reimbursed by the cooperative members at the going rate in the factory. The position of elder is generally considered to be lucrative because tradesmen at the stores where the elder buys provisions charge him a little less than the full amount of the bill.

Generally, each worker in the cooperative gets by for around eight rubles and twenty-five kopecks a month. This includes rent, food, the cook's wages (in this case the cook was the elder's wife), and reimbursement of the elder for lost working time. This does not include tea, and whoever wants it has to buy it for himself. In the morning, each worker takes about a pound to a pound and a half of black bread with him to work. This will be his "breakfast," which he will usually have with tap water instead of tea. Lunch consists of a sour cabbage soup, a small piece of meat, and wheat kasha.[10] The meat is rarely served in one piece but rather is chopped up into tiny bits and poured into the soup. (Does the reader realize just what a treat it is for a Russian peasant or worker to eat a piece of meat? Meat on the table is an extraordinary event and a sign of affluence. I clearly

[9]The Russian word for *elder* is *starosta* (the root is *star*, meaning "old"). Originally the *starosta* was the elected leader of a village commune, but the term was subsequently applied to elected leaders in other situations as well. In 1903, for example, a law was passed legalizing the establishment of factory elders in industrial establishments to improve communications between workers and management. As Timofeev observes, the members of an artel elected an elder who assumed responsibility for paying bills and providing food. Further on, Timofeev describes the election of an elder to oversee the maintenance of the icon on the shop floor. See below, pp. 95–101.

[10]Kasha is made from oat, wheat, or buckwheat groats that are cooked with either water or milk. It was one of the most important items in the Russian diet.

recall a certain stoker who could never forget the time he was sent away on a job where he was given as much meat as he could eat. "I would eat it on its own," he said, 'without any bread. I'd pick the fattiest piece and let the grease run down my beard.")

On holidays, a plain broth is made, along with buckwheat instead of wheat kasha. On both workdays and holidays, all the kasha is usually gone after lunch, leaving only meatless cabbage soup and black bread for dinner. This is how it is day in and day out.

One artel where I happened to spend some time was made up of peasants from two adjacent villages in the province of Novgorod, so they were all neighbors. Either because they came from the one place, or for some other reason, they got along surprisingly well together. There were hardly ever any quarrels or fights. If someone drank too much and got out of hand, then his comrades would immediately knock the troublemaker down on his bunk, tie his hands and feet with a belt, and leave him like that until he slept it off. The close regional ties bound them together into one large family, and many members sacrificed a lot to remain in this cooperative. One of them, for instance, had to get up at three o'clock every morning in order to walk from the Narva gates to the Nevskii factory, a distance of roughly eight miles both ways.[11] Someone else worked in the Vyborg district and had a similar journey to make every day.

"Why don't you find lodging near the factory?" I asked.

"Why, we like it here."

"But don't you mind having to walk so far?"

"We don't mind, we're used to it."

Yes, I thought to myself, you have to get used to things to survive here.

---

[11]This was an exceptionally long commute to work for a St. Petersburg factory worker. Since public transportation in the city was both expensive and poorly suited to workers' needs, workers usually made their journey to work on foot. For this reason, most workers tried to find housing close to their workplace so that they could go home over the lunch break and not extend the workday with a long commute. As industry expanded in St. Petersburg, however, housing for workers became more scarce and commuting distances to the workplace increased. See James H. Bater, "The Journey to Work in St. Petersburg 1860–1914," *Journal of Transport History*, NS, III, 2 (September 1974): 214–233.

SKILLED WORKERS AND THE VILLAGE

When a worker manages to get out of the "menial brigade" and move onto the shop floor, he has an incomparably greater sense of belonging to the factory. He is now paid twice a month rather than every day. The numbered identity tag which he receives serves for him as visible proof that he too, just like the skilled workers, is a numbered cog in the enormous machine called "the factory."

Sometimes the new arrival on the shop floor may be singled out by the foreman and given some monotonous but well-paying piecework. If that happens, his wages will rise considerably, almost to the level of the skilled workers' wages. However, he has to keep his distance from the skilled workers because they often see him as an unwanted competitor and are therefore not particularly friendly.

Once a worker starts earning thirty to thirty-five rubles a month and has almost become a skilled worker, he is no longer so willing to send money back home to the village. I have often heard of disagreements between parents in the village and their children working at factories in the town. Often the disputes even end up in court when a father refuses his son a passport for failing to send money back to the village.[12]

As for skilled workers, the majority probably feel that the village is nothing but a burden. At least, this was the opinion I personally heard from most of them. The only exceptions were those with such good land in the village that they didn't have to send money home, and those who were the sons of prosperous village artisans and merchants. All the rest said that the village was more of a hindrance than a help.

---

[12]Internal passports first made an appearance in Russia during the Time of Troubles in the early seventeenth century, but they were only introduced on a large scale by Peter the Great as part of his military and financial reforms. Internal passports remained a constant feature of Russian life from Peter's time on. Following the Emancipation Act of 1861, the village commune was vested with the authority to issue passports to those peasants who wished to leave the village. Men under the age of eighteen and women under the age of twenty-one needed parental approval to get a passport, and married women needed the consent of their husbands. A father could compel an absent member of his family to return to the village by convincing the authorities to revoke that person's passport. Without a passport, it was not possible to secure factory employment, since the law required workers to present their passports at the time of application.

There are many skilled workers who have never seen a wooden plow and do not have the slightest idea how to plant wheat because they have lived in a town and worked in a factory for the past twenty-five to thirty years. Their only connection with the village comes when they need to obtain a passport or when they have to pay taxes for land which is nominally theirs but is actually worked by other people.

While talking with one such worker recently, I heard the most unexpected opinion about workers who kept their ties with the village.

"These 'villagers' have hurt us a lot in the last strike," he told me decisively.

"In what way?" I asked.

"Well, they all shouted, 'Strike! Strike!' so we went on strike until the factory closed down."

"Then what happened?"

"Then they all packed up and went back to the village, leaving us high and dry. The landlord threatened to throw us out of our rooms, and we had no money and no food."

"Well, what do you make of this?"

"They're just holding back the worker's cause. They don't feel they have to organize the way we do, and why should they? Once they see that things are getting bad, they head for the village right away, saying, 'The rest of you, boys, you can just make do the best you can.' That's why the bosses don't give us unions—because not everyone demands them."

As I got to know a number of workers who hadn't broken their ties with the village, I noticed that they would send their families off to the village for the summer and would go back there every year or two themselves. Once I happened to mention that they probably could save up some money while their families were away since they would be spending less on room and board.

However, all my arguments immediately fell to pieces. They objected that when the family went away, they had to spend even more money. Even with the wife gone, they still had to rent the apartment because what could they do with all the furniture? In addition, there was the expense of the trip. They had to have decent clothes to go back to the village, otherwise people would say, "Look! They live in the city and dress worse than beggars." "Here we get by somehow," they said, "but in the village you have to show off. Then you have to take everyone a present: a dress for your mother, a jacket for your sister-in-law, a shawl for your mother-in-law, and shoes for the kids. On top of that, as soon as you arrive, everyone tries to get drinks out of you. They know that no one comes to the village broke."

From such conversations, I finally came to the following conclusions. If things are going well in the village, the skilled worker will maintain his ties to it and will send back relatively large sums of money. Thanks to this, he can send his wife there for the summer or even go there himself to recuperate from work. However, by doing this, he spends a lot of money unproductively and has no chance to accumulate even the slightest savings. If things aren't going well in the village, the skilled worker is inclined to break his ties. The small sum which he could send back robs him of an extra piece of bread and really cannot help the village very much.

The position of the unskilled worker is even more complex. Simply by virtue of the fact that he is an unskilled worker, one can assume that his relatives in the village are poor. Nor is he exactly well off in the town on his seventy kopecks a day. Yet he has to send money back to the village because his wife and children are there and also because he could be thrown out of work at any time. In that case, so as not to die of hunger in the town, he would have to go back to the village to eat bread made of the last seed grain.[13]

LOOKING FOR WORK

I shall now try and describe the ordeals which the worker has to go through to get a job. How does a worker find work in the factory?

Here in Russia, everything is done by means of "family" connections. Let us suppose you are a metalworker, and you have arrived in a totally strange town. The first thing you have to do is find a factory. In order to do that, you walk several miles to the outskirts of the town. You can always tell when you are getting close to a factory because of the buildings: the dirty taverns and the even dirtier shops and beer halls. A little further on you

---

[13]Peasants put away part of their harvest each year to use for planting in the following spring. In times of dire need, this seed grain would be eaten, and then the peasants would have to borrow money for grain in order to plant in the spring.

notice smoke rising from the factory chimneys; then you see the chimneys and finally the factory building itself.

Along one of these walls you will find the factory gates and next to them a small building called the "entry office" where you have to go. If it is early morning or around lunchtime, you will probably find several people dressed like yourself waiting there. They are also looking for a job and probably waiting to find a foreman or friend who can give them a reference. You go up to them and start a conversation.

"Hi, pal. You got a light?" Then you go on to ask where he worked before, what his trade is, and so on, and finally you ask the question: "Do they need any metalfitters here?"

It turns out that several workshops employ metalfitters, mainly the locomotive assembly shop and the machine shop. Metalfitters are usually paid quite well in these shops, since they work for piece wages.[14] In the other workshops, like the electrical workshop, the pig iron foundry, the steel foundry, or the rolling mill, metalfitters are also used, but in a limited way. Usually you are paid by the day there, and the wage is seldom more than one ruble and thirty kopecks. Sometimes you are paid an additional percentage, say ten to fifteen kopecks per ruble, but not always. Knowing this, you obviously want to try to get into the locomotive assembly shop or the machine shop. However, there are always lots of people trying for the same job, even metalfitters from different workshops in the same factory. Obviously you need a recommendation, so you go over in your mind all the workers you have worked with, looking for those who might be working here. If you can think of someone, you wait until the workers start leaving the factory and then ask around if so-and-so is employed there.

If you don't get a positive answer, then you have no choice but to try and speak with the foreman yourself and to plead with him. The watchman

[14]There are two basic methods of paying workers for their labor: by the time they work and by the piece. According to the former method, a fixed wage is paid for the time an individual works, that is, by the hour, week, or month. Alternatively, there is payment on a piecework basis, according to the quantity of work accomplished. Generally speaking, piecework is considered more disadvantageous to the worker than a fixed wage. Yet there are some exceptions, for example, the skilled metalfitters referred to in the text whose piece rates were high enough to provide them with earnings that were better than average in the industry.

will point him out as he leaves the factory and will tell you his name. You head toward him, but the foreman knows in advance what you are going to say before you get there and will either wave you away as if to say don't bother, or else he will try to frighten you away. If you are still possessed by the demon of pride, you will probably be equally rude in return; or you will plead with him until he either calls the watchman or disappears behind the doors of his own apartment.

Of course, this is not the only possible outcome. I have only given the worst example. If, for instance, you are a good skilled worker, you don't start by asking at the factory gates but instead make every effort to get inside the factory and into the workshop. This in itself often presents difficulties. You have to get hold of an identification tag and go inside with the other workers or, if you have any money, discreetly bribe the watchman. If that doesn't work, then you have to think up some kind of trick. You wash your face, put a ruler into the top pocket of your jacket, get hold of a sheet of drafting paper, and with the serious expression of a draftsman, boldly walk through the gate reserved for office personnel. The watchman will let you through because he does not know all the office workers by sight, and if he did, he would probably assume you are new on the job. However, if the watchman decides to ask you something, you have to be very careful. One false word and the game is up. They would ask you into the office where you, of course, would have to confess. Sometimes this even works in your favor and they send a boy to show you the way to the shop. However, this happens very rarely. Usually they just ask you to leave the factory, and that's all.

But let us assume you are inside the factory and are confidently walking toward the first workshop you see. At the door of the shop you hide your sheet of drafting paper and put the ruler into your pants pocket. This is important because only foremen, foremen's assistants, and draftsmen carry rulers in their top pockets. Ordinary workers put their rulers into the lower pocket of their jacket or in their pants. It may seem strange, but it is really the case that any worker carrying his ruler in full view would be mocked by his fellow workers.

At the entrance to the workshop you drop your air of importance and assume the appearance of an ordinary worker once again. Of course, the noise—the roar of the machines and the moving cobweb of transmission belts—does not bother you at all. You go straight up to one of the workers and ask him which workshop you are in, where the metalfitters are, and who their foreman is. With this information, you make your way between the machines in a corner of the workshop where the metalfitters are working at benches set up with vises. You approach them, say hello, and start talking. Is there any work here? Is anyone being taken on? They will ask you some questions too, like where you worked before, how long ago you left your last job, and so on. Usually at some point during the conversation the names of people who used to work at your previous factory come up; you find mutual acquaintances, and they start to see you as one of the crowd, at least to some extent. If you don't find anyone among these new acquaintances to put in a good word for you with the assistant foreman, then you have to talk to him yourself. Usually the assistant foreman does not have the power to hire or dismiss people. You know this perfectly well, but you go up to him nonetheless because nine times out of ten, the foreman will ask his assistant whether they need to hire anyone or not. This is the case because there is usually only one foreman in the shop but there are several assistants who are in a position to know whether a particular work team is short of people. You will usually get the following answer from the assistant foreman:

"Ask the boss himself. It's not my job."

"Yes," you say, "I know. But just in case he asks, put in a word for me, Egor Vasilevich."

"O.K.," the assistant replies, and you go off to the foreman.

You find the foreman drinking tea in his office, which is located in the workshop itself. You walk up and stand outside the door respectfully.

"Hey, you, what do you want?" he asks. His form of address will depend on your clothes. If you are well dressed, he might address you politely.[15]

[15]As in many European languages, Russian has a familiar *(ty)* and a polite form *(vy)* of address. The familiar form implies personal intimacy and is used with children, some family members, and close friends. In prerevolutionary times, it was also customary to use the familiar form when speaking with members of the lower classes. Workers expressed resentment against this condescending form of address and demanded polite treatment by their superiors at the workplace. This demand became especially wide-

6. Machine shop in a Petersburg shipbuilding plant around 1900. The shop mainly employed metalfitters.

You bow to him and start talking. "I'm a metalfitter. I've worked at this factory and that factory, but left to come and work for you." If you have some kind of written recommendation with you, then it's worth mentioning it, but don't put big hopes on it. If the foreman was once a worker himself, and he hasn't forgotten it yet, he's likely to say, "Don't show me any recommendations. Let's see how you handle this hammer and chisel." Of course, there are some foremen who think recommendations are very important.

When you have finished talking, the foreman will either send you away or tell you to come in tomorrow. Then again, he may call over his assistant, with whom you have already had a word, and ask, "We've got a metalfitter

---

spread during the 1905 revolution and in the years that followed. In this passage, Timofeev calls attention to the importance of visible signs of status among workers. A skilled worker was likely to be more prosperous and better dressed than one who was unskilled or semiskilled, and the foreman could be expected to show him respectful treatment accordingly.

here. Can you use him?" "O.K.," the assistant answers. "I can use one." You can now congratulate yourself on having been hired at this factory.

It is usually much better to ask for work inside the factory rather than at the factory gates. You are able to explain things properly, and, if necessary, you can demonstrate your skills on the spot, none of which is possible at the factory gates. In addition, when the foreman gets to the factory gates, he is hungry and hurrying home to eat, and everyone knows that hunger is the main reason people are in a bad mood. On the other hand, if he is on the way back to the factory from the lunch break, he is probably hurrying so he won't be late for work.

In this way, you have successfully participated in the process known to political economy as "the supply of labor." This is the most common and widespread method of finding a job, and it is used practically everywhere. Everything depends on the impression you make on the foreman. If he likes you for some reason, or if you have a friend who works closely with him and will put in a good word for you, then you can count on getting the job. If not, then you can get a job only under exceptional circumstances.

FIRST DAY ON THE JOB

When the foreman hires you, you receive a factory pass. The next day when you come to work, you show this pass to the watchman or bring it to the entry office. Then you go to your workshop.

Work hasn't started yet, and the workers are scattered around in small groups, chatting among themselves. You go over to a group of metalfitters that you know and wait for the third whistle. Soon all the other workers gather around to say hello, to ask whether you have found lodging yet, and to talk about the kind of "test" you will be given. Finally, the third whistle blows and everyone goes off to work while you remain standing there, leaning against the workbench.

About ten minutes later, the assistant foreman comes up to you and says, "Well, we'd better give you a test." He goes out and returns a few minutes later, placing a bearing and a gauge in front of you. Then he says, "Here's a bearing which needs calibrating. You can get the tools from the toolkeeper. I'll write you a note." He tears a sheet from his notebook and jots down a few words. Then he shows you the vise which you will use and directs you to the tool room.

You take the note from him, pick up your tools, and get right down to work. Around nine o'clock, a boy comes up to you and says you are wanted in the office. There they give you your passport and employment paper,[16] although sometimes this doesn't happen until after the test is over. The clerk tells you that your number is 727 and that you must proceed to the entry office to present your passport and employment paper, and then go on to the doctor for an examination. That's exactly what you do. By the door of the entry office you notice a sign above a window which says "Passport Division." You hand in your passport and employment paper there. Sometimes they will ask you if this is the first time you have worked at the factory. If the answer is no, then they will ask you what your number was before. But this is all for show because they won't take your word for it anyway and will look it up in the books. If you haven't worked there before, or if you have but quit on your own accord leaving no bad record behind, they will write on your employment paper: "This office has no objections to the employment of metalfitter no. 727." Then they write a receipt for the passport, noting its expiration date, and return both the passport and the employment paper to you.

From there you proceed to the infirmary, where you present your employment paper and get in line. There are usually a few newcomers like yourself at the doctor's. You join them and wait.

Finally, everyone is called into the doctor's office. You get into a single file and enter the reception room one at a time. Then they ask you to take off your clothes and show off your physique. The doctor rejects very few people. I do not really know whether this is because we Russians are a particularly healthy people or whether it is because this examination isn't considered very important. You only get a thorough examination in state-owned factories or in the railroad workshops. There they take your chest measurements, check your eyesight and hearing, and give you a color test. By the way, there is a simple explanation for this. After a worker has spent

---

[16]This employment paper *(priemnaia zapiska)* was a document issued by the factory certifying that a worker was employed there.

twenty years on the job, state factories are supposed to provide him with a pension, but private factories do not have to.[17]

At the end of the examination, the doctor writes "Healthy" on your employment paper and sends you back to the entry office. There you exchange your paper for a pass which has your number 727, your name, and the length of your probation period written on it. The probation period is usually somewhere between three to six days. While on probation, you have to use your pass instead of the identity tag which workers use to get into the factory during the appointed times.

At this point, I have to make one more digression. This pass and probation period have been introduced only in the best factories. If for some reason you decide not to keep the job after finishing your probation period, then you are entitled to be paid according to the rate determined by the factory regulations. There are, however, some factories that will not pay you for the probation period, so whatever work you do costs them nothing. I can name one railroad coach factory in Petersburg as an example. A worker there won't find out what his pay will be until he has finished his first test job, which can take from a day and a half to two days. Then let's say that instead of the ruble and twenty kopecks he thought he was worth, they only offer him eighty kopecks. If he doesn't want to work for that wage and leaves the factory, he won't get a cent for the work he did, while the factory gets a job done for nothing.

I don't think that this is a deliberate abuse on the part of the factory, but some workers I know argue convincingly that it is. Why else, they point out, would the factory go on hiring new people even in a time of unemployment?

[17]Enterprises in Russia were either privately or state-owned. The state-owned enterprises could be found in various sectors of the economy, with heavy concentrations in transportation (e.g., railroads) and the manufacture of military-related products. At the turn of the century, about one-third of the metal and machine workers in St. Petersburg were employed in plants owned by the state. The laws governing the terms and conditions of work in these state-owned enterprises were more comprehensive than for private firms. The pension provisions referred to by Timofeev were part of the law of June 3, 1894 (which was revised on June 2, 1903), establishing pension funds for workers employed by the state-owned railroad industry. Contrary to Timofeev's assertion, the law required fifteen rather than twenty years of employment in order to qualify for a pension.

Someone once said that a Russian peasant was made up of three elements—a body, a soul, and a passport. If we are talking about a factory worker, then we must add one more element: his identity tag. In the factory, this tag is usually more important than the other three. If the tag is in the factory, then the worker is in the factory. If the tag isn't there, then the worker isn't there. So if Grigorii Noskov gets his hand torn off while his tag was missing, he can't even think of getting compensation. As far as the factory is concerned, he wasn't there at all. Therefore you have to watch out for your tag and report it immediately if you lose it.

One paragraph of the factory regulations states: "There is a fine of fifty kopecks for losing the identity tag, a fine of twenty kopecks for leaving it at home, and a fine of one ruble for leaving it in the factory." The fine is high in the latter case because they assume you left work early and didn't pick up your tag (tags aren't handed back until five minutes before the whistle, and workers can be fined for leaving the factory without permission), or they think that you left the tag intentionally, hoping to get paid for the extra night shift.

After finishing up in the entry office, you return to the workshop and get back to work. By now, there's not too much time left until lunch. In less than an hour, the other workers finish off their work, wash their hands, and get their tags from the boy in charge. Just then the lunch whistle blows. You hurriedly hide your tools and leave the workshop with the other workers. They frisk you at the factory gates and when nothing is found, they let you out into the street.

After lunch you go back and work undisturbed until evening. The job you have been given is a test of your skill and knowledge, and therefore you try to work as quickly and efficiently as possible. In most cases, the quality of your work will determine the rate at which you will be paid.

Sometimes you won't feel fully competent to do the assigned job and will doubt whether you can finish the test, but don't despair. Look around at your fellow workers and pick out the friendliest-looking one. Go up to him and say, "Well, friend, I'm afraid that I can't do it. Can you please help me?" In such cases, workers are always willing to help. When they see that you have a problem with something, they will teach you how to do it, or if necessary do it themselves. Just don't put on airs and act like you know

7. Canteen in the early 1900s where Petersburg workers took their meals.

more than the others. In short, you should try to act like one of the crowd right from the start and admit it openly when you're not sure of something.

Many people think that workers are not motivated by simple generosity in such cases but by the hope of getting a bottle of vodka out of it. This isn't true, however. If vodka has anything to do with the issue at all, it is simply a way of saying thank you. In my opinion, vodka is a lot better than the money bribes customary among other social classes.

Once the assistant foreman brought us a new worker and set him to work on his trial job. The job was fairly easy, but it soon became obvious that the new man was having a hard time with it. One of the workers went up to him and asked, "Where did you work before?"

The newcomer gave us the name of a small factory.[18]

[18]The Russian term *kustarnyi zavod* connotes a small enterprise that relied mainly on hand labor. Often these small factories manufactured products on a subcontracting basis for larger firms. Timofeev describes the working conditions in one of these small firms

"Were you a metalworker there?"

"Yes, I was a metalworker, but all I ever did was assemble things. Then I was fired and I haven't had a job in three months. I've sold everything and my wife's hardly got any clothes left on her back. I'm lucky that Ivan Gavrilovich agreed to get me in here for ten rubles. I hope I can finish this."

"Why can't you?"

"Well, you can see what kind of metalworker I am."

"Who is this Ivan Gavrilovich, anyway?"

"He works in the office at the locomotive assembly shop."

At this point, several other workers came over, and one of them asked, "Have you given him any money yet?"

"Not yet. I promised to do it in three days. I was hoping I could borrow it from someone."

"Listen here, tell your Ivan Gavrilovich to go to hell. Just keep an eye out for the foreman. Now, boys, who has a sharp saw? Let's have it, and we'll get this job done."

"Dear brothers," the newcomer cried, "if we pass the test then there's a bucket of vodka on me."

"Now, you don't have to promise any buckets," one of the men said seriously. "A quart and a dozen beers would be plenty. And that's not why we're helping you out, pal."

Everyone pitched in on the job. After about an hour and a half, the newcomer came up and whispered, "Ivan Gavrilovich is coming."

"Which one is he? The one with the gray beard?"

"Yes, that's him."

"O.K. Just let him get a little closer."

He was about ten paces from the newcomer's workbench when one of the men yelled out at the top of his voice: "Hey, look, here he is coming for his tenner!"

Then the whole workshop joined in with the most frenzied whistling and hooting. Of course, Ivan Gavrilovich had no choice but to get out of the workshop as quickly as he could. The trial job was approved, and the newcomer was given a permanent job.

below, pp. 109–112. A description of a comparable firm in St. Petersburg can be found in Kanatchikov's memoir, pages 68–71.

I can also remember another case when a worker who was not very good at his job started at the Putilov works.[19] The workers helped him finish his test job in just the same way, even though two workers were fined a ruble by the foreman in the process. However, this time it didn't work because the foreman noticed what was going on and gave the newcomer another job, harder than the last, and then he stayed to supervise, making sure that no one could help.

There is still a custom for new workers to provide drinks for the whole shop. In some factories, the new worker will not even be addressed by his real name but will be called "Taras"[20] instead until he has done this. The custom is indisputably pernicious, and there can be little justification for it. Having endured a period of more or less prolonged unemployment, the worker is broke anyway, and then suddenly there is this new expense. But old customs die hard. It is common everywhere to conclude business transactions with a drink. In this respect, workers are no exception.

The cost of this initiation runs anywhere from two to five rubles; usually it is somewhere between two and three. There are cases when the cost is higher, even up to fifteen rubles, but that's only when the worker gets a relatively well-paying job that doesn't require any special skills. However, most workers find this kind of initiation shameful. I remember that at one factory the furnace workers were teased for a whole month because they drank themselves senseless on one poor fellow's fifteen rubles. Furnace workers can earn in a month anywhere from twenty-five to fifty rubles.

THE ELDER

At one factory, every time a worker is hired, he is asked whether he would like to donate two to three percent of his monthly wages to build a "new stone church." Often he is not even asked but simply given a special form to sign. Considering the circumstances, it's understandable that the new

[19]Founded in 1868, the Putilov works quickly grew to be the largest plant in St. Petersburg. At first producing mainly railroad track, it subsequently diversified and expanded under the stimulus of government contracts to produce munitions and other metal products. By the turn of the century the Putilov works employed nearly 12,000 workers.

[20]The meaning of this name, beyond what appears in the text, remains obscure.

workers always sign. In this particular case, the administration not only said it was building a church, but even had plans drawn up and distributed to the workshops, and would tell the workers every month how much money had been received. There was a large watercolor picture hung by the factory gate depicting the church with a belltower. It showed the workers standing around it in red shirts and new boots, with their wives wearing shawls and carrying parasols.

Not only do workers make donations for wreaths if the factory boss dies; they also have to contribute money for presents to managers who are very much alive. Even though these contributions are made in a familial way—that is, the money isn't deducted directly from paychecks, but is contributed by each worker independently—the recipient will sometimes demand to see the subscription list. Of course, there will be some consequences for those not on the list.

It is hard to say how often such collections are carried out, since it depends on the workers' level of development and whether or not there are workers in the factory who are willing to organize donations of this kind. However, it should be pointed out that the workers fully understand the impropriety of such gifts, and it often happens that these collections are organized by a small group which carefully conceals its activities from everybody else to avoid being laughed at. Once at the P—— factory[21] there was a collection, and not for the usual watch or silver tea service, but instead for a photograph album with pictures of all the contributors inside. Even this relatively innocent collection was hushed up, and I found out about it only by swearing myself to secrecy. This is at least a step forward, and it probably won't be long before the workers at this factory follow the administration's example and simply offer thanks or condolences rather than watches and tea services, as the management does when dealing with its own losses.

More often, however, it is the workers who have to help those in their midst who for some reason can no longer work or just need help. In such cases, the deductions are either made by the office at the workers' request or else collected by someone chosen by the workers to keep a list of contributions. There are cases where entire families of deceased workers

---

[21]It is likely that Timofeev is referring here to the Putilov factory.

are supported by these donations, but this only happens in long-established factories where the workers have settled down, know each other, and are sure that they too would be helped in time of need. I haven't noticed the same kind of solidarity in new factories.

There is also a collection for icon oil, undertaken in most cases unofficially. That is to say, the factory office doesn't have anything to do with it. Instead, the workers themselves contribute directly from their wages on payday, putting in ten to twenty kopecks a month. Each workshop has its own icon, usually of St. Nicholas, who for some reason is considered the patron saint of factory workers.[22] There is supposed to be a permanent flame in front of the icon and the workers make sure that this flame keeps burning.

For the sake of convenience, the workers elect an elder who is responsible for filling the lamp with oil and dusting the icon from time to time. Usually this elder is an older worker who knows enough about church services to hand the priest incense at the right time during prayers. He also must be trusted by his colleagues since he handles their money for the purchase of oil, wicks, and so on.

Let me try to describe how the elder is elected. Work is almost over. They are finishing up in the foundry. Some workers unmold the red, barely cooled castings and then pour water over the earth molds, causing hot dust to rise and cover them from head to toe. Other workers have already cleaned their work area and are busy washing up. A few workers, surrounded by dust and steam, are raking out the last red-hot coals from the furnace, working in unbearable heat. The electric crane, with its chains clanking, moves from one corner to the other for the last time, coming to a halt at the workshop gates by the cast-iron spiral staircase.

Workers gather by the office, and minute by minute the crowd keeps growing until everyone in the workshop is there. They should have received their identity tags already, but the office boy still has not arrived with the keys. Someone tries to open the office door, but it is locked. Then the whistle blows and workers start pouring out of the other workshops. Still the boy has not shown up. Someone suggests trying to pick the lock of the

---

[22]Workers in different occupations commonly chose a patron saint. St. Nicholas was an extremely popular choice.

cabinet where the tags are kept, and a moment later the cabinet doors fall open.

Now the confusion starts. Many people try to grab their tags quickly and leave unnoticed since there is a ruble fine for taking your own tag and leaving the factory without permission. But the noise and commotion don't go unnoticed in the office. Just then the door opens, and the office boy comes running out.

"Who opened it? Who opened it?" he cries, trying to close the cabinet doors again. The foreman comes right in behind him.

"What's going on here? You tried to get the tags for yourselves, didn't you?" the foreman shouts angrily at the workers. "Write down the names of those who left," he says to the boy, heading toward an unused casting mold standing nearby. Apparently he wants to make some kind of speech. He climbs on top of the mold and begins, "Well now."

The crowd immediately falls silent.

"You all know that Vasilii Diakov has been our elder until now. He's done a good job, but now he wants to resign."

"He doesn't need the job any more," someone from the crowd called out. "He's already built one house. That's enough!"

"He's given me a record of his accounts for the year," the foreman said. "If you want, you can check it for yourselves." He handed out several pieces of paper with some figures marked in pencil. "I kept you here after work because we have to elect a new elder. So, who do you want?"

The workers began scrutinizing each other carefully.

"Well, we could always ask Diakov again," the foreman continued.

"Who needs Diakov? To hell with him," someone said. "He only knows how to build houses for himself."

While all this was going on, Diakov was at the other side of the room doing something at his workbench. He probably already knew what the meeting was going to be about, and since he did not expect many compliments to come his way, he had decided not to take part.

"Come off it," the foreman said. "You can't build a house with such small sums."

"Hey," someone shouted from the crowd, "let's elect Kuzmich Martynich."

A weak old voice said, "How could I do it?" But by then several other voices picked up the cry, "Martynich, Martynich!"

"How can I do God's work?" Martynich objected. "You need someone younger for that."

"What's there to talk about? Let's elect Martynich. He knows all about the church service."

"He's got fewer sins to answer for," someone else said. "He's an old man and can always touch the holy icon."[23]

"No, friends, I really can't. If my health were better I would, but I just couldn't manage. I'm going now anyway. I don't want to miss the church service. Please excuse me."

"He's right," the foreman acknowledged. "No matter what you say, being elder does require some work. He has to buy the oil, keep everything clean, and nobody's going to do it for him."

"Besides, I'm illiterate," Martynich added, "and there are always things that need to be written down."

"Well, who's it going to be then?" a voice cried from the crowd.

The workers again looked at each other inquisitively.

"What about Ivan Vasil'ev?" the foreman suggested.

"No, Ivan Vasil'ev is no good. He's an Old Believer,[24] and you can't expect him to look after a Russian icon."

"Our icons are a lot cleaner than yours," the Old Believer retorted angrily from the back of the crowd. "But I wouldn't do it anyway, even if you asked me."

---

[23]The implication of this remark is simply that an old man, presumably nearing the end of his life, is more likely to lead a pure life and avoid sin than someone younger. This circumstance would enhance his suitability for tending the icon.

[24]In 1652, the head of the Russian Church, Patriarch Nikon, undertook to purify religious rituals in the Russian Orthodox Church (such as making the sign of the cross with three fingers instead of the traditional two) and to correct mistranslations in Russian holy texts. Nikon's efforts met with opposition from the church hierarchy, but after considerable debate the reforms were officially accepted in 1666. Part of the church hierarchy and numerous followers refused to accept the changes. These Old Believers, as they were called, clung to the old customs and subsequently suffered persecution for their defiance of both the state and the official church. See M. Chernyavskii, "Old Believers and the New Religion," *Slavic Review*, 25 (March 1966).

"Who'd want you to!"

"I wouldn't do it if you gave me two hundred rubles," Ivan Vasil'ev persisted.

"What about three hundred?"

"Oh, leave him alone," a third voice interrupted. "Let's get on with it, comrades. How about Vaniusha Voldyrev?"

"Are you crazy? The guy just got married, and you want to make him look after the holy icon."

"You're right, I guess I forgot. Well, who's got another idea?"

Finally, after many suggestions, they turned to Andrei Slesarev, who operated the electric crane. Even then there were problems. At first he himself objected, saying that he was too young and didn't have any free time. But they finally persuaded him. Then someone argued that since this was the foundry, a foundry worker and not a machinist should get the job. But since there were no other candidates, Slesarev was elected.

The meeting lasted for an hour and a half, and it was already getting dark by the time the workers got their identity tags and started leaving the factory in large groups.

"Hey, Andriusha!" one of the workers shouted, running over to join the group surrounding the hero of the election.

"What is it?" Andriusha asked.

"What are you going to do? Don't you think we ought to celebrate?"

"Celebrate what?" Andriusha asked, as if he didn't understand.

"You know what. Now you're the elder. That's coming up in the world!"

"Well, it wouldn't be a bad idea," the elder answered, "but I don't have any money."

"Haven't you got your paybook with you?"

"No, it's at home. And my wife wouldn't give it to me anyway."

"Too bad!"

At that moment, the workers passed through the factory gates. As always, the watchman frisked them, but of course he didn't find anything.

"So that's how it is. Well, we'll have to think of something," the worker insisted, refusing to give up. An alert policeman overheard his words and dutifully came to inform the workers that it was illegal to hold meetings in the street.

"Move along, move along now. What are you doing out here in the street?" But as soon as he noticed that there were too many workers for him to handle, the upholder of law and order softened his tone. "Your wife has probably gone to bed ages ago and you're still hanging around out here."

The workers started off again slowly, stopping every so often to argue among themselves.

"The shopkeeper will give us something, by God he will," one worker insisted. "Just offer him half a kopeck on your commission as elder and he'll give us ten rubles right away."

"We'll need at least ten rubles for a crowd this size," the elder said. "Should we go in and see what he says?"

"Let's all go in together," someone said. And they all made their way to the small store huddled right outside the factory walls.

THE FOREMAN

In the ten years that I have lived with workers, I have rarely met anyone who did not dream of changing his occupation. The only exceptions were those whose association with the factory was determined by some higher ideal, but such people were rare. All the rest lived in the hope that they would some day scrape up enough money to leave the factory behind so as not to be bound by any bosses or factory whistles. Some dreamed of owning their own little house in town, some dreamed of the village, and others dreamed of setting up some kind of business. Of course, these dreams rarely came true. Those who start out as "workers" remain "workers" and spend all their lives in the factory, even though nothing about the factory appeals to them. Far from it. They can be dismissed and thrown out into the street at a moment's notice. Therefore, it is not surprising that the worker's desire for independence only grows stronger with every passing year. This desire is perfectly natural and logical.

There is a big difference between railroad and factory workers in this respect. Those employed at the railroad, though by no means all of them, have a chance for significant promotion and a higher salary with the passage of time. The most a factory worker can hope for is to become the leader of a work crew, then assistant foreman, and finally foreman.

Work crew leaders are found only where a particularly monotonous job is done by a team of workers. The crew leader is still considered a worker and gets his wages either by the day or by the piece just like the other workers. But his wages, of course, greatly exceed those of the other members of the crew. Otherwise, the crew leader is no different from the rest of the workers, and he treats them as equals. It is very rare for anyone to hold the job permanently. The slightest disagreement with the foreman, or an argument about pay rates, can end in dismissal. Then the crew leader becomes just an ordinary member of the work crew again.

The assistant foreman is in an even more delicate position. He is attacked from two sides every moment he is on the job. On one side there are the workers who worked together with him until recently. They come to him expecting support and solidarity. On the other side is the foreman, who constantly urges him to be stricter with the workers and to report every infringement of the rules. It requires a lot of tact and skill to avoid hostility from both sides. For this reason, the assistant foreman usually tries to stay neutral, siding neither with the workers nor with the foreman.

After holding the job for some time, an assistant foreman may occasionally prefer to go back to the workbench with his comrades rather than have them turn against him. But that rarely happens. Usually he manages to avoid the dangers on both sides more or less successfully. Then when the foreman retires or dies, the administration appoints the assistant foreman to take his former boss's place. For the ordinary worker, it is almost impossible to become foreman through hard work alone. One cannot even think of it without "friends" in high places. In order to acquire such "friends," one often has to go against one's conscience, a price not everyone is prepared to pay.

Here is the most reliable way of acquiring "friends" in high places. Let's assume you have just arrived at a factory and decide to do whatever it takes to get ahead. First of all, you have to show diligence in your work. You don't fight with the foreman, you accept the going rate without argument, and you don't ask for a raise. You are never late, and if you have to take a day off for some reason, you let the foreman know two or three days in advance and hand in your absence slip the night before. In a word, you make yourself a model worker. But that's not all. There are many model workers in the factory who stay that way all their lives. The most important step is yet to come.

You find out from private sources that the foreman has a daughter who is old enough to marry. You use all your cunning to get to know her, and after a suitable length of time you propose. If she accepts, then it's in the bag.

If your foreman doesn't have a daughter, don't give up. Keep your eye out for another foreman who does, because all the foremen stick together. If worst comes to worst, just marry anyone and then invite the foreman to be your best man.

It is even better if you can get in with the management. I know a foreman who got his job by marrying the maid of an engineer who was a bachelor. This man was immediately promoted to foreman, although he was probably no older than twenty at the time. It is also an advantage if you have some special talent—other than literary—like music, for example. Then you can offer your services in organizing the factory orchestra or workshop choir. I heard of one worker who, thanks to his musical talent, became foreman in a workshop he did not even know existed. Another worker was promoted to foreman thanks to his aunt who rented her house to the engineers employed by his factory.

It is interesting how people who become foreman in this way feel when they first start work.

"I came into the workshop," one such foreman told me, "took a look around me, and sat down for a while to think over my new position. At that moment the work crew leader came up to me and asked, 'What kind of copper should we use for these fittings?'

"How the hell should I know, I thought to myself, but I replied nonchalantly, 'Well, friend, use the same as you did yesterday.'

" 'But we didn't cast any fittings yesterday, sir,' he answered with equal nonchalance.

" 'Well,' I replied, 'use whatever you think best and we'll discuss it tonight over a drink. Tell all the foundry workers that the foreman will buy everyone drinks tonight after work.' The crew leader went away, obviously very happy with my instructions about the copper. That evening I had to treat him and all the factory workers to drinks and have them all over to my apartment on top of that."

The custom of celebrating the appointment of a new foreman is widespread, although nowadays, as relations between the foreman and the workers become more formal, it is losing ground. Most of the younger workers are against trying to ingratiate themselves with the foreman, and they no longer see the point of this old custom. Foremen who are good at their jobs, and therefore do not need to sweeten up the workers, also reject the custom.

I remember one instance when a new foreman started work in the foundry. Of course, we immediately found out everything there was to know about him: where he had worked before, whom he was married to, what kind of man he was. The general consensus was that he was excellent at his job and could run rings around anyone. As a person, however, he was what the workers called a "dog," who would bite your head off as soon as you came near him. Despite this assessment of his character, the older foundry workers decided to give him a "benefit" and welcome him according to the old custom on the shop floor.

This custom goes as follows. When the first dipper is ready to be filled with pig iron from the furnace, one of the foundry workers invites the foreman over and hands him a long metal rod tipped with a piece of clay. For the occasion, the rod has been decorated with pieces of colored paper and the handle has a handkerchief wrapped around it. The furnace tender punches a hole in the mold waiting to receive the hot metal. When the molten pig iron has come down the chute and filled the dipper, the foreman must fix the hole in the mold himself. Afterwards, of course, he has to pay for the honor bestowed upon him.

All the preparations had been made the night before. Although the younger workers told the organizers that it would be the worse for them if they interfered with the foreman, the old men would not listen. When the moment arrived the next day, they went up to the foreman, who greeted them very sternly.

"Well, what do you want?" he asked.

"Allow us to ask you for a moment of your precious time, Egor Egorich."

"What's up?"

Everyone fell silent. The elder Martynich, stepped forward. "Egor Egorich," he said, "as is the custom here. . . ."

The foreman shot at the lean old man such a threatening look that Martynich became flustered. "You know it yourself," he mumbled, in a voice suddenly pathetic and trembling, "the custom, the way things are done."

At that point someone in the back of the crowd lost patience and said, "Are you going to buy us all drinks or not?"

"What for?" said the foreman.

"To get acquainted, according to the custom."

The foreman didn't say anything for a moment and then replied, "I'll give you a get-acquainted drink you won't forget for a long time. The nerve of you. Get back to work at once."

The workers trooped out of the office, looking very despondent. All the young men were waiting for them in the workshop and could tell by their expressions what kind of reception they had received. The jokes started up right away.

"Well, was there enough booze for everyone?"

"When are you going to get acquainted, today or tomorrow?"

As I have mentioned earlier, the foreman plays a huge role in every worker's life. For instance, the foreman can force a worker to leave the factory by systematically lowering the rate at which he's paid. When the worker finally leaves, the foreman will write in his paybook that the worker left "of his own accord." The foreman can also increase the wages of anyone he likes by paying him at a higher-than-average rate. An intellectual once asked an unsophisticated worker what he thought of the foreman. It's no wonder that the worker replied, "The foreman is a person who can make anyone happy."

Since he is completely free to change the pay scale at will, the foreman can decide how much each worker earns. The majority of workers put up a fight against this system, but there are some who give into it and try to make things better for themselves by currying favor with the foreman. I vividly recall an incident which shows what most workers think of this kind of behavior.

Last autumn, a few new workers came to our factory. One of them was a lathe operator named Panov. He was no better or worse at his job than anyone else, but he suddenly decided to get ahead by putting himself in the good graces of our foreman, Ivanov. Panov was already married, so he couldn't use that trick, and Ivanov never took bribes. Then one day a rumor began circulating in the workshop that the foreman himself was getting married. Someone suggested getting him a present, but the majority of workers refused to have anything to do with such tricks. So a small clique led by Panov decided to give him a present secretly.

The first problem was what to give him. Some wanted to get him a watch, some a cigarette case, and others a set of dishes, but the group was too small to handle such a large expense. Finally, someone suggested giving the traditional bread and salt.[25] This was agreed upon unanimously. They ordered a silver salt shaker and bought some bread. The day after the wedding ceremony, Panov and two other workers went off to congratulate the newlyweds. The foreman met them in the hallway of his apartment and asked them what they wanted.

"We would like to offer this bread and salt to congratulate you on the occasion of your marriage," Panov said.

"Oh, thank you, thank you," the foreman replied. He turned and called, "Matrena, my workers have come. Take them to the kitchen and give them a glass of vodka."

It isn't clear whether they went into the kitchen or not. Nonetheless, the next day they were shocked to discover that the story was all over the shop floor. Now that was something! The entire exchange between the foreman and his "deputies" was told in great detail. It was said that the foreman called in his bride to show her *his own* workers and that they were given two glasses of vodka instead of one. The unhappy well-wishers were tormented beyond belief. The workshop artist made a drawing on a sheet of metal showing Panov bowing with a small bundle in his hands. Behind him were the two others carrying canes and in the distance the foreman with a carafe of vodka. Several poets combined forces to compose some suitable verses for the occasion, and these were popular in the workshop for quite a long time. This is the usual treatment for those who try to get on the foreman's good side.

As recently as fifteen years ago, the workers' attitude toward the fore-

---

[25]The offering of bread and salt as a symbol of celebration and welcome is a traditional Russian custom.

man was very different. Suffice it to say that it was not uncommon for a foreman to use his fists on adult workers. Older workers tell many stories of this kind, and I have no reason to doubt them. Russian workers did not have the same sense of self-respect and personal inviolability that they do now. All that mattered then was money. The more a foreman let them earn, the more they respected him. An old worker once told me how everyone in his workshop stopped working and accompanied the foreman on his long way home after he had been dismissed. They did this in spite of the fact that the foreman was so free with his fists that "he'd sock you in the face the moment you didn't do his bidding." The only reason for his popularity was that he set high pay rates. "With him you could make up to a hundred rubles. Look at our foremen—there isn't a single one like him," the old man concluded regretfully.

It is true that one cannot find this kind of foreman any more, but it is also true that one cannot find the same attitudes toward foremen. Today workers demand both good wages and respectful treatment. A foreman would only have to shake his fist or push a worker for the whole workshop to erupt immediately, as if at the flick of a switch, and the conflict might spread to the rest of the factory. Recent reports about Russian industry show that many strikes and disorders are originally caused by the insulting behavior of a foreman. However, a strike is often not to the workers' advantage; there's too high a price to pay. Therefore, another tried and true method, known as the wheelbarrow treatment, is frequently used to keep in check a foreman who abuses his power. This method is worth describing in detail, since it is used all over Russia from the Urals to Siberia, from the North West to the Caucasus, and in the Central Industrial Region.[26]

A group of like-minded workers usually gets together to plan their revenge in advance. First, they find a wheelbarrow and a sack. They either smear the sack with oil, soot, and dirt, or else they simply use a coal sack. They wait until the foreman walks through the workshop, and then one or two workers creep up behind him and throw the sack over his head. At that

[26]Timofeev is referring here to some of the different industrial regions in Russia. The Urals and Siberia, rich in mineral deposits, were centers for the mining industry. The North West region refers to St. Petersburg and the adjacent area, which had a heavy concentration of the metalworking industry. The Central Industrial Region encompasses the provinces surrounding Moscow, where textile production predominated.

point, several others come up to help tie the sack around him. It won't help him to cry out or struggle, but it's a different matter if he is apologetic. If he says things like, "It's not my fault, I have to follow orders too. I never meant to insult anyone," then the workers might let him go. However, they make sure that he cannot tell who was involved. Many a foreman will change his attitude toward the workers after such a lesson, and the workers will say to one another, "You see, it worked. Now he's as gentle as a lamb."

If the workers are really angry, then all the foreman's protestations will not help him. After being bundled into the sack, he is dumped into the wheelbarrow like so much cargo and then wheeled around to the accompaniment of hoots and whistles. Usually he is taken to the gates of the shop and left there until some compassionate soul comes to untie him. But in the Western Region[27] where the people are not so kindhearted, they cart the foreman out of the workshop and dump him into a canal or a river.[28]

Sometimes even the apprentices[29] decide to carry out the operation on their own, but this only happens when they have at least the tacit approval of the adult workers. In some instances, the mere threat of the wheelbarrow is sufficient to produce the desired result. I remember that the following notice once appeared on the workshop gates: "Unless foreman N. leaves the factory voluntarily, we will take him out in a wheelbarrow. If anyone takes down this sign, we will have his head. The wheelbarrow will be painted black for the occasion." After reading this notice, foreman N. chose to hand in his resignation. Of course, such conflicts do not always turn out so well for the workers. At times the management will take steps to protect a foreman whom the workers dislike. In such cases the conflict escalates, since the workers have to deal not only with the foreman but also with the entire factory administration.

[27]The Western Region refers to the industrialized area of Russian Poland.

[28]This practice was not confined to the metalworking industry alone. In 1906, for example, the contemporary trade union press reported that four bakery workers at the Filippov firm in St. Petersburg were arrested for having carried a foreman out of the enterprise in a wheelbarrow after he turned a worker over to the police. See *Listok bulochnikov i konditerov*, no. 8, Nov. 18, 1906, p. 6.

[29]Skilled work in factories and in artisanal occupations generally required apprenticeship training, usually lasting from two to five years. See pp. 8–10 above.

PAYDAY IN A SMALL FACTORY

These sketches, as I have already pointed out, are mostly about workers employed in large enterprises. I have only occasionally worked at smaller so-called *"kustarnye"* factories, and I cannot speak about them in detail. I would like, however, to share with the reader one episode that gives some idea of what these factories are like, without making any claim to generalization.

Imagine a small factory surrounded by a high wooden fence. In the yard, there's one building partitioned into three sections. The first is the machine shop, with a small kerosene engine, the second is the foundry, and adjacent to it the furnace. Smoke rises from the coals, which have just been doused with water: the workers have finished the day's casting. Further on there is the forge. A little to the side is the workers' "dormitory," and in the corner there is the stable for the owner's horses. Next to the gate, you see a neat stone house—the home of the owner himself. The tidy front entrance of the house faces the street; the back door opens into the factory yard. About twenty workers are gathered at the back of the house.

It is already dark. The workers are dressed in ragged soiled jackets and blouses, and they stand shivering from cold in the autumn dampness. They have been waiting for about two hours, but nobody appears at the window. Finally, the kitchen maid appears at the window. Catching sight of her, one of the workers calls out, "Matrena, hey, Matrena!"

Matrena presses her face against the window pane.

"Tell the boss he shouldn't just let people freeze like this!"

"What do you want?" asks Matrena, as though she doesn't understand why they are there.

"What do we want? We're waiting for our wages. We waited last Saturday, waited and waited, and all for nothing. Is he trying to get away with that again?"

"But he's not home," says the kitchen maid, thinking she can fool them. "He's gone to the railroad station."

"Cut out the lies. What kind of horse did he take with him? They're all in the stable."

"O.K., O.K., I'll tell him you're waiting," and the kitchen maid disappears.

The workers become more animated. Some imagine a good glass of vodka, while others who have been sitting silently all this time suddenly begin complaining indignantly, "What kind of damned life is this? You've worked and worked all week long, days and nights, so you think that you'll rest on Sunday. But no, you sit here and freeze like a stray dog."

Then the kitchen maid appears again. "He says you should come tomorrow. He says it's too late today."

"Why the hell did he keep us here so late?"

The kitchen maid vanishes again.

"Well, guys, shall we go?"

"Yeah, let's go."

They all get up, moving slowly from fatigue, and walk out of the factory yard.

"Oh, boy, I wish I could have a drink now!" someone declares loudly as they walk past a Georgian tavern, "Kuki," tucked in right next to the factory.

"Shall we go in? Who knows, maybe he'll trust us on credit."

But the Georgian who owns the tavern already knows where these workers are employed, and as soon as the group appears in the doorway, he dashes from behind the counter and yells, "Get out, get out! You guys never have any money and today I sell for money. Credit is tomorrow."

The workers understand, however, that both tomorrow and the day after tomorrow they will receive the same treatment. They take the promises of the tavern keeper with complete equanimity and gloomily depart for home.

The next day, about seven o'clock in the morning, the workers again gather at the same back door and again begin to wait for the owner to appear. Today is Sunday, and for this reason some of the workers, mostly married ones, wear clean shirts. But there are also those who sport the same dirty linen which they'll wear continuously until it's completely in shreds. Today, again, they will have to wait two to three hours. Finally, the owner appears.

"What do you want?" he asks them.

"You know what we want, Matvei Grigor'evich—money," several voices reply to him.

"Money, money," the owner mocks them. "But what the hell do you need your money for? Drinking—that's all you want."

"Why drinking?" the workers interrupt him. "We have to pay rent, the shopkeeper. We need new boots. It's a torture without money, Matvei Grigor'evich. Give us even a little bit."

"And where will I get the money if I don't have any?"

"If you haven't got the money, why do you employ us?" exclaims one of the workers who has recently been hired.

"Who's keeping you here? Do me a favor, please, you can leave this moment."

"And how about paying up?"

"Paying up for what? Do I owe you anything?"

"And what do you think? Did I work for you for nothing these two weeks?"

The worker begins to get angry, but his comrades do not intend to hear the argument to the end, and they interrupt with their repeated pleas to give them "at least a little bit."

Finally, the owner decides to pay married workers a ruble each; the bachelors get half of that. Like it or not, they have to accept even that small sum. No paybooks or pay sheets are required here, and the owner simply checks off the names of the workers in his own notebook.

"Next Saturday," the owner promises, "if I get some money, then I might give you more."

Now the question is: what can a worker buy for this miserable ruble or fifty kopecks? All he can do is spend it on drink at a tavern.

The most interesting event in the life of such factories is, of course, the counting of workdays. I have already mentioned that no paybooks or any other documents—not even identity tags—exist at these enterprises. Therefore, the owner has a perfect opportunity to cheat his workers any way he wishes. For example, the owner may ask, "Mishka, how many work days have you accumulated?"

"Twenty-four and a half."

"Cut out those lies. You are trying to pass twenty-one for twenty-four and a half."

"God be my witness, Matvei Grigor'evich. I have twenty-four and a half days. Look, Vaniushka also has twenty-four and a half days, and we've been working as a team."

"You both lie. Both of you have only twenty-one days."

What does one do in this situation? God is too high, and the Tsar is too far away. Complaining to the police will yield no result, and so the worker reconciles himself, asking God to help him in getting "even that much."

Perhaps the word *court* has already crossed the reader's mind. Indisputably, this is a good word and the institution is wonderful. But to get involved with it is, alas, very very unpleasant. First, one has to be an expert in these matters. Second—and this is the most important—is it possible for a proletarian worker in the full meaning of this term to survive without work, even for a month? Consequently, the only thing that is left for the worker to do if he is, as they say, "fed up" with working for one particular owner is to forget about his money and to look for work elsewhere, or, as the workers put it, "take a shot" at other factories.

I have already referred to the fact that the factory I am now describing had a workers' dormitory. Only bachelors lived there, and in my time there were about a dozen such people (the factory employed twenty-five to thirty workers). The dormitory cost them each fifteen rubles a month. In the summer, they slept in the yard where they also ate. But now autumn had arrived, and the workers were forced out of necessity to move into the dormitory. It was built recently, so the dampness made itself felt right away: five workers got sick. One of them went so far as to hint to the owner about calling a doctor.

"What is this? Are you going to give birth at my factory? Maybe you'd rather I called for a midwife!"

I left the area shortly after this incident, and I do not know whether any of the workers recovered, but the memory of this factory will stay with me for a long time to come.

Part Two: Textile Workers

III

F. P. Pavlov

Ten Years of Experience
(Excerpts From Reminiscences, Impressions, and
Observations of Factory Life)

INTRODUCTION

During the last ten years, Russian society has taken a lively interest in the many problems associated with the growth of industry in our country. Yet we still lack an awareness of the nature and peculiarity of our factory life, a circumstance that has led to the author's humble attempt to relate a few observations and impressions, accumulated in the course of a decade of factory experience in our central region, in the hope of satisfying the curiosity of a rather limited circle of readers. It was this ambition that guided the author as he began compiling his "Ten Years of Experience," which first appeared as a series of essays in the newspaper *Russkie vedomosti (Russian Gazette)*.[1] In the author's opinion, the same ambition justifies their present publication in a single volume.

---

[1]*Russkie vedomosti* was a Moscow daily newspaper with a liberal outlook, founded in 1863. Its readers "were mostly professional people over thirty with a higher education and quite traditional literary expectations." See Jeffrey Brooks, "Readers and Reading at the End of the Tsarist Era," in *Literature and Society in Imperial Russia 1800–1914*, ed. William Mills Todd III (Stanford, 1978), p. 118.

For the sake of brevity, the author will omit his reasons for presenting these impressions in a semifictional form. Suffice it to say that within the confines of this form, the author has sought to depict only those aspects of factory life that were known to him from first-hand experience. Although he has worked in many factories at different locations, the author has placed his observations in one composite location, represented by a large and well-run textile mill.

THE WORLD OF THE TEXTILE MILL

Today is a holiday. Sitting with my samovar,[2] I feel especially content that there is no need to rush, that I can do as I please, and do not have to listen to the noise of the looms and other factory hubbub. Having finished my tea and turning to get a box of tobacco, I am unable to avert my eyes from the view outside my window. Beyond the fence that surrounds the small yard outside my house, I can see the enormous factory site, bound on one side by a river. Right now, all its imperfections, the ruts and the dirt, are concealed under a bright cover from the first snowfall. Even the piles of broken bricks, old logs, metal scraps, and other trash which for some reason have not been removed from the main yard since the spring, somehow look attractive under the cover of snow sparkling in the last rays of the setting winter sun. The river has not frozen yet and seems especially dark between the white snowy banks. Behind the river, there is an ordinary central Russian winter landscape, which is always dear to the Russian heart: the white cloth of the meadow, a gently sloping hill with a few patches of green winter wheat, a village in the distance, and the blue bank of a forest on the horizon.

This picture is abruptly interrupted on the left by a massive five-story textile mill. Behind it, by the river, I can see the smokestack of the dye works, also part of our enterprise. Further to the left, on a hill above the factory, a row of dormitories begins. The factory is separated from the workers' dormitories by a wide road, which leads to a small grove. The

[2]A samovar is a large metal urn used for making tea. It contains an internal tube into which hot coals are placed to heat the water. Usually a small pot of very strong tea is placed on top of the samovar. Hot water is then removed from the urn and used to dilute the strong tea.

church and the infirmary are here, set apart from the other buildings. The view to the right ends in an enormous garden, or rather three adjacent gardens. In front of me stands the small cottage of the factory director, surrounded by recently planted trees. Next to it is the garden and park of the owner's mansion which, except for the roof, is concealed by tall leafless trees. Still further, there is a small grove with a school building next to it. I complete this picture of the factory site by imagining other parts that are not directly in my view: whole streets of houses for the rest of the personnel, the club house, the tea house, the workers' library, the large grocery store, the slaughterhouses. These structures are situated behind the apartment buildings for technicians, and I am standing by a window in one of these apartments.

Even though it is completely familiar to me, the enormity of this factory complex captivates my imagination against my will and causes the same chain of thoughts to run through my mind for the hundredth time. I have never been able to interrupt this chain somewhere in the middle before following it from the first link to the last, and now I submit again to its flow.

This factory employs some 5,500 workers and nearly 250 clerical, technical, and managerial personnel. Not more than 750 workers live outside the factory gates. The rest of the workers, many of them with families, live in the factory complex which houses over 8,000 souls, if one counts the old men and children. According to the latest census, the whole of the Russian Empire can boast of only 138 towns with a population exceeding that of our factory.[3] There is even one provincial capital, Yakutsk, with a population of only 2,000.[4] The lives of these 8,000 inhabitants, not to mention several thousand of their relatives, are tied to the factory in the most intimate way. To me, this tie seems so powerful that I cannot help but ask whether there is an administrative or political power anywhere in the civilized world that can control an individual so completely, down to the last detail, as does the director of a Russian factory.

The director designs the rules and the schedule to which the worker must adhere. At the sound of the factory whistle the worker gets up, goes

[3]A reference to the national census conducted in 1897.
[4]Yakutsk is situated in the northeastern region of Siberia.

8. Moscow's Prokhorovskaia Trekhgornaia textile mill in the early 1890s.

to work, has lunch and supper. The same director alone decides what living quarters to assign and determines the conditions for their use. For example, the director may require that workers return home by a specific hour and may also restrict the number of people allowed to gather for a social occasion in the room of a friend. It is true that all such rules are, to a certain extent, controlled by the Factory Inspectorate,[ ] but, by necessity, this control is of a formal and therefore only negative nature. The inspector must make sure that the factory administration does not include anything in its regulations that would violate the law. The law, naturally, is only concerned with direct violations of a worker's rights. It does not protect him from a whole mass of regulations, sometimes necessary but often quite unnecessary, that are considered part of his contract. For example, if a worker's contract states that he must return home by ten o'clock at night, he will be subject to a fine if he returns at eleven. Or if a worker plays an accordion in his room longer than the regulations allow, he is also subject

[ ]See Ch. 1, n. 51.

to a fine. It will not strain the reader's imagination to prolong this list almost indefinitely.

Apart from work and living quarters, the administration supplies the worker with almost everything that he needs for his existence. And if it chooses to do so, the factory administration can fulfill all his needs. The factory maintains a store where the worker receives the necessities: flour, sugar, a horsewhip, a kettle, boots, a shawl, firewood, and mittens. The quality and price of these products, even their availability, are completely controlled by the administration, and a worker has little chance of receiving credit anywhere but the factory store. Besides, the factory store is often the only place of this sort for miles around. Workers often spend up to 70 or 80 percent of their wages there.

The factory administration not only determines the extent to which a worker's material needs are satisfied; it also reigns supreme in the sphere of rational and spiritual needs. It is the owner who builds the church, and it is the same owner who decides whether to build a school and hire the teachers. Likewise, the administration decides which worker will send his children to the factory school and which children will be allowed to receive an education. Libraries and workers' reading rooms are also set up according to the administration's wishes, and even the tickets to an occasional play are distributed in a manner designed to reward the most productive workers. Needless to say, the power to enact all of these regulations is minor compared with the power that is inherent in the administration's right to deny a worker employment and income, no matter how much this right has been circumscribed by law.[6]

Consequently, each step, each hour of the worker's life and the life of his family can be controlled by the factory administration, which is headed by one omnipotent person who governs the factory—its director. The director is the single autonomous legislator, the judge and the executor of his

---

[6]According to government factory legislation, the employer was required to give two weeks' notice in order to terminate a contract, except in cases of poor behavior such as unexcused absence from work, criminal activity, or insolence toward the factory administration.

own regulations. The fines that the director imposes on workers cannot be challenged or appealed if their amount does not exceed the legal limit.[7] Once the contract runs out, which happens no more than twice a year,[8] the law allows the director to take away a worker's living quarters, terminate his credit at the store, prevent his son from attending school, and, finally, deny him further employment forcing him onto the job market and possibly to starvation.

The Factory Inspectorate, albeit only in a formal manner, controls to some extent the relationship between the director and the worker. As to the technical, clerical, and managerial personnel, especially the lower ranks, they are subject to the director's absolute power. With the exception of the chief accountant and the two or three chief managers presiding over our ant hill, the rest of us do not receive any regular contracts from the administration. As a result, we can all be dismissed on a day's notice without any opportunity for legal recourse.

I can easily picture the familiar figure of our director, a small man with broad shoulders and penetrating eyes. One has to do him justice: he is very intelligent, knowledgeable, and hard working. But how spoiled he is by his unlimited power over all of his subordinates! He can barely tolerate even minor disagreements, and a serious difference with him is tantamount, in his eyes, to committing a crime. The workers, of course, are worse off. They never actually resort to impertinence or rudeness, but the director considers even an insufficiently respectful tone to be a transgression meriting the maximum fine, if not a summary dismissal. I can only compare the discipline reigning at our factory with military discipline, and I believe that on the scales of authority, the power of our director will outweigh that of any commander of a brigade or regiment.

---

[7]Fines were imposed on workers by the factory administration for infractions such as lateness and poor workmanship. Before 1886, there was no legal limit on the amount of these fines. The labor law enacted in that year decreed that fines could not exceed one-third of a single worker's monthly wage or one-quarter of the monthly wage of a married worker.

[8]Labor contracts were usually drawn up so as to expire twice a year, prior to the Easter holidays and on October 1.

It is possible to tolerate such power if it happens to be combined with intelligence, knowledge, and diligence. The factory population, from the lowest worker to the highest-ranking manager, greatly values these qualities and always respects the man who possesses them, submitting to his will without resistance and easily forgetting an occasional grudge. But what can happen if such power falls into the hands of a man who is neither intelligent, experienced, nor honest?

By now my cigarette has already burned my fingers. I extinguish it and automatically roll another, and then another, but the bothersome thoughts still refuse to go away.

If you decide to open even a small school for ten pupils, you have to submit petitions, obtain a permit, certify your credentials, and show diplomas which entitle you to become a teacher. In order to find employment even as a petty government official, say, a game warden or a tax collector, you have to finish a special school and satisfy specific educational requirements. But what kind of *formal* requirements do you have to satisfy in order to become a factory director? Not a single one! An official letter, informing the Factory Inspectorate that the owner has appointed Mr. So-and-So to be the factory's director, is sufficient to entrust one individual with the power to decide the fate of a few thousand people. It would not even occur to anyone to question this man's literacy, not to mention his education. Quite incredible! However surprising, this is the true state of affairs.

It is reasonable to suppose that a desire for profit will prompt the owner to find a man who is both intelligent and an expert, and this supposition is borne out by experience more often than not. Nevertheless, we technicians know of factories with hundreds and sometimes thousands of employees that are run by directors who can barely sign their names. Besides, a factory owner is looking, at most, for someone with technical expertise and skills. But these attributes alone do not qualify one to be the unchallenged ruler of a population numbering five or six thousand souls. Those of us with experience in the field are already familiar with the names of factory directors who, due to judicial reports on recent factory disorders, are gaining notoriety in all of Russia. These people, and particularly the foreigners among them, failed to take into account the customs, rights, and needs of Russian workers.[9] As a result, they precipitated incidents of a highly undesirable nature.

If an omnipotent director gives us such food for thought, his opposite, the "disenfranchised" director hired to serve as a figurehead, presents an even bleaker picture. In this case, it is the owner who runs the business while the legal responsibility belongs to this figurehead director, who must pay the fines imposed by the legal system out of his own pocket.[10] He even bears the brunt of any criminal prosecution, including imprisonment, for which he is sure to receive appropriate remuneration from the owner. Yes, we even have directors of this sort in Russia.

WORKERS' HOUSING

"Look at that view!" my friend observed. "The whole factory is spread out before us. What a picture! Just get rid of these smoke stacks," he went on, "they can spoil any landscape. But apart from them, you won't find a better view in the whole of Russia. Those red buildings against the green background of the fields are so lovely, and so are the small houses, almost drowning in the greenery, and the sparkling river. Not bad, not bad at all. It's a holiday, and there is no smoke or noise. Our ant hill is so picturesque, so positively lovely!" He paused for a moment and continued.

"Just think how many people live there—8,000! What a rich colossus we have! I can never help admiring the economy of space that can be achieved by such a concentration of human resources. I am sure that even our peasants will soon follow the workers and move into dormitories in order to increase the amount of land under cultivation. Their lives will become happier and more efficient."

I disagreed, and we began to argue. But I failed to convince my friend

[9]Following a massive strike of St. Petersburg textile workers in 1896, a government report stated that one reason for worker dissatisfaction was the prevalence of foreign factory managers who had little respect for Russian labor laws and social customs. See *Rabochee dvizhenie v Rossii v 19-om veke. Sbornik dokumentov i materialov*, ed. A. M. Pankratova and I. M. Ivanov (Moscow, 1963), IV, pt. 1, p. 236.

[10]Labor legislation of 1886 contained provisions fining factory administrators for violations of labor laws.

that workers flee such close quarters at the first opportunity, and not merely because of some old-fashioned prejudices. We fell silent, and my friend was soon asleep, but I kept thinking about our conversation.

Last summer, the factory administration asked me to supervise the installation of central heating in the dormitories, and I had plenty of opportunity to observe the workers in their living quarters. Now, when I look at these buildings from afar, I no longer see them as the picturesque "red spots" that appeal so much to my friend's aesthetic sensibility. Before my eyes there now pass scenes and memories of that other, different life which I observed in those enormous dormitory buildings.

I clearly remember the gruesome feeling of nagging monotony that overtook me when I went inside the dormitory for the first time. All three of them were designed according to a single pattern, each of the four stories resembling the others in every minute detail. A long corridor separated the two rows of "cells," which are formed by thin partitions. Each small room measured 10.5 feet wide, 19.8 feet deep, and 11.7 feet high. It had the capacity of 4.14 cubic *sazhen*,[11] and could easily accommodate four people, given the legal requirements. "One cubic *sazhen* per person," the factory owner used to say, distinctly pronouncing each word. Our chief accountant, who remembers the old days, once assured me that they used to put eight people in a room of this size. Because the factory operated round the clock, the night-shift workers had occupied the room during the day and the day-shift workers at night. This way the owner saved on mattresses as well, since both shifts could sleep on the same mattress. But the factory owner laughed off this kind of calculation, saying that it was not for him and that he wished to provide his workers with decent living quarters.

It is true that our dormitories are decent compared with others. They are well ventilated and have other excellent facilities. The factory administration is relatively generous when it comes to keeping the dormitory in good order: the interior is painted once a year, the corridors, the kitchens, and the stairs are always well swept and generally clean. Nevertheless, each time I

[11]One *sazhen* equals slightly more than seven feet, and 4.14 cubic *sazhen* would have been 1,420 cubic feet. There is an error in the figures for room dimension. Other evidence in the text indicates that the room length was only 11.6 feet, not 19.8 feet as stated above.

enter one of these buildings, I have the impression of entering either a military barrack or a prison. Monotony is everywhere. Each floor has a corridor 315 feet long. Each corridor is lined with thirty cubicles on one side and twenty on the other; the rest of the space is taken up by the staircase and those facilities that usually remain unmentioned in print.

Each building has a special annex in the middle containing an enormous stove heated by the central furnace. On the stove there are two rows of small burners, twenty-five altogether, one for every two rooms. Each room has two beds, one to the right and one to the left of the door, and there is a table surrounded by four stools by the window. If the rooms had not been numbered, I think the tenants themselves would have had difficulty finding their own quarters, because these fifty rooms on each of the four floors of each of the three buildings are so much alike. The only variety is in small details. In the rooms inhabited only by women workers, it is cleaner; when there are children, you can see cradles that make the already crowded space even more confined. The rooms occupied by weavers—workers who earn considerably more than the average wage at the mill—sometimes have curtains on the windows and a plant or two on the window sill.

The cheap prints covering the walls allow one to form an opinion about the aesthetic sensibility and intellectual potential of the inhabitants. Some rooms have religious themes; others have didactic prints such as "sayings in pictures" or the well-known "stages on life's way." For some reason, this product of a Nikolskaia Street[12] artist's imagination enjoys the most popularity. This strange picture depicts two sets of stairs meeting at the top. On one side there is an infant ascending the stairs who then turns into a youth, and then into a man with a stupid face wearing a top hat. This same man descends the stairs on the other side, finally reaching a coffin that is skillfully depicted in the lower right-hand corner. It is a rare room that does not have a print or two.

Unless the room is occupied by a single family—and most rooms have two—light curtains are all that shield the beds from each other. For some reason, I remember one of those curtains quite well: a cotton print with white specks against a red background. The first few times I went into

[12]Nikolskaia Street, located near the Kremlin, was known for the sale of religious artifacts. See *Ushedshaia Moskva. Vospominaniia sovremennikov o Moskve vtoroi poloviny XIX veka* (Moscow, 1964), pp. 78–79.

those little rooms inhabited by two families, I was very surprised at the calm way the tenants accepted such close cohabitation, living a mere half dozen feet away from the other couple. Whenever I asked them whether they felt uncomfortable sharing such close quarters, the men usually replied, "We don't mind, only the women quarrel," or "No, sir, why should we? We're all from the same village, almost kin."[13]

Sometimes the old men piped up, "You don't know how we lived before! Before we didn't even know what a room was like. We all slept together in one row."

"Do you like it better now?"

"How can you ask! Of course it's better!"

Yes, at least now in central and western Russia, those barracks where everyone—men, women, and children—slept in one place without any partitions between them are now part of the past. When we young technicians began our careers, such conditions had already ceased to be the order of the day. But even now one can get some idea of the old days by visiting the factory barracks for unmarried workers. Today these barracks are divided according to sex and age, and most owners pay attention to ventilation and general hygiene.[14] Yet the basic features of the "common barracks," which I would rather call a common boxcar, remain unchanged. There is the same large, often enormous room. Depending on the width, it contains one or two uninterrupted rows of scaffolding raised less than one foot above the floor. The rows themselves, extending from one wall to the other, are about thirteen feet deep. A single beam, elevated some seven inches above the scaffolding, runs the whole length of the row. On both sides of it are filthy bags filled with straw which often serve as the only bedding. Dozens and dozens of people sleep on these bags, with their heads facing the dividing beam. In these so-called "living quarters" there are neither tables nor chairs. Apparently, this room is not meant for people to sit down, to relax, or to read something. By day, you work at the factory;

[13]The term here is *zemliak*, discussed in Ch. 1, n. 4.

[14]As Pavlov implies here, conditions in factory barracks had once been much worse. Laws promulgated in the 1880s required factories to provide separate accommodations for unmarried men and women. Before that time, it was not uncommon for all workers to sleep together in a single room.

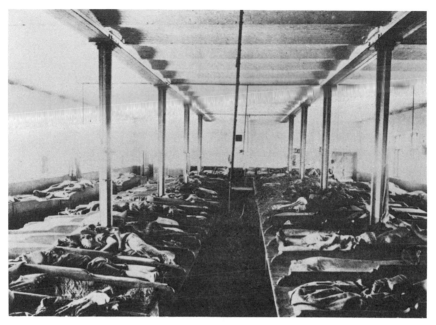

9. Factory barracks at Moscow's Prokhorovskaia Trekhgornaia textile mill in the 1890s.

at night, you sleep on the common plank bed; and in between, you eat in common dining rooms.

Once, at the very beginning of my career, I said in the director's presence that it would be a good idea to have carpenters make tables and stools for the common barracks. "And where are you going to put them?" the director asked. "Do not let the size of these halls mislead you," he went on. "According to our calculations their space has already been filled to capacity—one cubic *sazhen* per person. There isn't any floor space for such frivolity." True, when the standard density is one cubic *sazhen* per person, and the height of the room is usually 11.7 feet, you have only 29.2 square feet of floor space per person. After you subtract about 16 square feet for the bed, you are left with no more than 13 square feet of unoccupied floor space per capita. Obviously, this leaves little room for what the director calls "frivolity."

At first glance, it may appear that our workers are completely indifferent to their constant lack of privacy. They do not seem to care that they have to share their living quarters with strangers, be it in the common barracks or the less crowded dormitory cubicles. I thought so, too, until a chance incident changed my mind. This took place when the factory was under expansion. In the course of building new quarters for additional workers, the director decided to experiment by replacing the traditional dormitory with fifteen or so small cottages, each modeled after a simple peasant hut. The cottage was to be divided into two sections, each occupied by a single family. You should have seen the demand for those houses, and the impatience of the lucky few who had been selected to live in them, as they anxiously awaited the completion of construction. Our factory charged twenty-five kopecks a month per person for lodging in the dormitory.[15] This is a very decent rent. At other factories a worker often paid four or five times more for the same accommodations. Our workers were willing to pay twice as much, and even more, to get one of the new cottages, which were finally allocated to workers who had been at the factory longest and to a few of the most privileged workers, selected by the administration. Unfortunately, this project was the last we saw of such experimentation. It turned out that the cottages cost the employer 40 percent more to construct than the more traditional dormitories.

As I have already mentioned, soon afterwards I was given an assignment to supervise furnace repairs in the workers' dormitories. At one point I asked some women gathered in the kitchen why they had all been so anxious to move into the new cottages.

"Of course, we all want to live there, that's why!" one very energetic weaver answered on everyone's behalf. "You've got freedom there, you can do what you please. And here, may the Lord forgive me, you can't even spit without everybody noticing it! All sorts of things happen between a husband and wife, but you can't even exchange a couple of words here—right away, the neighbors sharing your room will spread the news all over the corridor!"

[15]In 1901, the average monthly wage for a textile worker in Moscow Province was 14 rubles and 48 kopecks. See Iu. I. Kir'ianov, *Zhiznennyi uroven' rabochikh Rossii* (Moscow, 1979), p. 126. Thus, lodging in a dormitory at this factory consumed roughly 1.7 percent of the average monthly wage.

"Don't listen to her, Fedor Pavlovich," an old woman interrupted, speaking in a sweet, ingratiating voice. "All of us here like everything. We've got nothing to complain about. She's just saying that 'cause her husband gave her a good beating last week, and she didn't like it when we all found out, so she's smarting!"

"Shut up, old liar. You just envy me 'cause you've got nobody to beat you any more!" the angry textile weaver retorted. She slammed the damper on the stove, grabbed her pot, and ran out.

10. Women workers at a Moscow silk mill in the 1890s.

Later in the day, I discussed this conversation with the metalfitter Krasnov, who was working with me on the furnace.

"Why don't these women like the barracks?" I asked.

"They've already told you why, haven't they? Why should they like them? Fedor Pavlovich, let me tell you about the time I worked at a glass factory. There we had real quarters. It was really nice. We had a whole village of cottages, only they were bigger and better than the ones we have here. The big huts were divided in half and shared by two families, but a single family could have a smaller one all to itself. Each hut had a little barn for cattle, a vegetable garden, and the workers were allowed to mow the grass in the woods nearby and take their cattle there for grazing. Before you knew it, you already had a couple of pigs, chickens. . . . It means a lot to the working man to have something of his own. I don't understand why our factory isn't building more of these cottages. They say it takes up too much land, but our owner has 15,000 *dessiatina*.[16] That's land enough! And if the village gets too big, you can have horse-drawn streetcars, like people say they have in Poland. Sure, it will cost more, but the worker will gladly pay for it. I wish we could have it so good! And what do we have now? Sure, it looks nice. The floor's asphalt, and there's ventilation if you please. But you can't tempt the worker with such things. Barracks are barracks, and that's that!"

True enough, barracks! I've heard that foreigners, and especially Frenchmen, find our barracks and dormitories too much like prisons. Individualists by nature, they thoroughly disapprove of our barracks. They maintain that the strict regimen our workers are subjected to, both on the job and during their free time, robs them of their individuality and has an enormously negative effect on their capacity for work. It is difficult to know for certain, but they may be right.

You have to imagine every detail of dormitory living in order to see the potential power it has to influence workers. Take our factory, for example. Twenty-four hundred men and women occupy rooms which are as similar as peas in a pod. They all obey the same factory whistle. They all get up at the same time, as though by order, and every day they have to perform the same or nearly the same task at their workplace. Those wives who remain behind all start to cook simultaneously at the call of the same factory whistle. At seven o'clock in the evening, all twenty-four hundred workers anticipate the same moment when half of them will leave for home and the other half will take their place at work. It will be the same tomorrow and the day after tomorrow, year in and year out, with only holidays to interrupt the routine. And during all this time there is never a moment of privacy, never a chance to have something different from your neighbor. Add to this the fact that your room is assigned by the dormitory supervisor, who can ask you to move into a different one at any time. And then twice a year,

[16]15,000 *dessiatina* equal 40,500 acres.

at Easter and the Feast of the Intercession,[17] when contracts are renewed, you may be turned out of the dormitories altogether. Ponder this, and you will understand Krasnov's exclamation, "Barracks are barracks, and that's that!"

My friend, who had been ardently defending the dormitories an hour ago, was now awake. We decided to go home, and as we were walking down to the river we met an old respected worker named Kasianov, returning home from a hunt. He asked if he could join us.

"Don't you want to ask Kasianov to help us resolve our dispute?" my friend whispered into my ear. "That way, we can find out what workers think firsthand."

"I don't object if you want to pursue the subject."

"Kasianov," he began, "are you married?"

"Yes, sir."

"Does your wife work?"

"Of course she does."

"And where do you live?"

"In the second block."

"Do you like living in those dormitories? Do you find it comfortable?"

"More or less."

"Are the dormitories crowded?"

"No, not crowded."

"And how about your wife? Does she quarrel with your neighbors?"

"No, why would she quarrel with them?"

"You mean the women don't get into fights over pots or a place at the stove?"

"No, they don't quarrel at all!"

This conversation went on for a long time until I intervened by asking Kasianov whether he would rather live in the dormitory or in one of the new cottages.

Kasianov began to laugh.

[17]The Feast of the Intercession, a Russian Orthodox holiday, takes place on October 1. It commemorates a victory of the Greeks over the Saracens at Constantinople in the tenth century.

"How can you even ask! Living in the dormitory, we're just like this game in my game sack, rubbing against each other all the time. The cottages, that's another matter. There you can breathe freely."

We fell silent.

"Of course, life in the dormitory isn't so bad either. You can get by. Let me tell you, nine years ago in Moscow I lived in a factory run by a German where I had quarters that I'm ashamed to remember. We worked on hand looms and slept there too, right on top of the looms. Like birds. Birds nest on tree branches, we nested on looms."

"You mean to say you slept in the weaving shop, right on the premises?"

"Right in the same spot. That German had two shifts working for him. So I'd be sleeping on top of the loom while my partner below me was knocking about with his shuttle—bang-bang, bang-bang. The loom's shaking all the time. Come night, I stand behind the loom, he's asleep over me. The loom is very wide, so I hang a kerosene lamp right in the middle of it, and while it burns, my sleeping partner gets fried a bit. That's the kind of life I used to have. I remember going home for Easter, feeling my whole body aching from such uncomfortable quarters—all 'cause I hadn't slept through a single night the whole winter, lying and shaking on that cursed loom. Nowadays, people say such places are rare. Thank God!"

We parted from Kasianov at the gate. My friend and I had arranged to invite each other to dinner on alternate Sundays so that our servants could have every other Sunday free. As we entered his house, we heard the angry voice of his cook, yelling at us from the kitchen: "Where have you been all this time? I thought you'd drowned in the swamp chasing ducks. You promised to come home at one, and it's already three—now the cake's as dry as a log."

A VISIT BY THE FACTORY INSPECTOR

One day in February, my work was interrupted by a messenger boy who handed me an urgent note from the director. It read: "Unless something special has come up, ask your assistant to take over for you for a day. I need you to accompany the new factory inspector. He wants to inspect the whole mill, and I do not have the time to go around with him. I believe you have more time than the other technicians." I gave the appropriate orders, and five minutes later I was on my way to the director's office.

"Allow me to introduce you," the director said as I walked into his office. "This is our new inspector, and this is Fedor Pavlovich Pavlov, the specialist in charge of the weaving division. He'll show you everything. I'm sorry I can't be of much assistance myself. I'm too busy at the moment."

The inspector said that he did not wish to interfere with the director's schedule, but expressed a desire to discuss some matters with the director later on.

"At your service," replied the director drily. Then he turned to me and added, "Mr. Inspector would like to take a look at our entire operation, including the dormitory, the barracks, the hospital and the school—in other words, everything. I would like you to answer all his questions as you accompany him on a tour of the plant. I think the best place to begin is the scutching shop."[18]

"I beg to disagree," responded the inspector. "I know textile mills very well, and I am quite familiar with the technological process. I would like to go directly to where children are employed[19]—the spinning shops using self-acting spinning frames, or to the warping machines.[20]

"As you please, Inspector!" was the director's reply, and the inspector and I left the director's office.

"Look, my announcement is already on display," the inspector said with a smile, as he looked at the big board near the main entrance posting various factory rules, laws, and regulations. Amid the other notices, I saw a small announcement that Vasilii Vasilevich Dolgopolov, the inspector of

---

[18]Scutching is a process by which cotton and other fibrous threads are formed into a lap and made ready for spinning. The machines which process the cotton are called lappers.

[19]Labor legislation enacted in 1882 prohibited the factory employment of children under the age of twelve. Between the ages of twelve and fifteen, children were permitted to work eight hours a day, excluding night work, and at the age of sixteen an individual could be employed for the full adult shift. Employers were required by law to provide schooling for children employed in their enterprises.

[20]A spinning mule, or *sel'faktor* spinning machine, simultaneously drew, spun, and twisted the thread. Warping machines are described below.

11. Spinning room in a textile mill with two child workers in the early 1900s.

such and such district, would be glad to receive workers, factory owners, or other interested persons on Saturdays from noon to six.

"I sent it here only three days ago, and I didn't expect you to be so prompt."

"We always try to be prompt," I replied.

"Yes, of course. Large enterprises with enormous staffs, with offices large enough for a ministry, are always prompt when it comes to enforcing the letter of the law."

His emphasis on the "letter of the law" somewhat offended my loyalty as an employee of our factory.

"Why are you saying 'the letter of the law'? We also try to adhere to the essence of the law, to imbue ourselves with its spirit."

"Really? Well then, I beg your pardon. I am very happy to hear this. I mentioned the letter of the law only because my past experience has taught me to anticipate only superficial compliance. I must say, I've come across a number of factories where the essence of the law was understood in a very peculiar fashion, to say the least." The inspector, speaking in a dispassionate tone, smiled gently and looked me straight in the eye.

I wanted to argue with him, but he interrupted me.

"I don't want to argue. Let's get down to business. Please take me to where the warps are prepared."

After we passed through two long weaving shops, we entered an area that seemed remarkably silent and spacious compared with the din and overcrowding of the weaving rooms. About forty children, both boys and girls, were at work as we entered. In this shop the warps were prepared by drawing in threads through the heddles. A heddle is that long, slender part of the loom harness with an eye in its center through which one or more threads pass. The harness then lifts and lowers the alternate threads of the warp, allowing the shuttle to carry the yarn back and forth. This is how a cross weave is made, and all fabrics from sackcloth to finer cottons are produced this way.

In this particular shop, all that was being done was to thread the heddles. Two children sitting in front of one another would secure two heddles with a special device placed between them, and then, using special hooks, they would thread the warp, strand by strand, through the eyes of alternate heddles. All the odd threads are drawn through the eye of one heddle, and all the even threads through the eye of the other. At first glance, this seems like very easy work, but in fact it requires much concentration and puts quite a strain on one's eyesight because if two or three heddles are missed, the whole weaving process may be ruined. Since they are confined to a sitting position with their backs bent and eyes strained, these twelve- or fourteen-year-old workers become fatigued very easily. As a result, children in this shop look tired and unhealthy and have yellow, pale skin.

Vasilii Vasilievich looked them all over and asked some of them how many hours a day they worked and whether they were attending school. He looked quite unhappy when they answered that they worked a nine-hour day in two four-and-a-half hour shifts. After writing down the names and numbers[21] of the youngest-looking children in his notebook, he returned to the weaving shops. He asked several workers to show him their

---

[21]Upon entering factory employment, every worker was assigned a number; see Ch. 2, p. 90.

workbooks,[22] questioning them about when they started and finished work and about the length of their lunch break. I could not hear him very well since the looms were making their usual deafening noise. He was putting things down in his notebook all the time.

"Tell me," he turned to me, "have you heard any complaints from your weavers recently?"

"What do you mean, complaints?"

"I mean any complaints. Say, about problems with the supply of yarn."

"Yes, I've heard some."

"Did you find these complaints unfounded?"

"On the whole, yes. Only a few were legitimate."

"Do you mean to tell me that the yarn from the more recent batches was of the same quality as before and did not affect the earnings of the weavers?"

In November, the Director received two thousand bales of a new kind of cotton, cheaper than usual, that the factory had not worked with before. The yarn spun from this cotton broke easily, causing problems for the technical personnel and for the weavers. We began to get complaints that the "warp is weak" and frequently breaks. When even one thread breaks, the weaver must stop the loom to correct the problem. As a result, the weavers' productivity, and with it their earnings, had dropped considerably, since they are paid on a piecework basis.

"I don't deny that some of the complaints were quite legitimate, but on the whole the weavers are exaggerating the magnitude of the problem. Incidents of disruption are quite rare."

"I beg your pardon, sir, but I did not ask you how frequent such cases might have been—only whether there have been such cases at all. And now, judging by your answer, I see that such incidents did indeed take place."

"I would never deny it," I had to acknowledge his astute conclusion, "but how did you find out?"

"Well, I've had a few anonymous letters and a few complaints. Now let's go to the spinning shops." We crossed the yard and made quick rounds of the whole spinning section, stopping as before in those areas where children and adolescents were concentrated.

[22]See Ch. 1, n. 32.

This was the first time I had taken a tour of the factory with one of the factory inspectors, about whom I had recently heard and read so much. It intrigued me that this man, who like myself was a trained technician and spent half of his time surrounded by factory equipment, nonetheless looked at factory life with completely different eyes. For a moment I imagined that he was wearing some special kind of glasses that greatly magnified everything a technician considered to be a minor matter and, on the other hand, ignored all the important things that make a factory technologically and commercially sound.

Right away, even before we stepped onto the shop floor, I was surprised by the attention that the inspector paid to all those regulations, announcements, and laws which the factory was required to post. By contrast, I had never more than glanced at those printed notices, and over half of them were completely unknown to me. My co-workers treated them in much the same fashion. The director always smiled sardonically when he received a new announcement with a request, "Post this prominently in a public place."

"Soon we'll have enough of them to use as wallpaper. What on earth are they doing there at the Factory Inspectorate? I really wonder. Frames and glass alone are an enormous expense. Nobody reads them anyway."

When he passed by the machinery, Vasilii Vasilievich usually paid particular attention to those details that the factory administration either ignored altogether or, at best, treated carelessly.

"Why is the floor uneven?" he asked me when we left the weaving shop.

I looked back and suddenly saw how uneven the floor was, something that I had been quite accustomed to. Now it practically leaped out at me. I also noticed that it was slippery and full of holes.

"Yes, we'll have to take care of it."

"The sooner the better," the inspector added. "A worker could easily break his leg here or slip and fall under a machine."

Then we walked through the spinning shop. The carriages of the self-acting spinning frames rolled back and forth on rails, drawing the fiber as they went. Twisters,[23] and the spinner who was supervising the frame, adjusted the torn threads while following the moving carriage as it rolled

---

[23]The twisters worked at spinning mules, making sure that the thread was twisted after it was spun.

back and forth. These workers, especially the young ones, often stepped on the rail, and if they were at all careless the wheel of the carriage could run over their foot.

"Why is it that some of the frames have guards protecting the workers' feet and others don't?" the inspector wondered.

"I don't think any of our frames have guards, at least I don't remember any."

We went back, and true enough, six of the frames had guards. I was not very familiar with the spinning process at our factory, so I could not give the inspector a satisfactory answer. We had to ask the assistant foreman. It turned out that those were new machines that had just arrived from England.

"Well," I said, "it's not the factory's fault. We received the old machines from the manufacturer without any guards."

"All that's clear to me," the inspector interrupted, "is that these guards are very easy to make and install. Any of your metalfitters could do it. I cannot understand why you have not copied and installed these guards. It's incomprehensible, at least from my point of view."

I tried to say something in explanation, but the inspector was not satisfied with my weak reasoning, and we moved on.

After we left the spinning room, we got into a carriage that the director sent for us and rode to the dye works. Then, after a snack at the factory club, we went to take a look at the rest of the factory premises—the school, the dormitories, and the infirmary. The factory store took us the longest, something I had not expected. I had only a very vague idea of what this "department store," as our workers jokingly called it, was like. All I knew about it was that my cook bought groceries there, and I thought they were quite good. In a way, I was glad that the inspector had decided to have a good look at it, since it was a large enterprise, separate from the rest of the factory.

According to general opinion, the store was well run; in other words, the owners did not wish to use it to make huge profits as is often the case elsewhere. The store's turnover amounted to 400,000 or 500,000 rubles a year, and the modest profit margin of 5 to 15 percent was used to cover maintenance costs, pay the interest on the capital invested in it, and absorb the losses from food spoilage and the like that are inevitable in a retail operation of this kind. In other words, it was a popular store, used both by the workers and by the factory personnel, and there were even customers from outside the factory. Obviously, the store was never in the red, but the 10,000 to 15,000 rubles' profit that it yielded was insignificant when compared with the enormous commercial success of the factory. The store gave the factory a good name, and the owners were well aware that this kind of reputation would make the factory attractive to new workers.

When we approached the large structure which the store occupied, we were greeted by the manager in charge of the operation. The manager, Stepan Fomich, was a tall, stocky man, who had a thick salt-and-pepper beard and a clever look in his eyes. He was, in my opinion, a typical representative of the retail trade in large village markets and small towns of central Russia. He understood the importance of his position at the factory and knew that the owners expected him to run his business fairly and efficiently. This was enough to make "fairness" his motto. He was angry with his employees whenever he noticed even a minute deviation from the established rules, and he had recently fired a salesman for offering the customers spoiled herring. Once, I remember, he made a big scene when he discovered that one of his men had overcharged a workers' artel[24] for bread. He liked making noises about such incidents, liked it especially because he knew that both the workers and the owners appreciated such "noises." — *putting on a show*

But the more ardently Stepan Fomich observed all the established regulations and insisted on guarding his customers' interests, the more I felt that he needed only to give his salesmen a nod in order to turn their skill and energy in a completely different direction. Indeed, it would have been easy to transform this factory store into a means of exploiting all 8,000 factory employees, none of whom could get more than fifty kopecks' credit anywhere else, unless they obtained special references from the factory office or were willing to pay an exorbitant interest. All the store had to do was to purchase slightly inferior products and raise prices by a kopeck or two. Even the Factory Inspectorate was powerless to do any-thing about abuses like these, since it had no way of establishing a mini-

[24]See Ch. 1, n. 2.

mum price for any grade of a given product.[25] And how tempting it must be to increase the profit by a hundred thousand rubles a year, with so little effort! The factory is completely helpless against such schemes unless it decides to prohibit retail sales on credit altogether.

Our law does not favor factory stores in principle, and the general public shares this poor opinion of them. We Russians have even developed an effective way to combat their abuses by placing them under the supervision of the Factory Inspectorate, which has the power to establish profit margins. However, there is one radical solution to the problem which has been tested and adopted in the West—namely, the complete prohibition of retail sales on credit, coupled with the stipulation that the factory pay all wages in cash only. Until now, the approach has not been adopted in our laws or in our factory life. Needless to say, it would be better and simpler to close down factory stores altogether, since their very existence creates an opportunity for exploitation and abuse. One need only recall the violent destruction of such stores during recent factory disturbances[26] to appreciate how desirable this approach would be.

Nonetheless, it would be unfair to consider existing legislation as totally ineffective. The very fact that our workers do not form the mutual aid societies[27] so popular in the West already speaks in favor of our laws. We have neither properly run consumer cooperatives nor credit unions. A Russian worker comes to the factory alone, without any cash and without

[25]One of the factory inspector's many duties was to inspect the factory store, where his main task was to check and approve prices.

[26]One of the most famous examples of the violent destruction of a factory store occurred during a strike at the Morozov textile mill in Vladimir province in 1885. On the first day of the strike, workers raided the factory store and smashed its windows. See *Rabochee dvizhenie v Rossii,* III, pt. 1, p. 170.

[27]Although the movement among workers to form mutual aid societies was extremely feeble during the nineteenth century, some workers nonetheless took steps to establish these organizations, beginning in 1814. Over the decades that followed, a small number of mutual aid societies were organized among printers and other artisans, sales-clerical employees, skilled service groups, and even some factory workers, principally to provide material benefits in the event of illness or accident. The weakness of the mutual aid movement among Russian workers was not due to the salutary character of labor legislation, as Pavlov asserts, but rather to the government's highly restrictive policies and inhospitable environment for voluntary associations.

savings. In order for him to be able to feed himself before he receives his first pay, he needs to obtain credit. It is true that sometimes the worker's artel can supply him with the necessary credit, but not every factory has an artel, and the credit terms offered by a factory store are far more favorable.

The fact is that the worker needs credit very badly, because of both the low wages and the infrequency of paydays (once a month, as a rule). Thus the reality of our factory life justifies, to a certain degree, the lenient stance that our laws take toward factory stores. And it is even possible that the workers themselves would not be willing to give up the opportunity to receive food on credit while awaiting their first pay.

Stepan Fomich chatted continuously while giving us a tour of his enormous storage room, which had five large windows. He showed us the sparklingly clean bakeries where up to four hundred puds[28] of rye bread were baked daily, and the cellars containing enormous barrels of salted meat and cabbage. Finally, we left the storage area and entered a room where dishes and hardware were sold.

Stepan Fomich never stopped talking, and even the inspector, despite his usual reserve, began to show some impatience. We were now in the third and last room of the store, where enormous quantities of textiles, haberdashery, and cosmetics were displayed, something quite remarkable for a provincial store. Here you could find anything from cheap cotton to rather expensive French perfume.

"Why do you stock these things?" the inspector asked, pointing to the expensive perfumes and colognes.

"I can't help it—customers demand it. The Lord strike me dead, but even the workers ask for it. They like to present a gift of perfume or fine soap to their sweethearts. People living nearby buy it too, you know, the railroad clerks, the landowners. Needless to say, we don't sell these things to workers on credit. Strictly cash, just as the owners told us. You see, we know the rules. But I wonder why you keep making changes in our price list and even cross out some of our items. I have to say that the workers don't benefit from it at all. For example, we would like to sell footwear. Why doesn't the Inspectorate allow us to do it?"

"What do you mean, we don't allow it?" the inspector interrupted. "We

[28]400 puds equals 14,414.4 pounds.

prohibit the sale of such products on credit, but you may still sell them for cash."

"Just as I said, you don't allow us to sell these things on credit. So we don't do it. But all around the factory there are about a dozen shoemakers; they all sell to our workers, and all on credit. While we sell the same pair of boots for three rubles, they, curse their souls, charge five. And there is nothing a workingman can do. Let's say his boots fall apart today, but he won't be paid for three weeks. What is he going to do without boots, go barefoot?"

"Well, I can't solve that problem for you." Vasilii Vasilievich shrugged his shoulders. "You know that they run up their credit debt too easily. If we allow the workers to use credit to buy fashionable jackets and patent leather shoes, they won't have enough money left for necessities. If they want to buy these things, let them pay cash. And if you want to make life easier for them, have the factory pay their wages more frequently."

"How can it be more frequent? We already pay them every month!"

"But abroad they are paid weekly."

"No, we can't do that—they'd spend it all on drinking."

"Well, then, why is it that drunkenness has not increased in Europe where they are paid once a week? This is simply one of our old mistaken convictions that everybody repeats without giving any evidence." Vasilii Vasilievich was now talking to me.

"But just think," I tried to come to the defense of our system, "we have 4,000 workers who are paid by the piece. Can you imagine what the accounting costs would be if we had to pay them once a week instead of once a month?"

"But what about the West? They have factories just like ours, if not bigger, and they manage to pay their workers every week on the dot without any complaints."

I was not familiar with Western factory customs, so I merely shrugged my shoulders. Stepan Fomich, however, sensed that the conversation was moving toward shaky political ground and attempted to turn our attention to other matters. But Vasilii Vasilievich had already exhausted all his patience. He asked me to take him to his room so that he could rest before supper. It was seven o'clock, and he was beginning to feel tired after spending the whole day touring the factory.

"Until tomorrow," said the inspector as we drove to the rooming house where he was spending the night. "Tomorrow I am planning to visit the school and then have a talk with the director. I would like it very much if you could be present during this talk. You could help me remember certain details. Will you be free around eleven o'clock?"

All I could do was to agree, and then we parted. Now I had to go to see the director and report to him on the tour. As it turned out, however, the director had left for Moscow and was not expected back until late.

A MEETING BETWEEN THE FACTORY INSPECTOR AND THE DIRECTOR

The next morning, as usual, I was already at the weaving shop at six o'clock. We could never complain about a lack of work, and today, after spending a whole day elsewhere, I had even more business than usual. I had completely forgotten about my eleven o'clock appointment, and was even surprised when a messenger boy asked me to come see the director at a quarter to twelve. I had no desire whatsoever to leave my work again, having already spent too much time talking with the inspector. For a moment I thought of not going, explaining my absence by the urgent problems at hand. But then I decided that it would be both impolite and inappropriate to miss the inspector's discussion with the director, so I left for the office.

There was silence when I entered the director's office, which did not bode at all well. The director was leaning back in his chair and nervously thumping his fingers against the table. The inspector, sitting in the chair opposite him, silently and gloomily leafed through his notebook. On the desk in front of him there was a heap of workers' paybooks and to the left of them an enormous stack of ledgers.

"As I was saying, the worker's paybook, which represents the contract established between him and the factory, must be maintained according to regulations. I would very much like to see you adhere to the established form. I came across several paybooks that did not specify, for example, whether the worker received wages in cash or also in room and board. There are some which did not mention the wage schedule. I won't even go into the length of contract—this category is left blank in every paybook!"

The inspector spoke these words in a virtual monotone, as though repeating them for the hundredth time.

"But I have already told you that all our workers know that the factory employs them for a specific period of time and that all contracts are terminated twice a year—on Easter and on October 1."

"I know this also. But if a worker decided to lodge a complaint with either the Inspectorate or the courts, it is necessary for him to have the length of contract specified."

"This is specified in our internal regulations."

"Then you may choose to paste these regulations into the contract books, but you often fail to do so. In any case, I repeat that the established form requires. . . ."

"Form! But these forms have nothing to do with the way things are done, they are not important! It's just a formality." The director began to lose his temper.

"I don't agree with you. Such formalities can serve the worker very well."

"Mere form can never serve anyone! You are the only one who gives it any importance. The worker does not care about it at all. It means nothing to him," the director answered coldly.

"The worker does not care about it until the time comes when the factory fires him without any legally valid reasons. If he lodges a complaint about it with the courts, he will not have much chance of winning the case unless his paybook specifies the length of his contract."

"But believe me, if I or any foreman want to, we will always be able to find a legal reason to fire a worker. Come to think of it, any assistant foreman can decide to pester the worker so much that he will leave of his own accord."

"Do you really think that I don't know this?" the inspector asked, looking the director in the eye. "One can abuse the law and one can find loopholes in it—everybody knows that. Factory inspectors know it especially well. But our function is to create obstacles in the path of abuse, whether it is committed by the factory or by the worker, and to limit arbitrary actions. In other words, we have to help establish the *idea of legality*. Individual abuses will have to be dealt with on an individual basis. Of course, if you decide to get rid of a worker, you can easily do it even without breaking the law. I have come across cases where the factory simply prohibited a worker from touching anything, and the worker left the factory of his own accord. He'd be told that he would be able to earn as much money as before but that he would have to sit in the corner of the shop all day long without touching the machines, and that alone sufficed to make the worker leave. Needless to say, such cases are rare, at least I hope so. But right now I am not interested in exotic incidents; I would like to concentrate on general rules instead."

Vasilii Vasilievich fell silent and started leafing through workbooks and ledgers again.

"All right. You may prosecute the factory for violating the law, but what can you do to a worker who breaks it?" The director could not stand the silence. "Last year, for example, twenty of my spinners suddenly left the factory when I needed them most. Even my reserve workers were not sufficient, and I had to stop four spinning frames. These clever fellows knew when to quit. They saw that I needed them badly and thought that I'd raise their wages! You can't trick me so easily, though; I'm an old hand at these matters. But this is beside the point. I am asking you what kind of redress I have when I am confronted with such cases."

"Redress? Why, you could have filed a complaint with the factory inspector who was in charge of the district at the time. He could have taken them to court. The zemstvo officer[29] would have had them arrested."

"Thank you very much for help like that! Send them to the zemstvo officer? Those zemstvo people either would have acquitted them or, at best, would have kept them in jail for three days. That's not worth my trouble. For this kind of behavior I would have. . . ." The director tried to find an adequate punishment.

"You mean you would have sentenced them to forced labor?" the inspector joked. "Well, on this point, I am afraid we disagree. In my opinion, our law already treats the worker too severely. Just think, the workers didn't commit a felony by quitting your factory; they simply made you incur a loss. The fair thing to do in such cases is to have them compensate you for the loss, and not sentence them to jail or hard labor."

[29]The zemstvo, an organ of rural self-government, was established in 1864. By the end of the nineteenth century, the zemstvo had become a center for the growing liberal movement in Russia.

"But how can they compensate me for my losses?"

"That's for you to find out. However, I think that if a worker likes the factory and finds it *profitable* for himself, then he won't quit. He is too intelligent for that. It is up to you to arrange things so that the worker considers your factory more advantageous to himself than another enterprise. And if you run into workers who like to go from one factory to another without any reason—and some directors tell me that they have encountered such workers—then get rid of them as soon as you can and look for ones who will stay."

The director wanted to present a counterargument, but the inspector went on:

"Let's stop these abstract arguments. I have other matters to discuss with you. Here's another question. I found seven fines in the paybooks, and I would like to know when they were added to the fines fund and the ledgers."[30]

Vasilii Vasilievich stood up and began leafing through a thick ledger, filled with brief but significant records reading something like this: "No. 3,332—Matrena Karpova. 15 kopecks for breakage. No. 670—Prokopi Solokov. 30 kopecks for sleeping on the job," and the like. These fines ranged from 5 kopecks to a ruble. Every month the factory collected 600 to 800 rubles in fines. In the course of a year, this added up to the substantial sum of 8,000 to 9,000 rubles, which went into a special fund. On the average, each worker paid about 2 rubles a year in fines.

Two rubles a year? Perhaps the reader might think this is an insignificant sum. But if you remember that the average yearly income of a factory worker is about 110 rubles,[31] then the amount paid out in fines is equal to about two percent of that income, not an inconsequential figure. Besides, these two percentage points represent an average, meaning that some workers pay little or nothing at all while others pay much more than two

[30]The labor legislation of 1886 required that money taken from fines be placed in a special fund to finance projects for the workers' benefit.

[31]Even for the first half of the 1890s, Pavlov's figure here is unduly low. In 1897, the average yearly wage of a factory worker in Imperial Russia was about 183 rubles. In textiles, the average yearly wage in cotton, wool, silk, and linen enterprises ranged from about 133 to 155 rubles. See Kir'ianov, *Zhiznennyi uroven' rabochikh Rossii*, p. 104.

rubles. For the latter, the fines took a large part of their income, sometimes as much as eight rubles a year. According to the law, the factory merely serves as a depository for these sums and is allowed to spend them only for the benefit of the factory workers. This, of course, is a minor consolation for those who are fined most often. And how could it be otherwise? What would a clerk or a government official say if his superiors could deduct some fifty rubles for charity out of his 1,500-a-year income? And for a worker, this relative loss in income represents a greater hardship than it would for an official.

Minor but frequent fines irritated the workers and often caused confrontations, even though fines were levied in full accordance with the law. Regulations required that all the possible infractions be tabulated in monetary equivalents. These strange tables were then approved by the factory inspector, posted under glass, and displayed prominently in every shop. The director could remember times when fines were much greater, amounting to 30,000 or 40,000 rubles a year, and went into the general factory budget. Therefore he did not think that fines under the present system deserved any serious consideration. The director thought that the inspector's interest in these things was petty and ridiculous. At first he watched silently as the inspector compared the fines in the workbooks with the records in the fines ledger, but then he could not contain himself any longer and said ironically:

"I see you have counted a whole two and a half rubles there. Do you really think that we would want to lay our hands on these paltry sums, and that we illegally transfer the fines capital into our factory account?"

"Oh, no," the inspector answered quietly, but also ironically. "I hope that this does not happen. But this is my first time at your factory, so I have to make sure that your fines ledger is in good order."

The director fell silent, but his fingers were still thumping against the table as loud as ever. After finishing with the fines ledger, the inspector reached into his briefcase, took out an envelope, and handed it to the director. It was an anonymous letter from a group of weavers complaining about the decline in wages due to the poor quality of warps.

"This is why I asked Fedor Pavlovich to come here. He is in charge of weaving, so he knows about the matter firsthand."

The letter was written in a language as cumbersome and artless as the handwriting of the person who wrote it. Nevertheless, it made its point effectively, stating that beginning in January the weavers had been receiving poor quality warps, which had slowed down their production and, consequently, reduced their income severely. "Even before January," the letter went on to say, "we had hardly been able to scrape together enough to feed our families and pay the taxes that we peasants owe the treasury." The letter pointed out that weavers who had been making sixteen or seventeen rubles a month were now only making nine. Finally, the letter appealed to the inspector to "investigate the matter thoroughly in order to avoid any unpleasantness." They warned the inspector that if he ignored their petition, they would appeal to a "higher authority." Instead of ending with a list of signatures, the letter was signed with the customary symbol of worker solidarity—a chain of interlocking rings.

"This complaint is unfounded!" the director declared, making me lower my eyes in embarrassment.

I had no doubt that the letter contained a number of reasonable, well-justified requests, even though there were some that were arbitrary and made out of ignorance. Only now did I fully understand the significance of the inspector's questions the day before. I should have warned the director in advance to avoid this embarrassment. But now it was too late.

"To begin with, no weaver has ever made seventeen rubles on our cotton looms; secondly, no weaver, unless he's a drunkard, makes as little as nine. If he's not a drunkard, an average weaver makes twelve rubles a month or more."

"Of course, the petition exaggerates some things; petitions usually do. But don't you think that a few of the complaints are justified? What is your opinion, Fedor Pavlovich?" the inspector put his last question directly to me.

My position was becoming quite uncomfortable. Of course, I knew better than anybody else that the petition had much more than a grain of truth in it. Yesterday I had said as much to the inspector, although not without reservations. My technician's pride alone made it difficult for me to acknowledge that the production for which I was responsible had serious problems. Moreover, I would be acknowledging it in front of an outsider, a government official who was a technician like myself but one who had abandoned his training and switched from private industry to a government job. Finally, the director's categorical denial could not help me to make a clean breast of things unless, of course, I wished to destroy my future at the factory forever. So I tried, very awkwardly, to steer a middle course. I admitted that during the past months we had encountered a few weak warps, but said this was a temporary occurrence, an exception that could not have any lasting effects.

Apparently the inspector was expecting precisely this kind of answer.

"So you are not denying that there have been incidents such as the letter refers to. You see, Director, some of the complaints are justified, after all."

The director looked at me, sorely disappointed.

"For my part," the inspector went on, "I noticed a considerable lowering of weavers' income when I was going through their paybooks. Of course, this drop is not as substantial as the anonymous letter makes it out to be, but it is not insignificant either. Take this weaver, Ivan Eremin, for example. Look at his paybook. In November he made 15.20 rubles; in December, with five extra holidays, he made 13.40 rubles; but in January, with only two extra holidays, his income dropped to 11.50 rubles. Here is another paybook, here is a third, but the picture stays the same. What kind of explanation can you give me now, gentlemen?"

"Must be a coincidence," retorted the director.

"What is your opinion, Fedor Pavlovich?"

At this point, I was forced to admit that the weavers had gotten bad warps.

"What do you propose to do in such cases in the future?" Vasilii Vasilievich now asked the director.

"What do you mean? I'm not going to do anything."

"But these workers took a substantial loss in income because of someone else's mistakes or, to be more precise, because of the factory's oversight. And you propose to do nothing? After all, it is up to the factory to supply them with satisfactory materials. It's the factory, not the weavers, that is responsible for the substandard warps. You have to agree that this is the factory's fault.

"But I have told you that this is a mere confluence of unfortunate circumstances, a coincidence. The weavers know perfectly well that their income depends on the quality of materials supplied to them."

"You have to admit, however, that ordinarily a weaver's income does not fluctuate that much. I would insist that if such incidents recur with any regularity, then you should raise the rates for poorer quality warps by 12 to 15 percent."

"I can't do that," the director said. "Then everybody would ask for a similar raise."

It was becoming quite clear that the argument was not going to end in a mutually satisfactory solution, and the director, who had not been challenged for a long time, began to lose his temper. The inspector also started to lose his calm demeanor. Finally, he picked up a special notebook and recorded the results of his inspection. The report discussed the essence of the dispute, giving examples of the drop in the weavers' wages, including my admission that the warps received by the weavers were sometimes of very poor quality. He ended his report with an official suggestion to increase the rates for weavers so that they could maintain their income at a level equivalent to the average rate for the past three months.

The director read the report and then said that he did not consider the inspector's suggestion binding and did not intend to follow it up.

"As you wish," said the inspector, who had regained his composure while writing the report. "But you may encounter major problems as a result. As far as I am concerned, I have done my duty—I've issued you a warning."

"You know," the director began in a seemingly calm tone of voice, "I am very perplexed by the attitude of the Factory Inspectorate. You spend hours looking through paybooks and ledgers, pointing out petty deficiencies or oversights such as the omission of the length of contracts. You are also very interested in whether we have recorded a ten-kopeck fine into the fines ledger. Yet you are not even curious about the losses that the factory incurs due to workers' drunkenness or disorderly conduct. Three days ago, on Monday,[32] only forty out of seventy machinists showed up for work! What do you say to that?" The director was losing his calm tone now.

"There is nothing to say to that. It is your business to find sober workers and create an environment where heavy drinking is discouraged."

"You cannot blame us for the lack of such an environment. We have a

[32]On the phenomenon of Monday absenteeism, see Ch. 1, n. 15.

tea house, a theater, a library. We have spent thousands on all of this, but I have not seen any results yet!"

"It is unrealistic to expect a dramatic change in the course of a year or so. You have to be patient."

"I wish you were right, but I don't think you are. But I won't argue. Maybe someday somebody will benefit from all this effort. But I need good workers now! What do you suggest I do with the ones I have who miss work every Monday? My job is to manage the factory, not to educate future generations of workers."

"I have already told you that you have to make a special effort to select better workers. Finally, as a last resort, you have a right to fine them for not showing up for work."

"Fine them? But the most I can fine them is a ruble a day. What kind of machinist cares about losing a ruble? No. It's easy for you government officials to talk that way, but in my opinion, we have to use different measures, the kind our workers will understand. If I were a factory inspector, I would have done things quite differently." The director's voice was reaching a crescendo. "You should have. . . ."

"I beg your pardon," interrupted the inspector. "I have 150 factories in my district. Don't you see that if I were to do what the director of every factory told me, I would not be able to accomplish anything at all?"

After these last words, the inspector said good-bye and quickly walked out of the office. The director could hardly wait until the door had closed behind him.

"They don't like to hear the truth! They simply can't stand it! What preposterous ideas—to raise the weavers' rates by 15 percent because of bad warps! What nonsense, what stupidity!"

"I didn't hear much that was *stupid* from that man," I timidly contradicted the director.

"You didn't? Well, I am very sorry! I would also like to tell you that I found your remarks about the warps, at best, very strange. You could have given me some support, after all. Bear this in mind for the future. But now, excuse me, I do not have any more time."

I said good-bye to the director and promptly left his office, feeling very disappointed.

ON FACTORY BOREDOM AND THE QUESTION OF READING

A dull autumn holiday brings dull unfestive thoughts that cover the mind and soul with a cobweb of gray, monotonous, painful, and desperate feelings.

Workdays at the factory are uniformly boring. What are holidays like? Factory workers might go down to the river, but they have already been there. Yet they go a second time, without any purpose or goal, and a third time, and finally they have had enough. How, then, can they spend their leisure time?

Should they read?

The love of reading—I would even say infatuation with reading—has truly become more and more common. There is no doubt that at the present time the factory masses, at least as far as male workers are concerned, include a significant stratum of *intellectuals*. (I will leave it to the statisticians to find out how large this stratum is—whether it is 1, 2, or 3 percent.) I am talking about real intellectuals, the kind that did not exist among working-class people twenty or twenty-five years ago. Of course, then too there were more than a few intelligent, educated workers who liked to read. But they were scattered individuals, set apart from the crowd either by chance or by virtue of their special talent.

Today, one can sense the existence of a true *intelligentsia stratum* among workers—a stratum that includes intelligent people, people of average ability, and some who are not at all smart, as well as workers of different proclivities, temperaments, and views. All of these have received a certain amount of primary education and have developed a taste for reading and a striving for thought. Given their persistent work habits, these people—notwithstanding the primitive nature of their schooling—have developed a passion for reading, and are able to achieve remarkable results from time to time. Dissatisfied with *belles-lettres*, they begin to devour books on history, economics, and philosophy. Darwin and Tyndall and Byron and Mill and Gladstone and Bismarck and dozens of other great European figures, not to speak of major Russian writers and public figures, are known to them, and not merely by name. Believing in science and appreciating the great service that knowledge can render, they thirst for enlightenment. Considering their serious attitude toward life, toward their studies and the printed word, they should not be considered inferior to our so-to-speak privileged intelligentsia.

Just as among other classes of society for whom reading has become a pressing need, this stratum of educated workers constitutes a small minority whose number diminishes in those branches of labor where wages are lower. If you go into a machine tool plant, you will find many more educated workers (yes, reader, I mean *educated*) than among spinners. But spinners are more cultivated than weavers,[33] and unskilled workers cannot be considered on the same level as weavers. As to the leatherworkers and bricklayers, in terms of their intellectual interests they still occupy the same step on the ladder where they stood twenty-five or thirty years ago. In the latter groups, a well-read worker is even now—just as in the old days—an exception.

Reading undoubtedly plays an enormous role in the life of the worker-intelligentsia, but can the same be said about the masses as a whole? I have thought about this question more than once, but despite my desire to answer this question positively, I have to say no. For the mass of workers, just as for the mass of the middle class, books still serve, as a rule, merely as entertainment. And entertainment, for the majority to enjoy it, must of course be highly accessible. But how accessible are books to the workers?

How, from where, and by what means can a factory worker obtain a book? One can say with certainty that in four out of five cases the source is either a factory library or a reading room. The average worker who lives in a factory far away from the city is in this respect fully and directly dependent on the good will of the factory manager. One would look in vain in the vicinity of a factory for private libraries, reading rooms, or bookstores.

And let us suppose that a worker lays his hands on an interesting and meaningful book. Where will he read it? The library is not always convenient; not all libraries have a reading room and those that do make it difficult to use. It is open only at certain hours, and in order to go there the factory worker has to change clothes, since every worker, within the limits of his understanding and his custom, is highly sensitive to exterior pro-

---

[33]This statement by Pavlov is puzzling because weavers were widely acknowledged to be more highly skilled and cultivated than spinners.

priety. Therefore, he is more likely than not to look for a place to read at home. But where at home? In the barracks, where space has been calculated at one cubic *sazhen* per person, where there is neither a table nor a stool nor adequate evening lighting, and the only furniture consists of bunks intended for sleeping and not for reading? Or will he read in a little overcrowded room inhabited by two or sometimes three different families with children, where the atmosphere is stifling and women constantly quarrel and he has to encounter all the inconveniences of forced cohabitation?

So if you do not see genuine merriment among the holiday factory crowd, it is because the conditions of everyday life place a mass of obstacles and inconveniences in the path of reading, and physical exercise and sports have not become part of the custom, and aesthetic entertainment in the form of concerts, exhibitions, theater, and museums, such as open their doors to workers in Germany, England, and other Western European countries, are inaccessible to our Russian workers, and because communal activities, such as choral and mutual aid societies, do not exist in the factory milieu. Where, then, can the worker go? And how can he spend his rare day off?

Outside the windows of my apartment, workers wander around aimlessly, hour after hour, bored, sluggish, as though half asleep. On this gloomy autumn day I keep on thinking how much willpower and firmness of character a worker needs in order to avoid the temptations which, in the provinces, destroy thousands of people, even among the intelligentsia. I have in mind alcohol, cardplaying, and sexual promiscuity. Consequently, I am not surprised at the enormous quantities of vodka sold at the nearby taverns, nor at the reckless infatuation with cards and games of chance that is so prevalent among factory workers, or at the growing incidence of venereal disease and syphilis in the factory population.

Part Three: Artisanal Workers

IV

E. A. Oliunina

The Tailoring Trade in Moscow and the Villages of Moscow and Riazan Provinces: Material on the History of the Domestic Industry in Russia

The task that I have set for myself is to study the garment industry in the city of Moscow and in Moscow province and, more specifically, the conditions of work and life of male and female workers engaged in the manufacture of clothing. Until now, there has been no research on this subject. To collect material for my study, I personally went to workshops and interviewed workers and employers. In this way, I obtained more or less complete information on 129 enterprises in the city of Moscow, employing 3,709 garment workers.

The typical forms of production in the Moscow garment industry are: (1) the manufacture of custom-made clothing, (2) the manufacture of ready-made clothing, and (3) the domestic ("putting-out") system of production, which is closely connected to the manufacture of ready-made clothing. In made-to-order work, the employer deals with a specific individual, the consumer, for whom the garment is produced. In the manufacture of ready-made clothing, garments are produced according to a standard measurement for an unknown consumer. My study of the Moscow garment industry in 1910–1911 involved all of these types of enterprise [Table 4.1].

154

Table 4–1

Types of Enterprise Surveyed by Oliunina in 1910–1911

Type of Enterprise	No. of Firms	No. of Workers
Custom-made	22	905
Ready-made	19	1,769
Domestic	88	1,035
Total	129	3,709

Custom-made work—the basic form of artisanal production in the garment industry—has undergone certain changes under the impact of the general evolution of manufacturing. Thus, almost every custom-made firm has a workshop on the premises. The owner of the workshop knows the trade and is called a "tailor." By contrast, the proprietors of retail firms that sell ready-made garments call themselves "merchants."[1]

Custom-made tailoring shops produce men's clothing, women's dresses and coats. Custom-made women's clothing is sewn in the firm's own workshop and almost never sent out to a subcontracting shop.[2] By contrast, custom-made men's clothing is frequently sent out to subcontractors. As a rule, the firm's own workshop employs only a part of the labor force: the so-called *peredelochniki* who make adjustments if the size is not right, as well as a small number of workers who do high-quality work and fill rush orders. All garments distributed to subcontractors are precut. In custom-made work, attention to the measurement and cut of a garment is extremely important. The owner-tailor does the cutting himself, but when the volume of orders is large, assistants will be employed and even a staff of specialized fabric cutters.

The organization of ready-made production varies. Some employers

[1]Oliunina is drawing attention here to the distinction between the employer who was a skilled tailor—the *portnoi* or *portnikha*—and the employer who was merely a merchant or *kupets*. The latter had no training in the tailoring trades and took no part in the production process.

[2]The contrast is between the workshop on the premises of a firm, the so-called *masterskaia khoziaina*, and the subcontracting shop, or *masterskaia khoziaichika*.

maintain warehouses and cater only to the wholesale market; others produce only for retail stores; a third type of production is geared to both
wholesale and retail markets. The largest Moscow clothing firms cater to
both the wholesale and retail markets. Adjacent to the warehouse there is
often a central office which distributes fabric to subcontractors and collects
the finished garments from them. Most large wholesale-retail firms distribute precut fabric and trimmings.

In general, the definition of a large firm does not depend only on the
number of workers employed in the workshop on the firm's premises or on
the technology. The number of workshop workers in tailoring firms is
often deceptive because a great many workers are employed on a putting-
out basis in the countryside and in Moscow. For example, the Roizentsvaig
firm has 10 workers in the workshops at its retail outlets, but on the side
there are up to 200 subcontractors, some of them employing as many as 30
hired workers. In addition, 500 peasant huts in Beloomutovo[3] produce
year-round for this firm, not to speak of other places as well. At the Mandl'
firm there are 230 workers in the workshops on the premises; in addition,
the firm employs 600 subcontractors and as many as 2,000 peasant households in the countryside.

The technology in wholesale-retail firms is poorly developed. At one
firm, only one out of five sewing machines operates electrically. There are
only one to two sewing machines for every ten workers in wholesale firms.
The largest enterprise, Mandl', employs four sewing machine operators
who specialize in machine work. But there is no detailed division of labor,
even in the very biggest firms. Mandl' attempted to introduce a division of
labor into its workshops, but it did not take root and was abandoned.

The appearance of large-scale capital created a system in the garment
industry whereby tailors became directly dependent on capital. The general
characteristics of this system can be described as follows: (1) production in
the home with simple technology, (2) small scale of production, and (3) a

[3]Beloomutovo was situated on the Oka River, 140 kilometers southeast of Moscow,
not far from the city of Riazan. A subcontracting arrangement involving Beloomutovo
peasants first became established in 1883 when several Moscow tailoring firms, including Mandl', opened offices in the vicinity to coordinate the expanding putting-out
system.

12. Mandl' tailoring firm on Petersburg's Nevskii Prospect at the turn of the century. This branch of the Moscow-based Mandl' firm opened in 1886.

certain autonomy for the producer, who is simultaneously a worker and an employer.

At first, this organization of production was based on family labor—the husband, wife, children, and old people. Tailors who work alone or with their family at home in a room or garret, and take work on a piece-rate basis from a warehouse, store, or another tailor, are called garret-masters or pieceworkers.[4] In the provinces, for example in Baku and Rostov-on-the-Don, they are known under the name of "apartment journeymen."[5] With the expansion of production, each pieceworker aspired to establish a workshop; and indeed, for the capitalist it was burdensome to distribute

[4] The Russian term *odinochka* has been translated here as "garret-master" and *stuchnik* has been rendered as "pieceworker." It should be noted that the term *odinochka* is derived from the word *odin*, meaning in this case "alone," "by oneself." Thus the *odinochki* were garret-masters who worked individually on a putting-out basis, without assistance from family members or hired workers.

[5] "Apartment journeymen" is a translation of *kvartirnye podmaster'ia*.

work to hundreds and even thousands of putting-out workers. Over time, alongside the pieceworker-garret-masters appeared pieceworkers with hired workers, and they are called subcontractors or middlemen.[6] According to the 1902 Moscow census, the city had 6,550 garret-masters, of whom 5,469 were women; 102 tailors working with their families and 462 subcontractors with hired workers. There was a total of 16,137 tailors employed in the Moscow tailoring and subcontracting shops, and 7,298 apprentices. About one-half of these workers and apprentices were women.[7]

A TYPICAL GARMENT WORKER

Male and female tailors in Moscow are subdivided into two groups: master tailors and journeymen. At the present time these designations, although legally still in effect, have lost all practical significance. Article 402 of the Code for Artisanal Trades[8] gives the following definition of a journeyman:

[6]The Russian terms are *khoziaichiki* (subcontractors) and *posredniki* (middlemen).

[7]Oliunina's data on the number of tailoring workers in Moscow in 1902 include only those employed in the manufacture of men's and women's dresses, suits, and coats. She has excluded a substantial number of additional workers engaged in the manufacture of other types of apparel (e.g., underclothing) or other needle trades (e.g., bed linens, tablecloths). According to the 1902 Moscow city census, the number of workers in the Moscow apparel industry (all categories) was as follows: factory workers, 1,823; nonfactory hired workers, 29,065; garret-masters working with other family members, 3,429; garret-masters working alone *(odinochki)*, 8,186; workers in domestic industry, 921; apprentices, 9,973; total in all categories, 53,397. See *Perepis' Moskvy 1902 goda, chast'* 1, vyp. 2 (Moscow, 1906), pp. 117–159.

[8]The first laws regulating artisanal trades were promulgated in 1721 during the reign of Peter the Great. In accordance with these regulations, guilds *(tsekhi)* on the German model were officially established in Russia. More than a half-century later, in 1785, new regulations were drawn up setting the conditions for entering and practicing an urban handicraft. The *Remeslennoe polozhenie*, as it was called, became the basis of all subsequent legislation concerning urban artisanal trades. The laws applying to these trades, enacted at various times, were combined into the Code for Artisanal Trades *(Ustav remeslennoi promyshlennosti)*. The code was last issued in 1913. On the legal status of artisanal trades in nineteenth-century Russia, see Reginald E. Zelnik, *Labor and Society in Tsarist Russia: The Factory Workers of St. Petersburg, 1855–1870* (Stanford, 1971), Ch. 1; K. A. Pazhitnov, *Problema remeslennykh tsekhov v zakonodatel'stve russkogo absoliutizma* (Moscow, 1952).

"A journeyman is an artisan who has learned his skill according to all the rules of the trade; in order to achieve perfection in his art through experience he must remain in this status for at least three years." After this period in accordance with Articles 414–415, he may become a master tailor.

In the past, a journeyman employed by a master tailor would learn how to sew everything in the expectation of eventually running his own workshop. But the enhanced role of capital in the garment industry, together with the development of large workshops and heightened competition, has led to the disappearance of the journeyman's hope of becoming the owner of his own shop. The earnings of a master tailor have declined to such an extent that in his struggle to survive, he has become more concerned with the quantity and cheapness of his goods than with their quality. Under such conditions, professional training quickly becomes meaningless and artisanal labor increasingly resembles work in a factory. The patriarchal relationship between the master tailor and his journeyman is rapidly disappearing. And capitalism, with its division of labor, is transforming the journeyman into a worker specializing in only one aspect of a given craft, thereby destroying the very concept of what a journeyman tailor should be.

Tailors begin to learn their trade from childhood, passing through the hard school of apprenticeship. All tailors require training, but this training need not take five to seven years as used to be the case, but only two or three years due to the increasing specialization which reduces the time it takes for an apprentice to learn a trade. In factories such as K. Til' and Company or Mandl' and Raits,[9] where a more elaborate division of labor has been introduced and workers sew only one part of a garment, seven days to two weeks are needed to train a new worker.

The best tailors are employed in workshops specializing in custom-made clothing and in large firms which combine custom-made and ready-made clothing. Poorly trained workers can be found everywhere, but they are particularly prevalent among the garret-masters who sew at home and among those in subcontracting shops. With the spread of the ready-made clothing industry and the increasingly complex division of labor, the percentage of poorly trained workers has been growing. But fine and delicate work still demands a good knowledge of the trade and therefore highly

[9]K. Til' and Company employed 2,050 workers; Mandl' and Raits employed 470.

skilled tailors continue to exist alongside the mass of workers who are virtually without training.

In my investigation, I found that the male tailors were still strongly tied to the land. The majority of men employed in tailoring shops (54 percent) and subcontracting shops (61 percent) owned some land which was either cultivated by the men themselves or by their families and relatives. My data on workers' ties with the land are shown below [Table 4.2].

Whereas only about two-fifths of the male workers in tailoring shops belong to the urban proletariat, women tailors belonging to the urban proletariat constitute 99.1 percent of the female workers in tailoring shops and 94.2 percent in subcontracting shops.

Table 4.2

Ties to the Land of Male Workers
In Tailoring Shops and Subcontracting Shops[a]

TYPE OF WORKSHOP	URBAN WORKERS		RURAL WORKERS		TRANSITIONAL WORKERS	
	No.	%	No.	%	No.	%
Tailoring shops	43	37.3	62	54	10	8.7
Subcontracting shops	130	30.9	258	61.2	33	7.9

[a]Oliunina is using a tripartite classification that was commonplace in contemporary literature on the Russian working class. Those classified as "urban workers" had lost or severed all connection with the countryside. They were either born in the city or had lived there for a considerable period of time. "Transitional workers," by contrast, still retained certain ties to the countryside. Some owned a house or a parcel of land that was cultivated by family members or rented out. Others sent sums of money to relatives in the village. But "transitional workers" did not themselves engage in agricultural cultivation, and their immediate family (spouse and usually children) generally resided in the city. Their contacts with rural life had been attenuated but not yet severed. "Rural workers" maintained close and continuing relations with their native village. These workers often retained a house or land, returned seasonally to assist in cultivation, and in the case of male workers, frequently had a wife and children living in the countryside. Although they were sometimes employed in an urban workshop or factory for many years, these workers eventually expected to return to the village.

The seasonal character of the garment industry helps to maintain workers' ties to the village. The season is short, especially in subcontracting shops. In the off season, only women and apprentices remain in the work shops because the labor of women and children is preferred to that of men.

During the off-seasons, workers who do not have a permanent income and have not broken their ties to the village go back to the countryside. They return a number of times during the year and stay there for considerable lengths of time. More than half the workers in tailoring shops and over 78 percent of the workers in subcontracting shops go back to the village an average of three to five times a year. The length of stay varies, ranging from one week to six months. Two-thirds of the workers in subcontracting shops remain in the village for a maximum of two to four months at a time, especially those in shops manufacturing ladies' wear, overcoats, and other large garments. Workers in tailoring shops go to the village for shorter periods, usually not more than a few weeks, since their season is longer than in subcontracting shops.

During Christmas and Easter, the workers all leave for the countryside at the same time, but in the summers, when they leave to work in the fields, they do so at different times. Thus, a large number leave around St. Peter's Day and stay until September, while a smaller number leave at Pentecost and stay until the Feast of the Intercession.[10] Many go to the village only for the month of July, which is the worst month in the off-season period. Those who live close to Moscow go back and forth to their villages more frequently.

Workers' ties to the village are very strong if their families live there, and more than half of the male workers have families in the village. On the average, a worker's family (regardless of whether the family lives in the city or the countryside) consists of three children (one is the minimum and six is the maximum). Almost half (45.2 percent) of the women workers in tailoring shops are single, 53.9 percent have families in Moscow, and an insignificant number (0.9 percent) have families in the village. In subcontracting shops, 52.2 percent of the women are single, 42 percent have families living in Moscow, and 5.8 percent have families in the village.

[10]These are both holidays celebrated by the Russian Orthodox Church. St. Peter's Day falls on June 29, and Pokrov, or the Feast of the Intercession, takes place on October 1.

Almost all workers with ties to the village send money there. Workers in subcontracting shops who do not send money back (12.5 percent) either have just completed their apprenticeship and need money to set themselves up or else have such low wages that they can barely manage to support themselves.

Most male workers are separated from their families and have to travel back and forth between the city and the village. Workers must also contend with employment insecurity. During the course of a year, layoffs or poor wages often force workers to look for jobs in other shops. Only 45 percent of the men in subcontracting shops and about 56 percent in tailoring shops stay at the same job for an entire year. By contrast, two-thirds of all women workers remain at one workshop in the course of a year.

WORK TIME

It is extremely difficult to establish the length of the workday in a given tailoring shop, for there are great variations in work time depending on the form of payment, that is, whether the workers are paid by the piece or by the hour.

In tailoring shops, the average workday is almost eleven (10.7) hours long. In reality, however, this average only applies to workers hired by the month, and very few of these can be found in any one workshop. The average working day for women is nominally nine and a half hours. But the workday is actually longer, and for piece-rate workers it averages around thirteen hours. In subcontracting shops, 34.2 percent of the tailors work an average of fourteen hours a day, and 24.6 percent work even longer. In these workshops, work starts at six or seven in the morning and ends at eight or nine at night, without fixed breaks for lunch and tea.

The length of the workday depends on the size of the workshop and on the type of production. The fewer the workers employed in a shop, the longer they will have to work. [The smallest tailoring shops with fewer than five workers have an average workday of 12 hours; in the smallest sub-contracting shops it is 14.8 hours a day.] Tailoring shops with five to fifteen employees have an average workday of 11.5 hours. In medium-sized tailor-ing shops with fifteen to fifty employees, the average workday lasts 9.6 hours. [In large firms with more than fifty workers, it is 9.4 hours.] The figures for subcontracting shops are consistently higher, with an average of 14.1 hours in shops with five to fifteen workers and 13.6 hours in medium-sized shops.

The length of the workday is also determined by the type of production (ready-made, custom-made, or putting-out) and the type of garment that is produced. In tailoring shops that manufacture custom-made men's clothing, the average workday is 12 hours. However, in workshops that produce low-quality ready-made clothing, this figure rises to 15.6 hours per day, by far exceeding the average of 10.7 hours per day for the garment industry as a whole.

Working hours also vary in subcontracting shops. Overcoat makers work a 15-hour day, and only in dressmaking shops does this figure drop to 13.7 hours. In the putting-out industry, that is, where a subcontractor is involved, the hours are, as a rule, incredibly long. The lack of proper rest and lunch breaks makes these hours even more difficult for the workers to bear. The same thing is true of many tailoring shops, particularly those producing low-quality ready-made clothing.

In factories, by comparison, the workday is usually about 10 hours long, beginning at eight or eight-thirty in the morning and ending at six or seven in the evening. On Saturdays and the eves of holidays, factory workers have a 9-hour workday.[11]

[11]The law of June 2, 1897, restricted the length of the working day in factory enterprises to a maximum of eleven and a half hours on weekdays and to a maximum of ten hours on Saturdays and the eves of holidays. In a few industries, however, the average workday was considerably shorter. As Oliunina points out further on, the average workday in the Moscow printing industry was nine hours. It is noteworthy that most tailoring establishments were not covered by the 1897 law because they did not qualify as "factory" enterprises. Although the criteria tended to fluctuate, and were often inconsistently applied, an enterprise was generally considered a "factory" if it had engine-powered machinery and no fewer than sixteen workers. As indicated above in n. 7, only a small fraction of the workers (about 3 percent) in Moscow apparel trades were classified as employed in factories in 1902. The 1785 law governing artisanal trades (see above, n. 8) limited the workday in artisanal shops to a maximum of ten hours. But this law had lapsed completely until Jewish artisans drew attention to it at the end of the nineteenth century. On this subject, see Ezra Mendelsohn, *Class Struggle in the Pale: The Formative Years of the Jewish Workers' Movement in Tsarist Russia* (Cambridge, 1970). New provisions for regulating the worktime in artisanal shops were adopted in 1906. According to

In all artisan shops, the length of the workday is greatly increased by overtime. The use of overtime is advantageous to the owners but not to the workers, who are paid very little or nothing at all for working overtime. The general rate for overtime is between twenty and thirty kopecks an hour for men and fifteen to twenty kopecks an hour for women. In workshops producing women's clothing, there is often no difference between normal pay rates and overtime pay. This is the case, for example, at the City of Lyon on Kuznetskii Most Street. Another way of compensating for regular overtime work is by giving workers gifts of three to ten rubles at Christmas and Easter.

Three weeks to a month before Christmas and Easter, the rush period begins, and workers must labor even harder to complete all the extra orders. Men and women work to the point of exhaustion, especially in dressmaking shops. In the workshop R. on Kuznetskii Most Street, there is frequent overtime work on holidays and particularly before Christmas and Easter. Even on Holy Saturday, workers frequently work right through until six o'clock in the morning.

In the sixth week of Lent, I have seen women workers come into the refectory and fall on the benches in utter exhaustion, unable even to eat. They only wanted to lie there for a quarter or half an hour in order to rest their tired limbs and ease their headaches. By the time they are thirty, most of these women have been sapped of their strength through such long hours of labor and have lost the capacity for sustained work. This is why the labor force in the workshops is so young.

During the rush period, sweat runs down the workers' faces and falls onto the jacket, vest, or dress which they are making for the customer. It is not only water but also these drops of sweat that dampen the garments for ironing. A high price is paid for the customers' fashionable clothes.

WAGES

Turning to the topic of wages, there is a great difference between the method of payment in tailoring shops and subcontracting shops. The vast

---

the law of November 15, 1906, the work time in artisanal shops and sales firms was to be established by local boards composed of representatives of the workers, the employers, and the local government administration.

majority (over 70 percent) of the workers in tailoring shops are paid in cash, whereas a large percentage of workers in subcontracting shops receive their payment in kind, in the form of food and lodging. Over 57 percent of the male workers eat their meals in the workshop, and 27 percent receive room and board there.

In both kinds of workshops, the majority of women workers have their own lodgings but receive their meals at the shop. Since the founding of the Union of Tailors in 1905,[12] there has been a marked transition from payment in kind (room and board) to payment in cash. This change is especially noticeable in subcontracting shops. Nevertheless, to this day almost 27 percent of the male subcontract workers and 18 percent of the women receive both room and board at their place of employment.

Subcontract workers are generally paid less than workers in tailoring shops. In both kinds of shops, women earn lower wages than men. In subcontracting shops, women receive 85 percent of the wages paid to male workers, and in tailoring shops, they receive 55 percent.[13]

If we compare wages during the on- and off-seasons, we find that off-season wages in tailoring shops are about two-thirds of seasonal wages, although sometimes they remain at the same level. However, in subcontracting workshops, the average off-season wage is not quite half the seasonal wage. Thus the workers in subcontracting shops are most affected by seasonal work.

---

[12]The Moscow Union of Tailors dates from November 1905. Following the promulgation of the "temporary regulations" of March 4, 1906, legalizing trade unions for the first time, the Moscow tailors applied for legal status. The union acquired registration in June 1906 and in the course of the next eleven months, attracted nearly 2,500 of the city's tailors. It was closed by the authorities in May 1907, but the union subsequently succeeded in reregistering and resuming its legal activities. In the fall of 1911 there were about 900 members in the Moscow tailors' union, and it was reputed to be one of the liveliest and most energetic unions in the city. Oliunina herself was one of the founders of the Moscow tailors' union in 1905, together with another intelligentsia activist, K. M. Kolokol'nikova. For a history of the Moscow tailors' union, see Victoria E. Bonnell, *Roots of Rebellion: Workers' Politics and Organizations in St. Petersburg and Moscow, 1900–1914* (Berkeley and Los Angeles, 1983).

[13]Wage data exclude room and board, which are discussed below. On women's wages, see Rose L. Glickman, "The Russian Factory Woman, 1880–1914," in *Women in Russia*, ed. Dorothy Atkinson, Alexander Dallin, and Gail Warshofsky Lapidus (Stanford, 1977), pp. 63–83.

In tailoring shops, seasonal work lasts six months out of the year. The fall season begins in mid-September and lasts until mid-December. In the spring, the season extends from March until the end of May. The off-season lasts for four months: June, July, half of August, half of December, and all of January. The remaining two months are considered the slow season.

For workers in subcontracting shops, the season is much shorter. It lasts only three months, October, November, and March, when the orders for more expensive items come in from retail stores and all kinds of tailoring shops. The off-season lasts four and a half months: June, July, half of August, January, and February. During that time, the workers usually make ready-made clothing. Generally, there is no work during the period from Pentecost to St. Peter's Day. The slower months are April, May, half of August, September, and December. The length of the season depends on the weather to a great extent, especially in workshops producing custom-made clothing for women.

In order to assess how much garment workers earn, we must consider the value of the room and/or board they receive at their workplace. In cash terms, the room and board of tailoring shop workers is worth about five rubles per month and that of the subcontracting workers approximately three rubles. The cash value of the lodgings provided is about two rubles a month for both groups of workers.

If we add these figures to the average monthly wage during the season, we get the following results. [In tailoring shops, male workers earn an average of 37 rubles 20 kopecks per month, whereas female workers earn 23 rubles 10 kopecks. The figures for subcontract workers are 23 rubles 10 kopecks for men and 19 rubles 10 kopecks for women.]

At first glance, it would seem that the earnings of garment workers are rather high when compared with the wages of printing workers, for example. Printers earn an average of 34 rubles 70 kopecks a month, and they are one of the highest-paid groups of Russian workers. However, one must consider the differing lengths of the workday when comparing the wages of printers and garment workers. The majority of printers work a nine-hour day, whereas thirteen hours is the norm in the garment industry. The following table [Table 4.3] shows the difference in average wages between printers and garment workers.

Table 4.3

Average Wages of Moscow Garment Workers and Printers

Type of Workers	Monthly Wage	Daily Wage	Hourly Wage
Subcontract workers	23r.10k	96k	7k
Tailoring shop workers	37r.20k	1r.55k	12k
Printers	34r.70k	1r.44k	15k

The hourly wage for a garment worker in a tailoring shop is actually only three-fourths that of a printer. In addition, tailoring shop workers do not receive this wage throughout the year but only during the season of seven months a year. In the off-season, lasting approximately five months out of the year, their wages are only one-third of the average wage during the season.

In medium- and large-sized shops employing fifteen workers or more, the average wage is significantly higher than it is in smaller shops. The wages of male workers in these small shops average about 62 percent of the wages in the larger shops. Women's wages also increase in large shops and decrease in small ones. On the average, female workers in small shops earn about 86 percent of the wages paid to women in shops employing fifteen people or more.

Wage rates vary considerably for workers in artisan shops. In 1906, during the garment workers' strike at the Mandl' firm, the employers' union attempted to introduce a system of fixed wage rates. However, only maximum rates were established, and these were only applied to a few first-class shops. The most widely adopted rates were based on the average wages paid to tailors making men's clothing. These wages were barely sufficient for subsistence.

The widespread use of piecework in the garment industry is detrimental to workers. Because of the low rates, a worker must labor intensively for very long hours. Piece rates are generally so low that the worker either has to work extremely fast or else make the workday as long as possible, just in order to earn a living wage.

Piece-rate workers have practically no family life since they leave home early in the morning and do not return until late at night. In fact, a majority of them leave their families in the village. These workers live in constant fear of losing their jobs; for this reason, some of them work as hard as they can in an attempt to outdo the others. In workshops where some people are paid by the piece and others by the hour, there is no solidarity among the workers. The divisions among them come to the surface during strikes when workers are struggling for better wages and working conditions.

The effects of piecework are even more onerous for garment workers than for workers in other industries. In the first place, garment workers are predominantly seasonal workers. They must work as hard as possible during the season in order to earn enough to tide them over during the off-season when they will be without work several days a week. Workers in tailoring shops manage to get through this period in one way or another, doing alterations or small jobs on the side; but workers in subcontracting shops lead a half-starved existence during the off-season. Second, payment for labor by piece rate is closely tied to the putting-out system of large-scale industry. Particularly under our conditions, which make it difficult to form workers' organizations, the putting-out system creates the most unfavorable conditions.

A majority of the workers I questioned wanted to abolish the piece-rate system because of all the hardships connected with it. However, some workers were opposed to the introduction of an hourly wage, saying that the piece-rate system gave them the freedom to organize their working time as they pleased. In actuality, this freedom is illusory. Having labored nine hours today, the worker must labor fourteen or sixteen hours tomorrow, and so on. Only well-organized trade unions can come to grips with the problem of regulating wages.

FOOD AND CLOTHING

Having discussed workers' wages, we can now turn to the question of the workers' diet. The administration of the City of Lyon tailoring shop estimates that lunch and supper costs between four and six rubles a month per person. Lunch begins either with cabbage soup or with meat soup containing about two ounces of boiled beef per person. Two days a week the second course consists of beef in some amount; on the other days it is kasha[14] or potatoes. Supper consists of soup and kasha. At the Siberian Trading House of Mikhailov, garment workers receive only lunch, but the furriers can have dinner as well. The lunch menu consists of cabbage or some other soup as a first course. The second course is kasha with lard four times a week and fried potatoes the other two days. During the strike in October 1911, workers demanded that the owner serve beef twice a week. The owner refused, but did promise to give each worker his own plate.

In the other tailoring shops, the meals are very much the same, although some workshops offer more variety by serving noodles instead of kasha or potatoes. The owners take no interest in whether the workers' food is well prepared. Usually the potatoes are dried out and the meat is either over-cooked or burned.

According to a questionnaire distributed by the tailors' union in 1909, 68 percent of the workers who received their meals in the workshop ate meat one to three times a week. Thirty-two percent stated that the meals were of good quality. Of those workers not eating in the workshop, 45 percent had meat every day, 23 percent had it between one and five times a week and 32 percent ate meat "occasionally."

The workers who provide their own meals spend fifteen to twenty kopecks a day on lunch. In a canteen or tavern, lunch costs between five and seven rubles a month. This does not include the price of dinner or tea.

Workers in subcontracting shops usually receive their meals at the workplace. The meals are much worse than those described above. The only meat is in the soup, and then it is never more than two ounces per person. The main course consists either of kasha or potatoes, with noodles on Thursdays. For dinner there is a meatless cabbage soup or kasha. By evening, warm water is often added to the soup if it has cooked too long or if there is not enough to go around. There is only black bread and it is always stale. On Wednesdays and Fridays, the owner prepares a Lenten fare for the workers. For example, to feed fifteen workers he will buy four kopecks' worth of onions, some poor quality *kvass*,[15] cucumbers, and, on

---

[14]See Ch. 2, n. 10.

[15]*Kvass* somewhat resembles beer but has a much lower alcoholic content. It is made from bran, malt, bread, flour, and water.

rare occasions, two herrings at five kopecks each. This is then all mixed together. The workers call this kind of meal a "garbage heap."

In the subcontracting shops the workers all eat out of one large earthenware or enamel pot. In the smaller workshops, the owner and his family share the same pot with the workers.

In both types of workshop, the workers who eat their meals there are usually provided with tea and sugar. However, in some workshops, such as the City of Lyon on Kuznetskii Most Street, the workers must get their own. Subcontract workers often go out to a tavern or tea shop for their tea. They explained this by saying, "It's too stuffy in the workshop." On this they spend between one ruble fifty kopecks and two rubles a month.

Approximately 60 percent of the workers interviewed spent an average of three and a half rubles a month on vodka (a minimum of one ruble and a maximum of fifteen), that is, about 16 percent of their monthly wage. Six percent spent the equivalent of half to three-quarters of their wages on drink, and they went around with hardly any clothes on their backs. "It's very hard work. During the season, you work from seven in the morning to ten at night, and you need a drop or two," some of the workers said. "We don't drink for pleasure," others told me, "but as a release from the backbreaking grind." Others also told me they sought consolation in vodka from a life of toil and hardship. Drunkenness is most widespread in subcontracting shops, where the custom of beginning the week with a drink still persists.

In the tailoring shops some of the workers are trying to put a stop to the problem of drunkenness by introducing certain rules, such as preventing people who are drunk from entering the workshop, not passing around vodka during working hours, and so forth. This policy has only been deliberately pursued since the tailors' union became actively involved.

Workers with families in the countryside spend the smallest possible amount of their wages on food and clothing. They send everything they can back to their families. Tailoring shop workers and subcontract workers dress quite differently. The former, especially those working in the center of Moscow, wear suits, shoes, and different coats according to the season. The subcontract workers, on the other hand, wear quilt jackets and boots. In these workshops one can find half-dressed workers wearing nothing but a calico shirt, often torn and dirty, and a pair of faded pants or long underwear. They work barefoot. When they go out, they cover themselves with a jacket. As one worker complained, "There are eight of us. My family is in the village. Our plot of land is so small there isn't enough bread to last until Christmas. No one cares about us. The wages are miserable. You send everything back to the village and only spend the bare minimum on yourself. So you go around half-naked. You don't take part in 'Blue Monday,'[16] you don't drink, and still you can never get ahead."

Some of the heavy drinkers own only one shirt and one pair of long underwear which they wear all week long. On Saturday they buy a new pair for the weekend, but on Monday they will sell it for a drink and put on the old dirty ones again. I often met workers like this in the subcontracting shops of Tiurin, Mamontov, Konovalova, and many shops which made trousers and vests. In the winter, several workers often share the same overcoat or quilt jacket to go out. When they sleep in the workshop, they don't have pillows or blankets, and so they use the newly made clothing for cover.

There are also differences in the way that women workers dress. Those who are employed in workshops in the downtown area dress comparatively neatly and have fashionable dresses, hats, and overcoats. The women in subcontracting workshops almost always look untidy. They wear kerchiefs. Many women, especially the older ones, have faded, dirty, and torn dresses. After about the age of twenty-five, these women usually drink wine and smoke.

The workers' treatment at the hands of their employers is unenviable, to say the least. In tailoring shops, workers have to put up with all kinds of abuse from the manager or the senior-ranking master tailors. The latter, although themselves former workers, are often the most active defenders of the owner's interests. They never leave the workshop and are always on hand to push the workers to work harder. In my visits to the workshops, I often heard these taskmasters yelling, "Why are you yawning, damn you? Work harder!" They called the workers "drunkards," "idlers," and so on. The owners in many workshops were just as rude.

In subcontracting shops, the owners themselves or members of their family supervise the work. Here the workers often sew to the constant

[16]On "Blue Monday," see Ch. 1, n. 15. Further discussion of the subject follows below.

accompaniment of swearing and insults. Only the skilled workers are spared. Because the owner values these workers highly, he will only swear at them when they are drunk.

The workers in subcontracting shops do not go to the theater or attend lectures. As one worker told me, "Our only amusement is the tavern." Others said, "We don't get off work until ten at night, and where else can you go at that hour besides a tavern? The way we are dressed, they won't even let us into the Narodnyi Dom,[17] they just turn us away at the door." A third worker said, "Reading, the theater, these things aren't for us. We don't have time. Our workday is very long and we're too tired."

Everywhere I went, I heard only complaints about life in the sub-contracting shops: "It's a hard life." "It's a bad life." "It's a dog's life, no one should live like this." "It's hard to make it in the village, but it's no easier here. There's nothing but poverty and grief no matter where we are." "This isn't life, this is just drudgery." When one considers the nature of work in the subcontracting shops, the complaints and widespread drunkenness among workers are not difficult to understand. For three or four months out of the year, they must work "until their backs are wet," but during the off-seasons, they are barely able to survive.

The tailors' union was established to fight for improved working conditions, but it has had little success in attracting the stratum of the tailoring proletariat that is worst off. One of the main reasons for this is the tenuousness of the union's own existence.

SANITARY CONDITIONS

Sanitary conditions in workshops are extremely poor. The majority of tailoring shops that I investigated (69.4 percent) were separate from the owner's living quarters, whereas 86.3 percent of the subcontracting shops were situated in the owner's lodgings. In the workshops I visited, the greatest defect was the lack of proper lighting in the work areas. Work-shops were often in basements where the windows were continually

---

[17]The Narodnyi Dom, or People's House, provided edifying leisure-time activities and recreation for workers.

shaded by the walls of a neighboring building. I encountered some shops where tailors worked all day under electric lights.

I happened to visit one tailoring shop on Maroseika Street that specialized in men's custom-made clothes. This shop was situated in a dark room with two windows that had no sashes, looking onto a terrace that had been transformed into another workshop and heated by a gas stove.

At one rather clean and light workshop on Petrova Street, the workers had only 0.6 cubic meters of air per person. This workshop employed thirty-six people, including eighteen girls. Before lunch, when the gas stove was heating up in the kitchen, the women worked with flat irons, and after lunch, from two o'clock in the afternoon, they used coal irons that made the air even worse. In such an environment a person who is not accustomed suffocates from the lack of air. As for the women workers, they suffer from chronic headaches.

I was not allowed into many workshops. For example, Mr. Lazarus, the proprietor of the City of Lyon, which employs approximately three hundred workers, explained his unwillingness to allow me into the workshop by claiming a "trade secret." I discovered what this "secret" was quite by accident. The city governor ordered a sanitary inspection of the workshop. The report stated:

The "City of Lyon" workshop is located on the third floor of a large building at the corner of Kuznetskii Most Street and the Neglinnyi Proezd. There is no ventilation on any of the floors and fresh air only enters the building through small window vents. The floorboards throughout the shop are dilapidated, with pieces of the parquet missing. The floors are filthy and litter is piled up in the corners of the hallway. There is dust everywhere—on the shelves, the lamps, the packing boxes. Both the sink and the faucet are in terrible condition. The walls have lost all trace of paint. The kitchen has no ventilation, and the shelves where dishes are kept are filthy. There are no toilets in the workshop itself; they are located in the basement and are very filthy.

Sanitary conditions in the subcontracting shops are even worse. Many of these shops are located far from the center of town where lodgings are cheaper. The rooms are dirty and the wallpaper in shreds. The floors and benches are rarely washed. The dirty linen of workers who live on the premises is strewn about under the benches. Because of the filth, insects flourish: bedbugs, lice, and fleas. The stove used for heating irons, located either in the work area itself or in the hallway, make the workshop very hot. A stench from the toilet fills the air. It's stuffy, cramped! During the season, the rooms are filled to overflowing, and voices drone above the constant din of the sewing machines.

In one typical shop run by the subcontractor K., there are thirty-two workers. There is not an inch of free space in the two rooms of the shop. All the space is taken by tables and chairs, and mannequins with dresses stand in the hallways. The constant hum and din makes the workers so on edge that swearing and coarse language are commonplace. In this atmosphere, twelve young girls are living and learning the trade.

I encountered one shop where work was carried on in a kitchen that had one window and only 0.8 cubic meters of space per person. Here they heat the flat irons, here they keep the bucket with food garbage, and here they cook. Fumes and smoke fill the room. But if the window vent is opened, there is a draft. This shop serves as an eating and sleeping place for the workers. There are no mattresses and the workers sleep on the workbenches, covering themselves with whatever they can find. One such shop makes women's dresses for a certain large capitalist firm; another makes men's suits for the public market. All the workers complain of the filth in the shops, of the fumes from the irons: "We often get asphyxiated from these irons to the point of passing out," they said. In these shops, there is no one whose sole responsibility is to maintain the premises. In most cases, the burden of cleaning up falls on the shoulders of the apprentices.

The workshop is not only a place of work but also a place to eat and sleep. Consequently, many of the workers that I investigated slept at their place of employment. No beds or blankets are provided, so the workers must sleep on the benches, or under them, or wherever they can find room. In those workshops that are heated by the stove, it is very hot in the daytime, but freezing cold at night.

When entering a workshop one is immediately struck by the long, wide wooden planks alongside the window, the workbenches on which male tailors sit cross-legged. In tailoring shops, women workers do their sewing at tables. In subcontracting shops, however, all the workers sit on these benches, even the women, although work tables are now being introduced for them. From its inception, the tailors' union has demanded that benches

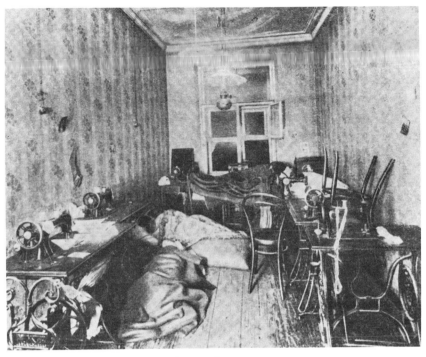

13. Tailors asleep on the workshop floor, 1890s.

be replaced by work tables because the workers' cross-legged posture on benches is very damaging to their health. Tables have now been introduced at some workshops, including Mandl', Zhak, Soldatskii, and others. The younger generation of tailors insists on this change, but older workers find it difficult to alter their customary ways. In one and the same workshop, you can find the young tailors working at tables while the older ones sit cross-legged on workbenches.

LIVING CONDITIONS

Having described sanitary conditions in the workshops where tailors spend half or more of their lives, let us now turn to a description of workers' living conditions. One can see from the following table [Table 4.4] how unenviable these conditions really are. The majority of male tailoring shop work-

Table 4.4

Housing of Tailoring Shop Workers (percentages)

TYPE OF ACCOMMODATION	MEN (PERCENT)	WOMEN (PERCENT)	COMBINED (PERCENT)
Room	65.2	55.6	60.2
Apartment	17.3	3.1	9.9
Live in the workshop	8.7	3.1	5.9
Bed only	7.9	0.8	4.1
With parents	0.9	37.4	19.9

Table 4.5

Housing of Subcontract Workers (percentages)

TYPE OF ACCOMMODATION	MEN (PERCENT)	WOMEN (PERCENT)	COMBINED (PERCENT)
Room	38.8	61.8	44.3
Apartment	0.4	—	0.3
Live in the workshop	28.5	18.3	26.0
Bed only	31.9	7.3	25.9
With parents	0.4	12.6	3.5

ers rent single rooms; only about one-sixth have their own apartments. About 37 percent of the women live with their parents or relatives.

For subcontract workers, the figures are shown above [Table 4.5]. Subcontract workers live in even worse conditions than their counterparts in tailoring shops. Only one-third of the men rent single rooms. The majority have no more than a bench in the workshop or a bed. Among women workers, the majority (61.8 percent) rent rooms; only one-fifth (18.3 percent) live in the workshop.

Male workers usually share rooms with two to five other workers. Frequently there is no bed in the room, so they all sleep side by side on the floor. Most women workers live two to a room.

In both kinds of workshops, the types of accommodations workers choose usually depend on how closely they are tied to the village where many of them still have families. A majority of tailoring shop workers rent rooms. However, those who still have ties to the village are more likely to live in the workshop or just rent a bed. Among subcontract workers, two-thirds of those with ties to the village sleep in the workshop or rent only a bed. Over half of those without ties to the village rent rooms. Many workers, subcontract workers in particular, have a very limited choice of accommodations because they send almost all of their wages back to their families in the countryside. With what remains from their meager earnings, it is not possible to find better lodgings.

Rented rooms are generally overcrowded and damp. There is constant noise and hubbub in such living quarters and workers can never find the relaxation they need after a hard day's work. There is an obvious link between drunkenness and these kinds of living and working conditions.

CHILD LABOR

The workshops that I investigated employed 885 juveniles, approximately 12 percent of the total number of children working in the Moscow garment industry, according to the 1902 census. Child labor is most often used in workshops producing ready-made clothing and in the subcontracting shops.

Children begin their apprenticeship between the ages of twelve and thirteen, although one can find some ten- and eleven-year-olds working in the shops. Apprenticeship can last from three to five years; usually it is four years. In the Lamanova shop, which employs 115 female apprentices (with an average of fourteen apprentices for every ten workers), and the City of Lyon with 150 apprentices, apprenticeship lasts five years.[18] In Germany,

---

[18]Since the City of Lyon tailoring firm employed about three hundred adult workers in its workshop, the presence of one hundred and fifty apprentices reveals the importance of these unpaid juvenile workers in the workshop economy. After a few years of training, apprentices were often capable of making a significant economic contribution to the employer for which, in most cases, they were paid virtually nothing except room and board.

apprenticeships last from three and a half to five years.* Apprentices work
without pay in all workshops, except in the City of Lyon where they earn a
ruble a month in the third year of their apprenticeship and three rubles a
month in the fourth and fifth years.

Girl apprentices learn the trade in the following way. Every female
worker gets her own "helper." First of all, the girls are assigned different
tasks. Some will be sent to the corsetmakers, others to dressmakers, and so
on. During the first year, they will all learn how to use a needle, make
special stitches, and use a sewing machine. In addition, they are taught
various skills according to their specialties. For example, if they are working
for a corsetmaker, they learn to make button loops, hem linings, and sew
on hooks. They must also put coals in the irons and take them to the
seamstresses. By the second year, the apprentices learn to tack on sleeves,
overstitch seams, sew on braids, hem petticoats, and make slips. By the
third year, the girls are making simple corsets and petticoats. In workshops
making streetwear for women, the young apprentices are given similar
small tasks during the first two years.

Not only do girl apprentices have to learn their trade; they also have
various domestic duties in the workshop. Depending on the size of the
workshop, one or two girls are put in charge of looking after the shop and
making sure everything is in order. They have to clean the work area and
the other rooms of the owner's apartment, tend the stove, and so on. The
girls who are assigned these chores come earlier and leave later than the
rest.

Boy apprentices are trained in a different way. For the first two weeks,
they are left to look around on their own. During this time, they are given a
few chores in the shop, but they do not have to start their work yet. After
this, each boy is given a place on the bench and set to work. His thimble
finger, the middle one, is tied down so that it stays bent. He is given some
rags and is taught how to make a proper stitch, take out stitching, prepare
cotton wool for linings, sew seams, linings, and sleeves, and use a sewing
machine. The boys are put under the supervision of adult workers. In many
cases, however, the workers simply show the apprentices how something is

*Protokoll über die Verhandlungen des elften ordentlichen Verbandstages des Verbandes
der Schneider, Schneiderinnen und Wäschearbeiter Deutschlands, 1910, p. 404.

14. Male apprentices learning to sew and to iron in a Moscow tailoring shop around the turn of the century.

sewn and then leave them to learn the rest by observation. The owner never gives any instruction. He is too busy cutting cloth, receiving customers, running around to stores to find new orders, or taking the finished goods back to distributors. The workers don't have the time either. Being paid by the piece, they have to work as fast as they can.

The boys' training lasts from two months to a year. In the second year, they are put to work making trousers and vests. In addition to sewing, they must tend the stove and heat the irons before the master tailors arrive at work. They have to sweep the shop, chop wood, go to the store, and carry water if there isn't a faucet in the shop. At times, they also have to take care of the owner's children. In order to get everything done, the apprentices get up at six in the morning. During the day, they are on the go constantly, taking orders to customers and picking up work from stores.

Under such conditions, the training proceeds very slowly. In those workshops that produce custom-made street wear for women, there is a continual rush to complete orders. Many tailors will work on one garment, each one preparing a different part. In workshops such as these, the training is quite unsatisfactory. Therefore, it is hardly surprising that there are so many tailors who do not really know the skills of their trade.

Regarding the living conditions of children, in tailoring shops 433 of the 472 apprentices lived outside the shop. However, in subcontracting shops, all apprentices, with only one exception, lived in the workshop itself. The majority of children live at the owner's apartment where there is rarely a separate sleeping area. In fact, only 18 percent of the subcontracting workshops had a separate sleeping room, and in those cases it was usually reserved for adults. The children slept on the benches, in the hallways, on boxes, in the kitchen, or wherever they could find room.

In one workshop I saw a room set up to accommodate five boys; there were two beds with mattresses but no blankets or pillows. During the day, the room was used by the owner to cut out patterns. There are many such examples. In another shop, two bunks with bedding, one in the work area and the other in the hallway, were provided for eight to ten young girls. Only in one shop, that of the subcontractor Kamov, were there enough beds to accommodate all the workers, and even here no bedding was provided.

Apprenticeship is generally very hard on children. At the beginning, they suffer enormously, particularly from the physical strain of having to do work well beyond the capacity of their years. They have to live in an environment where the level of morality is very low. Scenes of drunkenness and debauchery induce the boys to smoke and drink at an early age.

For example, in one subcontracting shop that made men's clothes, a fourteen-year-old boy worked together with twelve adults. When I visited there at four o'clock one Tuesday afternoon, the workers were half-drunk. Some were lying under the benches, others in the hallway. The boy was as drunk as the rest of them and lay there with a daredevil look on his face, dressed only in a pair of long johns and a dirty, tattered shirt. He had been taught to drink at the age of twelve and could now keep up with the adults.

"Blue Monday" is a custom in most subcontracting shops that manufacture men's clothes. The whole workshop gets drunk, and work comes to a standstill. The apprentices do nothing but hang around. Many of the workers live in the workshop, so the boys are constantly exposed to all sorts of conversations and scenes. In one shop employing five workers and three boys, "Blue Monday" was a regular ritual. Even the owner himself is prone to alcoholic binges. In these kinds of situations, young girls are in danger of being abused by the owner or his sons.

Conditions such as these make a deep impression on children. Especially in subcontracting shops, the environment fosters coarse manners and cynicism.

One subcontracting shop making streetwear for women employed twenty-six workers: eight tailors, six seamstresses, eight girls, and four boys. The workshop had separate but adjoining rooms, one for women and the other for men. On Mondays, the men would drink. Most of them were only half-dressed. Among the women there were prostitutes, and they openly discussed their adventures in front of the girls. Relations between men and women were extremely lax. When a woman walked past, the men would often embrace her and make provocations.* In another subcontracting shop on Pimenovskaia Street, two young girls, aged twelve and thirteen, who had just arrived from the village, lived and worked in a similar environment.

As I have described above, boys start making pants and vests by the second year of their apprenticeship. Girl apprentices begin making a profit for the owner by the third year, but their apprenticeship will last another

---

*I've repeatedly heard of cases where girls were raped by people who were supposed to look after them.

year or two. In subcontracting shops, the girls are already making cheap ready-made clothes by their second year.

The increasing division of labor has simplified the work process, thus reducing the time needed for training. The owners, however, intentionally keep their unpaid apprentices for the full term of the apprenticeship in order to take advantage of this source of free labor. Young workers prefer to leave shops such as these and go to ones where they are paid a minimal wage, from three to six rubles a month, and can get more experience in their particular areas of expertise.

The following figures show the extent to which child labor is used in different sectors of the garment industry. In shops producing custom-made clothing, there are ninety-eight apprentices to every one hundred adult workers. In subcontracting shops there are seventy-five apprentices and in shops making ready-made clothing seventeen apprentices to every one hundred adults.

Child labor is used most frequently in shops producing women's clothing. This is true both for shops manufacturing custom-made and ready-made clothes. One also finds children employed in shops making men's clothing for retail outlets at the Sukharevskii and Smolenskii markets, and the like. Shops which are part of a retail establishment seldom employ children.

The widespread use of child labor, when there are one or more apprentices for every adult worker, makes it impossible for the apprentices really to learn the trade well, especially in subcontracting shops where the owner himself doesn't know the trade. I've come across owners who were former cobblers, chambermaids, and so on.

My own observations confirm the general opinion that cheap labor and the master tailor's dependence on retailers make it impossible for master tailors to make a living. As one report noted: "The master tailor cannot survive if he only employs trained journeymen. The only chance he has to be successful is to build his shop on the unpaid labor of apprentices."

In order to protect themselves from the influx of cheap child labor, Western European workers have for a long time tried to restrict the number of apprentices in the garment industry.

In Russia, there have been no measures taken to improve the working conditions of apprentices. As I have tried to show, the situation in work-shops in no way provides apprentices with adequate training in their trade. The young workers are there only to be exploited. Merely limiting the number of apprentices would not better their position, nor would it eradicate the influx of cheap labor. An incomparably more effective solution would be to replace apprenticeship with a professional educational system and well-established safeguards for child workers. However, the only real solution to the exploitation of unpaid child labor is to introduce a minimum wage for minors.

Part Four: Sales-Clerical Workers

V

A. M. Gudvan

Essays on the History of the Movement of Sales-Clerical Workers in Russia

ASPIRATIONS OF SALESCLERKS

Salesclerks lived their lives in a world of unending profitmongering, cupidity, servitude, and brutality. It is not surprising, therefore, that they developed a particular view of the world and aspired to become shop owners themselves.

Already as apprentices, salesclerks learned the importance of money in the world of commerce. A fascination with money permeated the very air they breathed. Money could free the clerk from the deprivation and humiliation he had known since childhood and make him master over others. Thus money had to be acquired, no matter how. The shop clerk struggled to attain it: some by scrimping and saving, some by stealing from the boss, some by swindling and cheating, and still others by marrying into a dowry.

In the old days, as soon as a clerk had five or six hundred rubles, he would immediately quit his job, rent space in the market square or on a side street, and go into trade for himself. Thanks to activities of a purely criminal character (like declaring false bankruptcy or staging a fire after making sure that all the insured goods were tucked away the day before), a few of the salesclerks managed to make it and became merchants. The majority of Russian merchants, especially in provincial cities, were once salesclerks themselves. They had endured all the agonies of a clerk's subjugation and tried to outdo each other in tormenting their own employees. This apparent anomaly has deep roots and, at least to a certain extent, can be explained by the fact that subjugation fosters slave instincts and habits, which can turn into the most awful despotism when given a chance.

With the growth and concentration of capital at the end of the nineteenth century, small and medium-sized merchants could no longer compete with large department stores like Muir and Merrilees.[1] As a result, the former shop clerk who had just established his own business soon lost everything and became an employee once again. After seeing many such cases, most shop workers were disabused of the notion that "today I am a slave, but tomorrow I'll exploit someone else's labor."

Russian salesclerks were isolated and alienated from the rest of the proletariat because so many of them were children and juveniles. They were also set apart by their lack of opportunity to come together and find methods of struggle for improving their situation. They were always disunited. Even in the distant past, workers in factories and workshops who labored side by side found it much easier than salesclerks to gather at a moment's notice and decide what measures to take. Widely dispersed and working in groups of two or three under the watchful eye of the employer or his assistant, clerks had practically no opportunity to discuss their problems and needs and decide who were their enemies and who were their friends. Naturally, they had to wait for help from outside. As soon as that help came, they quickly broke with the past and joined forces with the industrial proletariat.

APPRENTICES

Conditions for children and adolescents were especially harsh in commercial firms. Driven from their families by poverty, these children usually came from the countryside. Rather than going to school, young boys from eight to ten years of age found themselves in a world where an individual

---

[1]Muir and Merrilees was a department store in Moscow located on the Petrovka opposite the Bolshoi Theater. The store was controlled by an English joint-stock company. Today it is the TsUM department store.

15. Apprentices and salesclerks in a Petersburg stationery store, 1900.

was valued only for the profits he could produce. Shop owners preferred to recruit apprentices from more distant provinces so that they could not visit their parents and the parents, in turn, could not visit them. In this way, a boy would fall under the full control of the owner, who became for him a master and a teacher. Without the employer's permission an apprentice did not dare to set foot outside the owners' home or store.

Before apprentices learned anything about commerce, they had to endure all kinds of ordeals and hardships that had little to do with sales work. Apprentices got up earlier than everyone else, frequently at four-thirty or five o'clock in the morning, in order to sweep out the store, bring in the wood, clean boots and clothing, prepare the samovar,[2] wash dishes, and help the cook in the kitchen. Then they were on the go all day long, delivering purchases, unpacking goods, or standing on the street, regardless of the season and the weather, to coax customers into the store. Apprentices got to bed later than anyone else in the shop, at eleven-thirty or midnight. Thus, the apprentice's workday lasted almost nineteen or twenty hours.

[2]See Ch. 3, n. 2.

The apprentice did not have the right to make any compla. supposed to know and remember eternally that he was funda mute being without any right to protest. For the slightest error (mistake, he was beaten not only by the employer but by the adu.. clerks, members of the owner's family, the cook, the coachman, and so on. Apprentices were often beaten by the owner and the clerks for the same offense. S. V. Kurnin, in his brochure "Sunday Rest," cited 172 incidents in which apprentices were beaten for such offenses as failing to sneak past the owner with vodka sent for by the clerks. First, the employer beat the apprentice for fetching the vodka; then the clerks beat him again for letting on to the employer about it. The beating of apprentices was practiced even in very large firms. Dr. S. I. Listov[3] reported that "in one of Moscow's best stores, a salesman told a boy to get him a certain piece of cloth from one of the shelves. When he was not given the piece he wanted, the salesman hit the boy on the head so hard that he fell to the floor, covered with blood. All this took place in front of the customers." While investigating incidents of beatings, I was able to help convict a number of Odessa merchants who had stolen incriminating police reports from the chambers of a judge who was about to try them for beating their apprentices.

Apprentices had no legal protection from physical abuse or inordinately long working hours. On the contrary, the Imperial Russian Law Code gave merchants the right to use the rod on minors apprenticed to them as punishment for bad behavior.[4]

Apart from the unlimited duration of the workday, which deprived apprentices even of the time necessary for sleep, work in a store often had other harmful effects on the apprentices' health. We have already noted that they had to run out onto the street in all kinds of weather to try and coax customers into the store. Numb with cold, these young "barkers" competed with each other in shouting praise of their employer's dubious merchandise and importuning passers-by to enter their stores.

[3]The author is referring to Dr. S. Listov whose reports, "K voprosu o polozhenii sluzhashchikh v torgovykh zavedeniikh," and "K voprosu o polozhenii torgovykh mal'chikov" were presented to the Moscow Branch of the Imperial Russian Technical Society on April 29, 1904, and March 14, 1905, respectively.

[4]A law allowing masters to birch their apprentices was first enacted in the eighteenth century. It was retained in the Russian Legal Code until 1902.

According to V. A. Mefodiev, a medical inspector in Kherson,[³] many sales apprentices worked in an extremely unhygienic environment. He asserted that "there are many health hazards specific to certain branches of trade. In tobacco shops, for example, both the apprentices and the adults work in an environment where the air is full of suffocating tobacco fumes. Workers handling flour get it in their lungs, and so on." Under these kinds of conditions, apprentices had to work nineteen or twenty hours at a stretch, just as in other stores.

Apprentices slept on filthy, smelly, and pest-ridden beds, usually in the kitchen, on boards covered with hard straw mats or bags filled with straw. In a majority of cases, the sleeping quarters, accommodating from five to fifteen boys, were small, damp, and cold. The lack of ventilation, especially in winter, made the air oppressive, filling it with the strong smell of sweat. According to Dr. Iavein, who was called in to treat a sick apprentice, "Prisoners in jail live in more hygienic conditions than the employees and apprentices of some shop owners." Some employers had the apprentices sleep on the floor in the front hall so they could open the door without delay if any member of the owner's family came home late at night. Dr. Listov reported instances where beds were not changed for four years, the entire duration of the apprentice's "training." According to his research, more than half of the accommodations in which adults and children were housed displayed various defects, most commonly overcrowding, dampness, cold, and insufficient lighting.

For breakfast, apprentices got a quarter pound of black bread and a glass of tea. They ate lunch either at the owner's home when they went to pick up food for the clerks or else in the shop after the others had finished. In either case they had to eat while on the move. Even in the best firms, the usual lunch was nothing more than cabbage soup or broth with a tiny piece of meat. In medium-sized and small firms, lunch consisted of a piece of black bread with herring or onion. There was tea four or five times a day, especially in the winter. The employer, his guests, and all the clerks drank tea made from a single pot, and then the apprentices got what was left.

To illustrate the position of shop apprentices, we will cite part of a letter

___

[³]Kherson is a city in southern Russia, located on the right bank of the Dnieper near its mouth in the Black Sea.

sent to the St. Petersburg Union of Sales-Clerical Employees[6] by Alexander Iakovlevich Griaznov, a peasant from Iaroslavl province. This letter, with its unpretentious words, gives a picture of the conditions facing apprentices. Published in the newspaper *Novaia Rus'* (New Russia)[7] in 1908, Griaznov's letter asked the union "to help protect the rights of his son, Nikolai Griaznov, who had entered into apprenticeship with an ironmonger at the New Alexandrovskii Market."

Nikolai Griaznov began his apprenticeship with the shop owner Kasatkin on March 5, 1908. According to the contract, the boy was to receive three rubles a month plus room and board. The father charged that not only had Kasatkin never paid the boy, but he also beat him mercilessly and forced him to do work that had nothing to do with the trade, such as washing floors or going to the market with the cook. His son had to sleep on a filthy floor in the pantry by the kitchen. Alexander Griaznov wrote:

I tried to take my son Nicholas away and put him in another shop, but his boss wouldn't let him go. He said there was some kind of law which let him keep my son until the apprenticeship was over, that is, for three and a half more years, and until then he wouldn't give him up. Kasatkin told me, "The law gives me the right to teach the boy to be a human being and to hit him and even beat him with a rod if he is disrespectful to my family. If you want your son back," Kasatkin said, "then you will have to pay me twenty-five rubles a month for the time he has been here and 300 rubles for my expenses in training the boy. Then I'll give him to you."

Now where is a poor peasant like me supposed to get that kind of money? I don't even have a crust of bread, not to speak of 625 rubles to give Mr. Kasatkin for my child.

---

[6] An illegal union of salesclerks was first organized in St. Petersburg in the spring of 1905. Following the legalization of trade unions by the law of March 4, 1906, the union applied for and was granted legal status (July 14, 1906). The union rapidly expanded, drawing 2,688 clerks into its ranks. Although the government rescinded the union's legal status in late December 1906, the organization functioned for a number of months thereafter and was eventually replaced by a number of smaller unions uniting clerks in specific types of enterprises. See Victoria E. Bonnell, *Roots of Rebellion: Workers' Politics and Organizations in St. Petersburg and Moscow, 1900–1914* (Berkeley and Los Angeles, 1983).

[7] *Novaia Rus'* was published in St. Petersburg between 1908 and 1910.

Griaznov ended his letter by asking the union to help him get his son out of Kasatkin's clutches.

In response to these charges, Kasatkin sent a letter to the newspaper, in which he stated:

> I would like to direct your attention to the following fact. I paid a middleman a good bit of money for Griaznov, just like all the other merchants who buy apprentices for their stores. These middlemen travel around to impoverished villages in Iaroslavl, Novgorod and Pskov provinces[8] during the winter months when food is scarce. They collect eight-to-ten-year-old boys and send them to stores as apprentices without obtaining the consent of either the parents or the children. An honest press should not attack particular individuals but should attack this system of buying and selling children, which exists in Petersburg and in other cities. I alone do not have the power to fight against the established custom. Competition forces me to use as much cheap and unpaid labor as I can.

History has recorded cases when apprentices refused to put up with all the beatings and other abuses any longer. They ran away from their exploiters and went back home to their parents or relatives. If their parents sent them back, some of the boys would run away again, this time going to the port of Odessa, the Khitrov market in Moscow, the slums of St. Petersburg or similar places. These runaways began their new life by begging and they would soon sink lower and lower into the swamp of vagrancy.

Even under the best of circumstances, it took from three to four years for an apprentice to begin earning a salary of three to ten rubles a month, depending on the branch of trade and the apprentice's abilities. Once he got to that point, his earnings would improve, but only at a slow pace since employers were not generous with pay increases.

FEMALE LABOR

After apprentices, female sales and clerical workers received the lowest wages in commercial firms, according to data for the years 1902–1903.

---

[8]These provinces were located to the north and northeast of Moscow in regions where poor land kept peasants in a state of chronic poverty, compelling many of them to seek employment elsewhere.

Female labor, like that of children, deserves to be considered as a separate subject because of its unique features.

Women began to be employed on a large scale in Russia immediately following the emancipation of the serfs, that is, in the 1860s. During this honeymoon in the employment of female labor, Russian capitalists relied heavily on the labor of women and children. Having emancipated the peasants from slavery "without [granting them] freedom or land," the government thrust a huge mass of hungry and ragged peasants into the insatiable maw of their exploiters. Women and children have always been easy objects for capitalist exploitation. The passivity of women workers and their lack of resistance, together with their almost universally low wages, make them particularly attractive to capitalists the world over.

Beginning in 1904, there was a sharp rise in the use of female labor due to the drafting of reserve troops for the Russo-Japanese War. But already by the following year, factory inspectors' reports[9] gave another reason for the increase in the employment of female labor, namely, the fact that women workers were calmer, more reliable, less likely to come under the influence of agitators, and also much cheaper than male workers. After 1905, the process of replacing male workers with females proceeded at an accelerated pace, and this continued until the 1917 revolution. In the twelve-year period from 1905 to 1917, the number of women workers [in all branches of Russian factory industry] increased by 50 percent.*[10] The number of children employed also grew significantly. In commerce, transportation, banking, insurance, and other firms, female and child labor replaced that of men to no less an extent than in factories. Precise data on the number of women and children employed in these nonfactory enter-

---

[9]On the Factory Inspectorate, see Ch. 1, n. 51, above. The findings of the factory inspectors were variously published between 1882 and 1886, but these reports revealed such scandalous abuses that their publication was halted. Factory inspectors' reports were not published again until 1903 (for the year 1901), and then only in summary form.

*In calculating the increase in female labor on the eve of 1917, it must not be forgotten that this was caused, above all, by the specific conditions of wartime.

[10]In 1905, the Factory Inspectorate reported that there were 457,900 women employed in factories under its jurisdiction in the Russian Empire. In 1917, 922,500 women were factory workers. Thus the number of women factory workers increased by 100 percent during this period, and not by 50 percent as Gudvan asserts.

prises are not available. Nor are there exact statistics on the number of individuals employed in commercial and related firms. This deficiency can, however, be rectified by data of an indirect nature.

In 1902, according to the Ministry of Finance, there were 1,100,000 commercial firms. Included among them were enormous department stores, banks and insurance companies with hundreds and thousands of employees, as well as small enterprises and independent trades. If we suppose that on the average, each firm employed no more than two workers, then we would reach a figure of almost two million employees in commercial firms. If we add to this figure office employees in factories (attendance supervisors, clerks, cashiers, accountants, typists) and those employed in countless government bureaus, institutions, departments of various ministries, and so on, then we reach a figure of 2.5–3 million sales-clerical workers in the Russian Empire around the turn of century.

The wages of women shop clerks were significantly lower than men's. Women's wages ranged from three to thirty rubles a month in the capital cities of St. Petersburg and Moscow and in large provincial towns. In Odessa, a female shop assistant earned only 41 percent of the wages of her male counterpart. In Warsaw, the figure was 43 percent, in Kiev 48 percent, in Kharkov 49 percent, in Moscow 50 percent, and in St. Petersburg 51 percent. As these figures show, female clerks in St. Petersburg earned the highest wage relative to men. The inequality of wages, together with other equally important characteristics of female labor in commercial firms, directly affected the participation of women in the trade union movement of sales-clerical workers. We must therefore give special attention to the position of women workers in shops and offices.

Earning an average of only fifteen rubles a month for sixteen-to-eighteen-hour days, female salesclerks were nonetheless expected to dress attractively. In most cases, women had to pay their prospective employers "in kind" to get a job in the first place. Their only recourse was to turn to prostitution, and what began as occasional prostitution would often become a permanent source of income.

A number of letters published in 1908 in the newspaper *Novaia Rus'*, in the section "The Salesclerk Question," bear witness to this fact. When writing about their miserable lives, women workers invariably referred to the problem of prostitution. These letters so vividly depict the situation of female sales and clerical workers that the reader will not hold it against us, I hope, if we quote extracts from them here for illustration.

This is how female shop workers described their life and work: "Work in bakeries," wrote one woman clerk in a pastry shop,

> begins each day at five or six o'clock in the morning and ends at eight or nine at night. In pastry shops, work starts at seven or eight and ends at ten-thirty or eleven at night. Year-round, we have to work a fifteen- or sixteen-hour day. We don't get any time off for lunch. We have to eat behind the counter. The wage of a female bakery shop clerk ranges from six to eighteen rubles a month; in pastry shops, it ranges from twelve to twenty-five rubles. Work this out for yourself—a fifteen to sixteen hour workday comes to about 450 to 480 hours a month. This means we earn from two and a half to four kopecks an hour.

> These long hours and low wages force us to turn to the shameful trade. Our wages do not give us enough money to survive, but the bosses still demand that we dress fashionably. We can't fight this because Petersburg is full of girls who are willing to work fifteen hours a day just to get a crust of bread. The bosses want only good-looking girls. Most shop girls are from seventeen to twenty years old, and a girl over thirty can very seldom be encountered, and then never in shops on the main streets.

A shop clerk named Aizenshtein described the situation of women workers in stores selling ready-made clothes in the New Alexandrovskii Market.

> This is what our working conditions are like. The stores open between eight and eight-thirty in the morning and close at nine in the evening. Both male and female shop clerks have to be at work at seven-thirty in the winter and seven in the summer. We never leave work earlier than nine-thirty at night in the winter and ten in the summer. Our workday in the winter is therefore thirteen and a half hours, and in the summer, fifteen hours. Before the store opens and after it closes we have to clean, sort and put away all the merchandise that was taken out during the day. When the store is open, we have to stand out on the street continuously to attract customers. If we let anyone go by, the boss swears at us in the choicest language. The customers also swear at us for trying to drag them in by the coat tails.

> We are very poorly paid; ten to fifteen rubles a month is considered a good wage for a salesgirl. They don't pay us each month, or every two weeks, so we

oss each day and beg him for enough money for food. And
mployer for money, you are insulted: "You're always asking
never sell anything. How much money did you earn today,
... asking you! Answer my question!" screams the employer. "If you want
money, you have to work. If you don't want to work, go stand on the Nevskii
and do it the easy way!" After a response like that, it's hard to approach the boss
again. But when you've gone hungry for a few days, you try once more. You
look around timidly, then go up to the boss again, and he either insults you or, in
the best circumstances, he gives you fifty or sixty kopecks saying, "Don't bother
me again!"

We don't get any time off for lunch. We eat behind the counter. A piece of
bread and a cup of tea—that's our meal. We're not allowed to sit down, even
when there aren't any customers in the store. This wouldn't be so bad if we
didn't have to carry around piles of cloth and other goods. When you ask one of
the salesmen for help, he replies, "It's good for you. It will help you to miscarry
what the owner has put into you."

The salesmen think we all are prostitutes. *And in fact, it is hard to find even one
virtuous girl at the New Alexandrovskii Market. The first thing the shop owner or
manager says when you ask for a job is "Are you ticklish?" If you bat your eyes or nod
your head suggestively, the job is yours. But if you don't agree, you might as well forget
it.*

*The boss will court you, pay you on time, treat you politely and give you presents, etc.,
until you "grow heavy in the waist." But when you "grow heavy," he will drop you and
maybe even fire you. After that you follow in the footsteps of many other salesgirls until
you get sick and wind up in the hospital.*[11]

A woman clerical worker, Osipovich, described the same problem.

Alongside the enormous number of salesgirls there is a group of women
engaged in clerical work. I am referring to women who earn their living as
cashiers, bookkeepers, secretaries, stenographers, and so on. Compared with the
tens of thousands of salesgirls, their numbers are small. But in spite of this, or
perhaps because of it, I would like to make society aware of their difficult and
dreary situation.

The vast majority of these workers are unmarried girls. In bourgeois circles,
material security is obtained through marriage. However, for the ever-increasing

[11]Italics in original.

number of needy young women this is not a viable solution. Their desire for freedom and independence is satisfied more and more often by the new professions which are opening up to them. If these girls do get married, their most precious dowry will be their ability to work, just as it is for working class women.

For women in the clerical professions, the workday ranges from seven to thirteen hours, depending on the place and the responsibility of the job. For example, women employed in banks work only six and a half to seven hours a day. In insurance offices, women work from eight to nine hours a day. In other kinds of offices, such as export or transportation firms, women work nine to ten hours. Finally, women employed in stores as cashiers, clerks or supervisors, work at least twelve or thirteen hours, and sometimes as long as sixteen to eighteen hours a day. Wages range from fifteen to sixty rubles a month. The average wage of women working in banks is thirty-five to forty rubles a month. In offices, the average wage is thirty to thirty-five rubles and in stores twenty to twenty-five.

As a result of these low wages, long hours and the very high cost of living in large cities, many of the less determined girls begin to follow the same course as the salesgirls. The income from an evening stroll helps many a cashier or secretary make ends meet.

To make matters worse, even the decent and well-paying jobs, for example, those in banks, are rarely available unless one first grants favors to the director, the manager, or some other individual. I could name dozens of women who have made brilliant careers in business thanks to their compliance in this area, but there's no point in doing that. It's a well-known fact anyway. The young girl, driven to such acts by need and hunger, is not to blame. The blame lies with those who use their strength and power to enslave women, body and soul. This sad state of affairs has caused more than one woman to take her own life.[12]

We could fill a whole book with letters like these and with similar responses to questionnaires, but the point has been made. Let us simply add that all the contemporary studies of prostitution show that before World War I, the majority of prostitutes were former salesclerks, servants or factory workers. In a study of prostitution in Berlin and other German cities, Dr. Grinberg found that 42 percent of the prostitutes were former shop girls or domestic employees (governesses, nannies), 36 percent were former servants and 16 percent were factory workers before turning to prostitution. In Germany, for every thousand saleswomen, there were

[12]Italics in original.

twenty-one prostitutes. For every thousand domestic servants the figure was seventeen and for factory workers thirteen. Dr. Grinberg found that thirty-two out of a thousand saleswomen in France became prostitutes, twenty-six in England, and twenty-nine in Austria-Hungary. According to other statistics 45.5 percent of all registered prostitutes in Russia were formerly either salesclerks or servants.

WORK TIME

Since wages and working hours constitute the very basis of a worker's life, the author has made every effort to collect the responses of all the sales employees in Petrograd,[13] Odessa, Warsaw, and elsewhere who participated in surveys concerning workplace conditions. More importantly, I have tried to ensure that the responses to these surveys were as accurate and complete as possible. Much time was spent investigating the issues of hours and wages and I can say with assurance that not a single statistic came to our attention that was not verified.

We will consider the ideal workday to be not eight hours but eleven and one-half hours, the legal maximum set by the tsarist government for factory workers, which included a lunch break.[14] By this standard, we will see how "shamelessly" long—as Webb and Cox put it[15]—was the length of the salesclerks' workday, not only in the above-mentioned cities for which we have data, but in the rest of Russia as well.

The average working day in wholesale firms fluctuated between 14.1 (the minimum) and 17.4 (the maximum) hours. In retail and wholesale-retail firms, the workday ranged from 15.57 (minimum) hours to 19.34

[13]Petrograd refers to the capital city of the Russian Empire, St. Petersburg, which was renamed in 1914 following the outbreak of World War I. In 1924, Petrograd was renamed Leningrad.

[14]This legal maximum for the workday in factory enterprises was established by legislation enacted on June 2, 1897; see Ch. 1, n. 19.

[15]Sidney Webb was a leading British socialist and social reformer; Harold Cox was an economist and journalist. Together they wrote *The Eight Hour Day*, published in England in 1891 and translated into Russian by D. L. Muratov under the title *8-chasovoi rabochii den'* (St. Petersburg, 1904).

(maximum). But it is necessary to emphasize the differences in the length of the workday for clerks in various branches of commerce.

If we exclude sales personnel in jewelry stores, who comprised only 1.45 percent of the sales workers in the cities surveyed, then the shortest workday could be found in commercial establishments of manufacturing firms (14.39 hours), furniture stores (14.66 hours), and in linen stores (14.71 hours). In these three branches of commerce, however, our data came mainly from old and trusted employees who turned in 90.1 percent of all the questionnaires. This stratum of the work force, called the "aristocracy," worked shorter hours than other employees and enjoyed a one-to-one-and-a-half hour lunch break with the right to leave the shop and go home. They also arrived at the store later and left earlier than other workers.

Even when we take this factor into account, salesclerks in dry goods, furniture, and linen stores worked comparatively shorter hours than other sales employees. The average workday was significantly shorter for these

16. Stores on Petersburg's fashionable Nevskii Prospect where many salesclerks found employment.

employees because almost all of them had lunch breaks as well as time off on Sundays and holidays (27.68 percent did no work at all on Sundays and holidays, whereas 72.3 percent worked only one or two hours on these days). As we shall see in the following section, these employees also earned much more than their counterparts in other trades. The only ones who fared poorly were the apprentices. In these branches of trade, as in others, apprentices worked to the point of exhaustion. In dry goods stores, they had to stock the store after it closed and then wash the floors and dust the counters before it opened in the morning. Unless the apprentice lived in the owner's home, he had to fetch the key in the morning and return it in the evening after closing the store. In many cities surveyed,* it was customary for the apprentices to open the store before the other employees arrived and then close it at night after cleaning up. Two older workers would be put on duty to supervise. These tasks added another two or three hours to the apprentices' workday, making it sixteen or seventeen hours long. When we consider that the apprentices, some of whom were only eight or nine years old, had to fetch tea and lunch for the adult clerks, deliver parcels to customers' homes, and unpack deliveries all day long, we can see how much child labor was exploited even in one of the best branches of commerce.

Shop clerks in haberdasheries, book stores, fur stores, the lumber business, stationery stores, shoe stores, and clothing and millinery shops worked the next longest workday—an average of 15 to 15.56 hours. In the section on female labor, we have already mentioned some of the special problems encountered by women workers in the clothing and millinery trades. Let me only add here that women workers in these shops lost their jobs during the off-season, which forced many of them to earn their living by taking to the streets.

Employees in the pharmaceutical business worked an average of 16 to 16.52 hours a day, making them the next group on our list. These workers were constantly in danger because fires and explosions of gasoline, ether, alcohol, and other flammable substances took place very frequently as a result of even minor mishandling of fire. The life of employees in pharmacy

---

*The author personally observed this in Petrograd, Warsaw, Kiev, Odessa, Nikolaev, and Kherson.

stores and warehouses was not pleasant. Apart from explosions, they had to endure air that was always saturated with poisonous fumes, they had no lunch break and they had to work on Sundays and holidays, as on ordinary days. But the longest workday could be found not among pharmaceutical workers but among clerks in tobacco stores, bakeries, grocery, and hardware stores. Their workday lasted from 17 to 17.4 hours.

Generally speaking, the workday in southern Russia was longer than in other parts of Russia. Partly for this reason, partly because of the revolutionary attitude of the Jewish masses in the south who suffered from pogroms and other abuses, southern workers took an active part in underground revolutionary activity in the early 1900s and in underground trade union work beginning in 1905. Salesclerks in the south were in the vanguard of a widespread movement for a special law regulating the working time of sales-clerical employees and they became involved in party work before their comrades in northern Russia.[16]

WAGES

No matter what aspect of the sales-clerical proletariat we consider—moral and intellectual development, work time or material welfare—we must address the fundamental factor of wages on which the entire life of the proletariat depends.

In the previous section, we surveyed the length of the workday for salesclerks and saw what long hours these twentieth-century slaves had to work. In this section, we will see how little they were paid for their efforts. A large majority of the clerks literally received only kopecks for their unbearably long hours of work.

[16]The campaign over work time to which Gudvan refers culminated in the promulgation of the law of November 15, 1906, which placed the regulation of working hours in the hands of local boards composed of representatives of workers, employers, and the local government administration. The law affected both sales firms and artisanal workshops. For further discussion of the political activities and labor movement among workers in southern Russia, see Ralph Carter Elwood, *Russian Social Democracy in the Underground: A Study of the RSDRP in the Ukraine 1907–1914* (Assen, The Netherlands, 1974).

The wages in commercial enterprises varied greatly. Some employees earned no more than an unskilled factory worker, while others were paid almost as much as employees of government ministries. Wages usually corresponded to one's position in the firm. The higher one stood on the ladder, the more one earned. As in other parts of the service sector, the payment received for one's labor often stood in inverse proportion to the quality and quantity of the work performed. Naturally, the employee's needs played no role whatsoever in determining wage rates. It was possible, for example, for someone with an enormous family to earn no more than a pittance, despite back-breaking labor. An employee in this position would often work for less than his fellow workers who were not in such desperate need of work. The laws of supply and demand, and the competition which they generated, all played a crucial role. As in the industrial sector, the bankruptcy of a firm presented employees with the sad prospect of finding another position.

The following factors were influential in determining how much sales workers earned: the size of the firm and the scope of its trade, whether the business was wholesale or retail, and the personal qualities or merits of the individual employee. Along with these general economic factors, local conditions also influenced earnings. As we shall see, workers in major cities earned more than those in remote towns, where lower wages corresponded to the relatively lower cost of living.

The highest salaries were paid to the directors, solicitors, and business managers of commercial firms. Their salaries varied according to the location and type of firm. In Moscow, for example, an annual salary of 6,000 to 10,000 rubles was typical for these strata of the labor force.

In comparison with the directors and managers, almost all of the other employees in sales firms were paid next to nothing. In fact, 0.72 percent of the women workers and 4.8 percent of the apprentices earned nothing at all and 2.59 percent of the women salesclerks and 20.04 percent of the apprentices earned only one to five rubles a month, as did 0.95 percent of male and female office employees. In the next salary range of five to eight rubles a month, we find 0.59 percent of male clerks with five to nine years of experience on the job, 1.95 percent of the female clerks, 21.98 percent of the apprentices, and 1.09 percent of all office workers. Even those male employees with more than nine years experience usually received a miserable wage; 11.75 percent earned fifteen to thirty-five rubles a month, while 13.08 percent earned thirty-five to fifty rubles. Apprentices and women salesclerks earned the lowest wages.

From the foregoing, it is clear that the wage rates of sales employees showed considerable variation. There is nothing surprising, therefore, that because of these variations, the ranks of sales employees included individuals at every conceivable level of affluence and poverty. But wages were not the only factor that determined a worker's state of material well-being. Other crucial factors included the cost of food, housing, basic necessities, and, most important of all, the number of dependents an employee had to support. Dr. Listov, whose work we have often referred to in this and the previous section, made a study of sales employees in twenty-five Russian cities, not including Moscow. He found that only 27.46 percent of the sales employees lived in housing provided by their employers. The remaining 72.54 percent rented lodgings. The majority of those who lived in their employer's housing were single (68.61 percent) and also poorly paid. However, some of the employees in this category who had families, 31.39 percent in all, received comparatively good salaries.

This section on wages would not be complete without a discussion of one very important factor, namely, the relationship between age and salary. It is well known that an employee's age is very important in determining earnings in every branch of business. Among factory and artisanal workers, for example, earnings increased with age because the longer they worked, the more skills and experience they acquired in their trade. A similar phenomenon can be observed among those engaged in intellectual work. For those engaged in sales occupations, age has a special meaning. Not only did clerks have to learn their job and do it well; they needed to learn something more besides. In prerevolutionary times, a salesclerk was valued for having the "knack," that is, the ability to attract customers and sell them goods for a high price. In the world of trade, the following rule applied: "If you don't cheat, you won't sell." This was the guiding principle of the Russian business world until the end of the tsarist regime. New apprentices were imbued with this spirit by their employers. Learning how to sell, which in shopkeeper's jargon meant learning how to fleece a customer, required a long period of time; this is why wages of sales employees went up as they got older.

LIVING CONDITIONS

It would be something of an understatement to say that the living quarters of a majority of sales-clerical workers were disgusting and unfit for human habitation. No words can possibly describe what it was actually like inside these hovels. To gain a picture of the living conditions of these workers, one would have to see the situation for oneself. Nevertheless, I will attempt to give the reader some impression by describing several places that I have seen during my investigations. Apartments on two streets in Odessa—Meshchanskaia and Staroreznichnaia streets—will serve as examples of dwellings which employees rented on their own. For illustrations of housing provided by employers, we will take various dwellings in Petrograd.

Some of the rented apartments that I observed were below street level. In order to get to them, you had to descend a slippery wooden staircase that had no railings. One needed the agility of an acrobat to get down these stairs without breaking one's neck. These basement apartments got no light at all. Little oil lamps burned night and day, spreading a thick black soot and stench over everything. Water streamed down the mildewed walls.

One apartment on Meshchanskaia Street (three rooms and a kitchen) was rented by Dain, a hardware store clerk in Odessa. Each room measured seven feet high, eight feet wide, and eight and a half feet long and was heated by one small brazier. Dain and his family occupied one of the rooms and the kitchen. Two salesclerks and their families occupied the remaining rooms: Rabinovich, who worked in a dry goods store, and Tsypin, who worked in a wholesale warehouse. There were eight people in the Dain family, five in Rabinovich's, and eleven in Tsypin's. In addition, the apartment accommodated a paralytic co-worker who had been fired when he became ill, together with his sister and her family. The sister's husband, a shoemaker, worked at home.

The preceding description of an apartment on Meschanskaia Street applies also to dwellings on Staroreznichnaia Street and other streets in Odessa, with the difference that on Staroreznichnaia Street the apartments had floors made of clay rather than dirt, and some of the basement apartments received a little light through glass doors opening on to the half-dark corridors. In every other respect, however, these apartments were just as damp, moldy, dark, and rank as the one described above. None of these dwellings had any furniture to speak of and a family of seven to twelve people would have one table, a few stools and a double bed.

Conditions were even worse for the salesclerks and apprentices who lived in lodgings provided by their employers in Petrograd. One employer named Koren'kov set aside a pantry next to the kitchen as a sleeping area for his thirteen workers. This room was nine feet high, three and a half feet wide, and six feet long. There were no beds at all. The workers slept on wooden planks arranged in three tiers. During the day, the upper boards were taken down and used as a dining table. Apprentices had to sleep on the floor.

The sausagemaker Migaev employed sixteen workers, eight "fellows," as he called his salesclerks, and eight apprentices. All of them slept on the floor without mattresses in the room where the sausages were made. Another sausagemaker named Zhirnov employed eight salesclerks and seven apprentices. All fifteen of them slept in their employer's apartment in a room next to the servants' kitchen. The grocer Zhukov had fifteen people (eight clerks and seven apprentices) sleeping in one room adjacent to the kitchen. At Zhukov's the clerks slept together with those employed in his bakery on the same street. All of these apartments, if such cupboards and pantries could be called apartments, were infested with bedbugs, fleas, cockroaches, beetles, lice, and other insects, which tormented the occupants.

We must also keep in mind the extremely long workday of sales employees, often without any breaks. Due to their low wages, they could often afford only the poorest quality food. In some trades, such as tobacco and pharmaceuticals, they worked in a suffocating atmosphere filled with fumes; in others, such as the hardware or butcher business, they had to carry heavy loads on their backs. One can easily imagine the combined effect of poor working and living conditions on the health of these workers.

The extremely long workday under unhygienic conditions, without adequate rest periods and regular meals, produced numerous and varied illnesses among sales employees. In the event of "illness, incapacitation and old age," as Dr. Listov has asserted, "they cannot count on anything except their own savings which, due to the low wages, they can hardly accumulate." Following the death of a clerk, his family always found itself in a still worse situation for the same reasons. Even if, in the course of fifteen to twenty-five years of employment, a clerk's wages increased somewhat (though to a very slight extent), his weakened condition and premature illness made it impossible to accumulate savings. Employers seldom put aside funds to assist disabled and ill workers. Consequently, the sick or elderly salesclerk had to find treatment and live at his own expense. This frequently forced him to sell or to pawn his last pieces of furniture, and if the illness persisted, then the unfortunate man joined the ranks of the beggars.

CULTURAL DEVELOPMENT

We have sufficient data on the levels of literacy and education among sales-clerical employees to describe their cultural development. These data, which were assembled by the author and published in a number of his studies, apply to the end of the nineteenth and the beginning of the twentieth century. Despite the fact that the information was collected at various times, it gives quite an accurate picture of the educational level of these workers.

On the basis of this evidence, we find that 12.33 percent of all sales-clerical workers in Russia were totally illiterate, that is, they could not read the labels on products or write a sales slip. Almost half (46.5 percent) of the illiterate workers were women, 43 percent were children of both sexes and only 10.5 percent were men. The rest of the workers, the remaining 87.67 percent, were literate: 47.76 percent could read and write; 37.37 percent had finished their primary education; and only 2.54 percent had completed some form of secondary schooling, usually at a commercial institute or trade school.

At first glance, this high rate of literacy makes quite a good impression. In reality, however, it would be difficult to find a more ignorant and unenlightened group. In the world of the shop assistant, ignorance, cowardice and inertia prevailed. Of course, this should not surprise us since these unfortunate people lived their lives in a state of complete submission and constant fear. Their basic human rights were continually ignored. After studying the daily lives, habits, and customs of sales-clerical employees over the last twenty-four years, I have come to the conclusion that their widespread submissiveness and ignorance were caused by the combined effects of long working hours and pitifully low wages. They lived in constant fear of tomorrow, and this fostered the submissive spirit which characterized the group as a whole. This kind of fear made it possible to survive in the present but robbed them of all hope for the future. We cannot really blame them for their attitudes, though it was precisely this slavish fear and ignorance which allowed all their urgent problems to remain unresolved until the time of the October Revolution. This is all the more striking since sales-clerical workers lived side by side with other groups of workers who frequently let their voices be heard.

The educational level of sales-clerical employees varied considerably according to age and sex. In some cases, the differences were quite substantial. Above all, literacy corresponded to gender. Illiteracy was greatest among female workers, followed by children and adolescents. Male workers were the most literate, and literacy rates showed a definite correlation with workers' ages [see Tables 5.1 and 5.2].

Since the overall literacy rate was 87.67 percent, only those workers between thirteen and forty years of age had a level of literacy that was higher than average. The first group, those workers who were nine years old or younger, were totally illiterate, and the remaining three groups had a literacy rate that was below average. After the age of thirty, the literacy rate declined as workers' ages increased. The oldest group of workers had the

Table 5.1

Percentage of Literate Salesclerks[a]

CATEGORY	% OF LITERATE WORKERS
Men	94.5
Women	85.5
Children and Juveniles	89.5

[a]Based on the data in this table, it would appear that the percentage of literate workers (all categories) was 89.8 percent and not 87.67 percent as stated earlier. It is not possible to resolve this discrepancy using the data provided by Gudvan.

Table 5.2

Percentage of Literate Salesclerks, By Age

AGE GROUP	% OF LITERATE WORKERS
9 and under	—
9–12	85.6
13–30	96.4
31–40	93.1
41–50	79.1
50 and above	65.6

lowest level of literacy. Only 65.6 percent of the workers over fifty were literate.

The vast majority of sales-clerical workers were poorly educated.[17] While everything around them was changing, these workers remained in the same sad state. It is only fair to add, however, that despite the many difficulties in their lives, most shop assistants would take advantage of a free moment to look at a newspaper or book, thus adding to their scanty knowledge of what was happening in the world in general and in their own class in particular.

As someone well acquainted with the lives of sales-clerical workers, I can testify that their desire to acquire education and culture was slowly increasing. Gradually they were developing a sense of dignity and an awareness of their own self-worth. Their attempts to attain some level of education were at first expressed by adopting only the most superficial trappings of a cultivated life. This was already a healthy sign which soon turned into a genuine concern for intellectual development. The data in the above tables confirm this. As the figures show, sales apprentices were illiterate when they entered the labor force. Yet despite their extremely long workday, most of them still found time to learn how to read and write.

[17]Compared to other groups in the laboring population, salesclerks had a relatively high level of literacy. In 1897, only 39 percent of the textile workers in European Russia were literate; among metalworkers the figure was 66 percent. See A. G. Rashin, *Formirovanie rabochego klassa Rossii. Istoriko-ekonomicheskie ocherki* (Moscow, 1958), p. 593.

Selected Bibliography

This bibliography consists of two parts. In the first part, the reader will find a comprehensive listing of the major publications by each of the authors whose work has been translated in this volume. Part Two includes all the works cited in notes to *The Russian Worker*, with the exception of reference books.

I. WORKS BY THE AUTHORS

S. I. Kanatchikov. "Kul'turno-prosvetitel'naia deiatel'nost' v Peterburgskikh professional'nykh soiuzakh," *Vozrozhdenie*, nos. 5–6, 1909.

25 let bor'by (1898–1923). Petrograd, 1923.

Rabochaia partiia i krest'ianstvo. Petrograd, 1923.

Istoriia odnogo uklona. Leningrad, 1924.

Lenin i krest'ianstvo. Leningrad, 1924.

"Moi vospominaniia o podpol'noi rabote v Nizhne-Tagil'skom zavode 1906 g." In *Sbornik materialov revoliutsionnogo dvizheniia v Tagil'skom okruge.* Vyp. 1. N-Tagil, 1925.

Iz istorii moego bytiia. 2 vols. Moscow and Leningrad, 1929–1934.

P. Timofeev [pseud. for P. Remezov]. "Zavodskie budni. Iz zapisok rabochego," *Russkoe bogatstvo,* no. 8, Aug. 1903, pp. 30–53; no. 9, Sept. 1903, pp. 175–199. [Published under pseud. initials P.T.]

"Ocherki zavodskoi zhizni," *Russkoe bogatstvo,* no. 9, Sept. 1905, pp. 19–24; no. 10, Oct. 1905, pp. 71–91.

Chem zhivet zavodskii rabochii. St. Petersburg, 1906.

"Rabochie i 'politika'," *Russkoe bogatstvo,* no. 8, Aug. 1906, pp. 165–182.

F. P. Pavlov [pseud. for A. N. Bykov]. *Za desiat' let praktiki. Otryvki iz vospominanii, vpechatlenii i nabliudenii iz fabrichnoi zhizni.* Moscow, 1901.

Fabrichnoe zakonodatel'stvo i ego razvitie v Rossii. Rostov-on-Don, 1906.

Germanskoe strakhovanie i drugie sposoby obespecheniia rabochikh. St. Petersburg, 1906.

A. N. Bykov [pseud. F. Pavlov]. *Fabrichnoe zakonodatel'stvo i ego razvitie v Rossii. Lektsii, chitannye v Spb. politekhnikume i v Tekhnologicheskom institute v 1908–1909 ucheb. godu.* St. Petersburg, 1909.

E. A. Oliunina. *Portnovskii promysel v Moskve i v derevniakh Moskovskoi i Riazanskoi gubernii. Materialy k istorii domashnei promyshlennosti v Rossii.* Moscow, 1914.

Organizatsiia vserossiiskogo soiuza rabochikh shveinikov. Moscow, 1927.

A. M. Gudvan. *Prikazchiki v Odesse.* Odessa, 1903.

"Professional'nye bolezni torgovykh sluzhashchikh." In *Russkoe obshchestvo okhraneniia narodnogo zdraviia.* 1904.

Prikazchichii vopros (Zhizn' i trud prikazchikov). Odessa, 1905.

Doklad komissii po vyrabotke obiazatel'nykh postanovlenii o normal'nom otdykhe sluzhashchikh v torgovykh zavedeniiakh, skladakh i kontorakh. Odessa, 1908.

V tsarstve t'my i eksploatatsii. St. Petersburg, 1914.

Besedy s kuptsami po voprosu o normirovke truda torgovykh sluzhashchikh. St. Petersburg, 1910.

"Svoboda soiuzov," *Sovremennyi mir,* April 1911.

"Gosudarstvennaia Duma i strakhovanie rabochikh," *Sovremennik,* 1912.

"Izbiratel'naia kampaniia i prikazchiki," *Prosveshchenie,* nos. 5–7, 1912.

"Khoziaeva i prisluga," *Sovremennik, 1912.*

Zakonodatel'naia okhrana truda prikazchikov. Odessa, 1912.

Sredi prikazchikov. St. Petersburg, 1912.

"Bor'ba s bezrabotitsei," *Gorodskoe delo,* no. 10, 1915.

"Gorodskie Dumy i prikazchichii vopros," *Gorodskoe delo,* no. 9, 1915.

"Normirovka truda prikazchikov," *Gorodskoe delo,* no. 6, 1916.

Normirovka truda torgovo-promyshlennykh sluzhashchikh. Petrograd, 1917.

Ocherki po istoriia dvizheniia sluzhashchikh v Rossii, Part I: *Do revoliutsii 1905 goda.* Moscow, 1925.

II. WORKS CITED IN *THE RUSSIAN WORKER*

Ainzaft, S. S. "K istorii professional'nogo dvizheniia torgovo-promyshlennykh sluzhashchikh," *Vestnik truda,* 2 [39] (1924): 222–230.

Anderson, Barbara. *Internal Migration During Modernization in Late Nineteenth-Century Russia.* Princeton, 1980.

Antoshkin, D. V. *Ocherk dvizheniia sluzhashchikh v Rossii.* Moscow, 1921.

Anufriev, V. M., P. I. Dorovatskii, and N. I. Roganov. *Iz istorii profdvizheniia rabotnikov torgovli.* Moscow, 1958.

Bater, James H. *St. Petersburg: Industrialization and Change.* London, 1976.

———. "The Journey to Work in St. Petersburg 1860–1914," *Journal of Transport History,* NS, III, 2 (September 1974): 214–233.

Belin, A. [A. A. Evdokimov]. *Professional'noe dvizhenie torgovykh sluzhashchikh v Rossii.* Moscow, 1906.

Belousov, I. A. *Ushedshaia Moskva. Zapiski po lichnym vospominaniiam s nachala 1870 godov.* Moscow, 1927.

Blackwell, William L. *The Beginnings of Russian Industrialization 1800–1868.* Princeton, 1968.

Bonnell, Victoria E. "Urban Working Class Life in Early Twentieth Century

Russia: Some Problems and Patterns," *Russian History*, 8 (1981): 360–378.

———. *Roots of Rebellion: Workers' Politics and Organizations in St. Petersburg and Moscow, 1900–1914.* Berkeley and Los Angeles, 1983.

Bradley, Jr., Joseph Crane. "Muzhik and Muscovite: Peasants in Late Nineteenth-Century Urban Russia." Ph.D. diss., Harvard University, 1977.

Brooks, Jeffrey. "Readers and Reading at the End of the Tsarist Era." In *Literature and Society in Imperial Russia, 1800–1914*, ed. William Mills Todd III. Stanford, 1978.

Buzinov, A. *Za Nevskoi zastavoi. Zapiski rabochego.* Moscow and Leningrad, 1930.

Chamberlin, William Henry. *The Russian Revolution.* 2 vols. New York, 1935.

Chernyavskii, M. "Old Believers and the New Religion," *Slavic Review*, 25 (March 1966).

Chislennost' i sostav rabochikh v Rossii na osnovanii dannykh pervoi vseobshchei perepisi naseleniia Rossiiskoi Imperii 1897 g. Vols. 1 and 2. St. Petersburg, 1906.

Druzhinin, N. K. *Usloviia byta rabochikh v dorevoliutsionnoi Rossii (po dannym biudzhetnykh obsledovanii).* Moscow, 1958.

Elwood, Ralph Carter. *Russian Social Democracy in the Underground: A Study of the RSDRP in the Ukraine 1907–1914.* Assen, the Netherlands, 1974.

Engelstein, Laura. *Moscow, 1905: Working-Class Organization and Political Conflict.* Stanford, 1982.

Gerschenkron, Alexander. "Problems and Patterns of Russian Economic Development. " In *The Transformation of Russian Society: Aspects of Social Change since 1861*, ed. Cyril E. Black. Cambridge, Mass., 1967.

Glickman, Rose L. "The Russian Factory Woman, 1880–1914." In *Women in Russia*, ed. Dorothy Atkinson, Alexander Dallin, and Gail Warshofsky Lapidus. Stanford, 1977.

———. *Russian Factory Women: Workplace and Society, 1880–1914.* Berkeley and Los Angeles, 1984.

Gohstand, Robert. "The Internal Geography of Trade in Moscow from the Mid-Nineteenth Century to the First World War." 2 vols. Ph.D. diss., University of California, Berkeley, 1973.

Gordon, M., ed. *Iz istorii professional'nogo dvizheniia sluzhashchikh v Peterburge. Pervyi etap (1904–1919 gg.)*. Leningrad, 1925.

Gruzdev, S. M. *Trud i bor'ba shveinikov v Petrograde 1905–1916 gg.* Leningrad, 1929.

Gvozdev, S. *Zapiski fabrichnogo inspektora: iz nabliudenii i praktiki v periode 1894–1908 gg.* Moscow, 1911.

Hogan, Heather Jeanne. "Labor and Management in Conflict: The St. Petersburg Metal-Working Industry, 1900–1914." Ph.D. diss., University of Michigan, 1981.

Istoriia rabochikh Leningrada, 1703-fevral' 1917. Vol. 1. Leningrad, 1972.

Johnson, Robert E. *Peasant and Proletarian: The Working Class of Moscow in the Late Nineteenth Century*. New Brunswick, N.J., 1979.

Kabo, E. O. *Ocherki rabochego byta. Opyt monograficheskogo issledovaniia domashnogo rabochego byta*. Vol. 1. Moscow, 1928.

Keep, John L. H. *The Rise of Social Democracy in Russia*. Oxford, 1963.

————. *The Russian Revolution: A Study in Mass Mobilization*. New York, 1976.

Kir'ianov, Iu. I. *Zhiznennyi uroven' rabochikh Rossii*. Moscow, 1979.

Koenker, Diane. *Moscow Workers and the 1917 Revolution*. Princeton, 1981.

Laverychev. V. Ia. *Tsarizm i rabochii vopros v Rossii (1861–1917 gg.)*. Moscow, 1972.

Listok bulochnikov i konditerov, no. 8, Nov. 18, 1906, p. 6.

Luninskii, N. "Soiuz prikazchikov Odessy (1905–1907 gg.)." In *Professional'noe dvizhenie sluzhashchikh Ukrainy (1905–1907 gg.): Sbornik*, ed. I. S. Stepanskii. n.p., n.d.

Mally, Lynn. "Russian Workers and Factory Legislation, 1882–1900." Seminar paper, University of California, Berkeley, Spring 1978.

Mamontov, S. "Dvizhenie rabochikh po obrabotke blagorodnykh metallov v Moskve v 1905 g. (po lichnym vospominaniiam)." In *Materialy po istorii professional'nogo dvizheniia v Rossii*. 5 vols. Moscow, 1924–1927, V: 180–199.

Materialy ob ekonomicheskom polozhenii i professional'noi organizatsii Peterburgskikh rabochikh po metallu. St. Petersburg, 1909.

Matossian, Mary. "The Peasant Way of Life." In *The Peasant in Nineteenth-Century Russia*, ed. Wayne S. Vucinich. Stanford, 1968.

Mendelsohn, Ezra. *Class Struggle in the Pale: The Formative Years of the Jewish Workers' Movement in Tsarist Russia.* Cambridge, 1970.

Moore, Jr., Barrington. *Injustice: The Social Bases of Obedience and Revolt.* White Plains, N.Y., 1978.

Muromskii, K. *Byt i nuzhdy torgovo-promyshlennykh sluzhashchikh.* Moscow, 1906.

Pazhitnov, K. A. *Problema remeslennykh tsekhov v zakonodatel'stve russkogo absoliutizma.* Moscow, 1952.

Perepis' Moskvy 1902 goda. Chast' 1, vyp. 2. Moscow, 1906.

Pipes, Richard. *Social Democracy and the St. Petersburg Labor Movement, 1885–1897.* Cambridge, Mass., 1963.

Pokrovskaia, M. N. *Po podvalam, cherdakam i uglovym kvartiram Peterburga.* St. Petersburg, 1903.

Professional'noe dvizhenie Moskovskikh pishchevikov v gody pervoi revoliutsii. Sbornik 1. Moscow, 1927.

Prokopovich, S. N. *Biudzhety Peterburgskikh rabochikh (po dannym ankety, proizvedennoi XII [Sodeistviia trudu] Otdelom I.R.T.O.).* St. Petersburg, 1909.

Rabinowitch, Alexander. *Prelude to Revolution: The Petrograd Bolsheviks and the July 1917 Uprising.* Bloomington, Ind., 1968.

———. *The Bolsheviks Come to Power: The Revolution of 1917 in Petrograd.* New York, 1976.

Rabochee dvizhenie v Rossii v 19-om veke. Sbornik dokumentov i materialov, ed. A. M. Pankratova and I. M. Ivanov. Vol. 3, pt. 1; vol. 4, pt. 1. Moscow, 1963.

Rashin, A. G. *Formirovanie rabochego klassa Rossii. Istoriko-ekonomicheskie ocherki.* Moscow, 1958.

Remeslenniki i remeslennoe upravlenie v Rossii. Petrograd, 1916.

Rimlinger, Gaston V. "Autocracy and the Factory Order in Early Russian Industrialization," *Journal of Economic History,* 20 (1960): 67–92.

Rozen, M. *Ocherki polozheniia torgovo-promyshlennogo proletariata v Rossii.* St. Petersburg, 1907.

S.-Peterburg po perepisi 15 dekabria 1900 g. Vyp. 2. St. Petersburg, 1903.

Schwarz, Solomon M. *The Russian Revolution of 1905: The Workers' Move-*

ment and the Formation of Bolshevism and Menshevism. Chicago and London, 1967.

Semanov, S. N. *Peterburgskie rabochie nakhanune pervoi russkoi revoliutsii.* Moscow and Leningrad, 1966.

Shelymagin, I. I. *Zakonodatel'stvo o fabrichno-zavodskom trude v Rossii 1900–1917.* Moscow, 1952.

Shevkov, N. *Moskovskie shveiniki do fevral'skoi revoliutsii.* Moscow, 1927.

Shuster, U. A. *Peterburgskie rabochie v 1905–1907 gg.* Leningrad, 1976.

Stites, Richard. *The Women's Liberation Movement in Russia: Feminism, Nihilism, and Bolshevism, 1860–1930.* Princeton, 1978.

Surh, Gerald Dennis. "Petersburg Workers in 1905: Strikes, Workplace Democracy, and the Revolution." Ph.D. diss., University of California, Berkeley, 1979.

Svavitskii, V. A., and V. Sher. *Ocherk polozheniia rabochikh pechatnogo dela v Moskve (po dannym ankety, proizvedennoi obshchestvom rabochikh graficheskikh iskusstv v 1907 godu).* St. Petersburg, 1909.

Tugan-Baranovsky, Mikhail I. *The Russian Factory in the 19th Century,* trans. by Arthur Levin and Claora S. Levin, under the supervision of Gregory Grossman. Homewood, Ill., 1970.

Ushedshaia Moskva. Vospominaniia sovremennikov o Moskve vtoroi poloviny XIX veka. Moscow, 1964.

Von Laue, Theodore. "Factory Inspection Under the 'Witte System:' 1892–1903," *American Slavic and East European Review,* 19 (Oct. 1960): 347–362.

———. "Russian Peasants in the Factory, 1892–1904," *Journal of European History,* 21 (March 1961): 61–80.

———. *Sergei Witte and the Industrialization of Russia.* New York, 1963.

———. "Russian Labor Between Field and Factory, 1892–1903," *California Slavic Studies,* 3 (1964): 33–64.

Walkin, Jacob. "The Attitude of the Tsarist Government Toward the Labor Problem," *American Slavic and East European Review,* 13 (1954): 163–184.

Wildman, Allan K. *The Making of a Workers' Revolution: Russian Social Democracy, 1891–1903.* Chicago and London, 1967.

Zelnik, Reginald E. "The Peasant and the Factory." In *The Peasant in Nineteenth-Century Russia,* ed. Wayne S. Vucinich. Stanford, 1968.

———. *Labor and Society in Tsarist Russia: The Factory Workers of St. Petersburg, 1855–1870.* Stanford, 1971.

———. "Russian Bebels: An Introduction to the Memoirs of Semen Kanatchikov and Matvei Fisher," *Russian Review,* pt. 1, 35 (July 1976): 249–289; pt. 2, 35 (Oct. 1976): 417–447.

Designer	Janet Wood
Compositor:	Computer Typesetting Services
Printer:	Vail-Ballou
Binder:	Vail-Ballou
Text:	12/14 Garamond
Display:	Korinna

\ Essay due the (5th)
- parenthetical cite
-first person acceptable